Get the eBook FREE!

(PDF, ePub, Kindle, and liveBook all included)

We believe that once you buy a book from us, you should be able to read it in any format we have available. To get electronic versions of this book at no additional cost to you, purchase and then register this book at the Manning website.

Go to https://www.manning.com/freebook and follow the instructions to complete your pBook registration.

That's it!
Thanks from Manning!

Algorithms and Data Structures for Massive Datasets

Algorithms and Data Structures for Massive Datasets

DZEJLA MEDJEDOVIC
EMIN TAHIROVIC
Illustrated by INES DEDOVIC

MANNING
SHELTER ISLAND

For online information and ordering of this and other Manning books, please visit
www.manning.com. The publisher offers discounts on this book when ordered in quantity.
For more information, please contact

> Special Sales Department
> Manning Publications Co.
> 20 Baldwin Road
> PO Box 761
> Shelter Island, NY 11964
> Email: orders@manning.com

Illustrated by Ines Dedovic

The author and publisher have made every effort to ensure that the information in this book
was correct at press time. The author and publisher do not assume and hereby disclaim any
liability to any party for any loss, damage, or disruption caused by errors or omissions, whether
such errors or omissions result from negligence, accident, or any other cause, or from any usage
of the information herein.

Manning Publications Co.	Development editor: Karen Miller
20 Baldwin Road	Technical development editor: Al Krinker
PO Box 761	Review editors: Mihaela Batinić
Shelter Island, NY 11964	Production editor: Keri Hales
	Copy editor: Michele Mitchell
	Proofreader: Melody Dolab
	Technical proofreader: Tim van Deurzen
	Typesetter: Dennis Dalinnik
	Cover designer: Marija Tudor

ISBN: 9781617298035
Printed in the United States of America

brief contents

contents

preface

The idea for writing this book took form while we were teaching together at the International University of Sarajevo. In discussion with our students, who were working for local companies, we realized that data structures for massive data were becoming pretty common in everyday use for data engineers and data scientists. It was not just the Googles and the Facebooks of the world that employed these techniques to solve their scalability problems; it was also the companies with much smaller data footprints whose systems were starting to face ever-increasing demands on data-processing speeds.

Over lunch, we would ponder where a student learning to deploy HyperLogLog or a Bloom filter into a working production system could go for an application-friendly overview of it. The original papers introducing these data structures were often mathematically very deep, but with little context for a data engineer trying to fit this data structure into a real system with real data. Aside from an occasional blog post featuring a data structure implementation, resources that bundled this massive data domain–specific algorithmic knowledge were scarce to nonexistent.

We wanted to write a book that could present these highly technical subjects in a friendly tone and also be able to give a better answer to the perpetual student question, "Where can I use this?" Marrying the probabilistic, streaming, and external memory data structures into a living, massive data ecosystem and showcasing practical use cases was no small challenge for two professors in corduroy jackets. We were not ready to give up on math entirely, so we made it a challenge to try to convey as much mathematical intuition as possible without including a single proof.

We were extremely fortunate to work with Ines, an illustrator with an advanced engineering background, who created actionable and charming drawings to illustrate some of the more complex algorithmic content. If you have ever explained an algorithm to someone, then you know they are inherently visual, yet the books on computer algorithms often do not feature many visual cues. We hope this book is one small step toward changing that.

Every good story needs a conflict, and the main one in this book is the tradeoffs arising from constraints imposed by large data—a major theme of this book is sacrificing the accuracy of a data structure to gain savings in space. Finding that performance sweet spot, and learning how to balance different competing goals in a complex data pipeline are the main challenges massive data brings to the table, and the key lessons to take from this book.

We are grateful to have had the opportunity to write a book on such an exciting and important topic. We feel incredibly thankful to all who provided feedback while the book was in development. We started writing the book as academics but finished it as engineers at data companies (this is a practical book indeed!). We hope that engaging with this material enriches your algorithmic tool kit and enables you to tackle your next big data problem with curiosity and confidence.

acknowledgments

A lot of things happen from the moment you start writing a book until the end, and producing chapters on a regular basis, while navigating all the vicissitudes of life and work, is not always easy. Luckily, we had a whole village of people who supported us, cheered us on throughout the process, and brought food during deadline nights.

First and foremost, we would like to thank our parents: Merdzana and Safer, and Zikreta and Esad. Your examples and your guidance throughout life have set us free to read, learn, and explore, and made us feel that we can—and should—write books. Without that, this book would have never happened. We would also like to thank our dear siblings and nieces who supported us throughout the writing process: Dzejra, Ensar, Ajla, Serif, Mersad, Dalal, and Lejna. Emin would also like to thank his aunt Indira for putting up with him during his studies in Frankfurt.

Second, we would like to thank our friends, who repeatedly asked about the progress on the book (even while knowing they needed to brace themselves for a really long answer). A lot of our friends come from fields other than computer science, so their eagerness to read through our early chapters counts for so much more.

We would like to thank our students from the Sarajevo School of Science and Technology and the International University of Sarajevo, who helped inspire this book and reviewed it at different times.

We owe the completion of this book to our editor, Karen Miller, who has done a superb job of guiding us through the process with an incredible mix of professionalism and kindness. Her insight and experience were crucial in shaping this book.

During the process of writing, we collaborated with many people at Manning. The Manning team has a dedication to perfection and takes an agile and early feedback approach to book publishing, something we found incredibly useful and invigorating as authors.

We would like to thank the reviewers at Manning: Alejandro Bellogin, Alex Gout, Anto Aravinth, Arno Bastenhof, Christopher Kottmyer, Chunxu Tang, Clifford Thurber, Daniel Vasquez, Diego Casella, German Gonzalez-Morris, Hilde Van Gysel, Jean-François Morin, Jens Christian Bredahl Madsen, Jim Amrhein, Juan José Durillo Barrionuevo, Juan Antonio Rufes de Vicente, Kelum Senanayake, Manu Sareena, Marcus Young, Mark Bower, Nick Vazquez, Raushan Jha, Rui Liu, Satej Sahu, Sébastien Janas, Stuart Perks, Tim van Deurzen, Travis Nelson, and Yuri Kushch. Your suggestions helped make this a better book.

Finally, we would like to thank our readers, whose engagement and input made the book significantly better suited for its intended audience.

about this book

Algorithms and Data Structures for Massive Datasets is intended to help you build scalable applications and understand the algorithmic building blocks underneath massive data systems. The book covers different algorithmic aspects of building massive-scale applications that include saving space by using probabilistic data structures, handling streaming data, working with data on disk, and understanding performance tradeoffs in database systems.

Who should read this book

This book is intended for readers who understand fundamental data structures and algorithms. A lot of the content in this book builds on the material that is usually covered in an early data structures/algorithms course: the majority of our chapters begin by exhibiting the traditional solution to the problem and demonstrating why that algorithm or data structure fails in the context of massive data. Even though introductory sections of the chapters offer some discussion of the basic algorithms, that material serves only as a brief refresher on topics that the reader should already feel comfortable with. A reader of this book should also have an intermediate knowledge of programming and know the fundamentals of probability. No knowledge of any particular system or framework is required (ah, the beauty of algorithms) aside from basic familiarity with Python and pseudocode.

How this book is organized: A road map

The book has three parts covered in 11 chapters. Part 1 is about probabilistic succinct data structures, part 2 is about streaming data structures and algorithms, and part 3 is about external memory data structures and algorithms. Here is a brief summary of each chapter:

- Chapter 1 explains why massive data presents such a challenge for modern systems and how those challenges shape the design of algorithms and data structures.

Part 1: Probabilistic succinct data structures

- Chapter 2 reviews hashing and explains how hash tables have evolved to meet the demands of large datasets and complex distributed systems (e.g., consistent hashing). Hashing methods are heavily employed in the coming chapters, so this chapter serves as a preparation for other chapters in part 1.
- Chapter 3 introduces the approximate membership problem and two data structures that help solve it: Bloom filters and quotient filters. The chapter exhibits use cases and false positive rate analyses, as well as the pros and cons of using each data structure.
- Chapter 4 describes the problem of frequency estimation and introduces count-min sketch, a data structure that solves frequency estimation in a very space-efficient manner. Use cases in NLP, sensor data, and other areas are discussed, as well as applications of count-min sketch to problems like range queries.
- Chapter 5 goes deep into understanding cardinality estimation and HyperLog-Log algorithms, along with their applications. The chapter uses a mini experiment to show the evolution in accuracy from simple probabilistic counting all the way to the full HyperLogLog data structure.

Part 2: Streaming data structures and algorithms

- Chapter 6 is a gentle introduction to data streams as an algorithmic concept, and streaming data (applications) as a real-world manifestation. Using several practical use cases within the streaming data architecture, we show how data structures from the previous chapters fit in the streaming data context.
- Chapter 7 explains how to keep a representative sample from a data stream or a sliding window on a stream. We explain when one might be interested in a biased sample and give code examples showing how biasing a sample toward more recently seen data tuples is implemented.
- Chapter 8 is concerned with calculating approximate quantiles on numerical data from a continuous data stream. We describe two sketch data structures or digests: q-digest and t-digest. We explain the algorithms behind them and showcase them against each other on a realistic dataset.

Part 3: External memory data structures and algorithms

- Chapter 9 introduces the external memory model and a number of examples that demonstrate how the I/O cost dominates the CPU cost when dealing with data on remote storage. This chapter is a perspective shifter for an algorithm designer used to thinking of optimizing algorithms in terms of CPU cost.
- Chapter 10 exhibits data structures that power mainstream databases, such as B-trees and LSM-trees, and covers different read/write tradeoffs in database engine design. Understanding, at a high level, how these data structures work should help you discern between different styles of databases and choose the right one for your application.
- Chapter 11 looks at sorting to the external memory and shows the optimal algorithms for sorting files on disk using external memory–optimized versions of merge-sort and quick-sort. Chapter 11 uses sorting as an example to demonstrate what sorts of optimizations are possible for batched problems when moving them to external memory.

Parts 1 and 2 are more related to each other than they are to part 3, as they both deal with in-RAM data structures and the theme of maximizing accuracy while saving space. Part 3 has an independent theme, and a reader interested solely in it can skip ahead and not lose much context. It is also not necessary to read part 1 before part 2, but a reader who reads part 1 first might be readier to understand part 2 than one who directly jumps into it.

Parts 2 and 3 start with a chapter that explains the model and the context (chapters 6 and 9, respectively), and it is highly recommended to read those chapters to understand the other chapters in the respective parts. With this in mind, feel free to explore the book on your own. We tried to write all the chapters in a self-sufficient manner as much as is possible. You can always flip back for more context if needed. We recommend that all readers read chapter 1, which explains why massive data causes such a paradigm shift when it comes to algorithms and data structures deployed in busy, large infrastructures.

About the code

Several chapters contain code, and for some of the more complex algorithms and those where the context would significantly complicate the code (e.g., external memory algorithms), we fall back to pseudocode. We use Python and R for most code snippets and to create mini experiments that demonstrate data structure performance in some of the chapters. A reader should feel free to implement the coding exercises in the language of their choice, as the topics covered are not specific to any particular language or technology.

This book contains many examples of source code both in numbered listings and in line with normal text. In both cases, source code is formatted in a `fixed-width font like this` to separate it from ordinary text. Sometimes code is also **in bold** to highlight code that has changed from previous steps in the chapter, such as when a new feature adds to an existing line of code.

In many cases, the original source code has been reformatted; we've added line breaks and reworked indentation to accommodate the available page space in the book. In rare cases, even this was not enough, and listings include line-continuation markers (➥). Additionally, comments in the source code have often been removed from the listings when the code is described in the text. Code annotations accompany many of the listings, highlighting important concepts.

You can get executable snippets of code from the liveBook (online) version of this book at https://livebook.manning.com/book/algorithms-and-data-structures-for-massive-datasets. The complete code for the examples in the book is available for download from the Manning website at https://www.manning.com/books/algorithms-and-data-structures-for-massive-datasets.

liveBook discussion forum

Purchase of *Algorithms and Data Structures for Massive Datasets* includes free access to liveBook, Manning's online reading platform. Using liveBook's exclusive discussion features, you can attach comments to the book globally or to specific sections or paragraphs. It's a snap to make notes for yourself, ask and answer technical questions, and receive help from the author and other users. To access the forum, go to https://livebook.manning.com/book/algorithms-and-data-structures-for-massive-datasets/discussion. You can also learn more about Manning's forums and the rules of conduct at https://livebook.manning.com/discussion.

Manning's commitment to our readers is to provide a venue where a meaningful dialogue between individual readers and between readers and the authors can take place. It is not a commitment to any specific amount of participation on the part of the authors, whose contribution to the forum remains voluntary (and unpaid). We suggest you try asking the authors some challenging questions lest their interest stray! The forum and the archives of previous discussions will be accessible from the publisher's website as long as the book is in print.

about the authors

DZEJLA MEDJEDOVIC, PhD, earned her PhD in the Applied Algorithms Lab of the Computer Science department at Stony Brook University, New York, in 2014. Dzejla has worked on a number of projects in algorithms for massive data, taught algorithms at various levels, and also spent some time at Microsoft. Dzejla is passionate about teaching, promoting computer science education, and technology transfer. Currently, she works as a VP of Data at Social Explorer, Inc.

EMIN TAHIROVIC, PhD, earned his doctorate in biostatistics from the University of Pennsylvania in 2016 and his master's degree in theoretical computer science from Goethe University in Frankfurt in 2008. His statistical methodology and theoretical computer science background make him an archetypical data science researcher at the crossroads of computing and statistics. He has worked for DBahn AG as an IT consultant, and he regularly consults on projects for pharma and tech companies. Emin worked as an assistant professor of software engineering at the International University of Sarajevo. Currently, he works at HAProxy Technologies as a senior data scientist.

DR. INES DEDOVIC earned her doctorate at the Institute for Imaging and Computer Vision in the Department of Electrical Engineering at RWTH Aachen University, Germany. She has worked as a researcher at the Research Center Jülich and is currently employed as a software developer for camera systems at an automation company, Jonas & Redmann. For over 10 years, Ines has also worked as a 3D animator, comic artist, and illustrator for textbooks. In this book, she uses her art and technical skills to create intuitive visuals of technical concepts.

about the cover illustration

The figure on the cover of *Algorithms and Data Structures for Massive Datasets* is "Roussienne," or "Russian woman," taken from a book by Jacques Grasset de Saint-Sauveur, published in 1788. Each illustration is finely drawn and colored by hand.

In those days, it was easy to identify where people lived and what their trade or station in life was just by their dress. Manning celebrates the inventiveness and initiative of today's computer business with book covers based on the rich diversity of regional culture centuries ago, brought back to life by pictures from collections such as this one.

Introduction

This chapter covers

- What this book is about and its structure
- What makes this book different from other books on algorithms
- How massive datasets shape the design of algorithms and data structures
- How this book can help you design practical algorithms at a workplace
- Computer and system architecture fundamentals that make large amounts of data challenging for today's systems

Since you picked up this book, you might be wondering what the algorithms and data structures for massive datasets are and what makes them different from "normal" algorithms you might have encountered thus far. Does the title of this book imply that the classical algorithms (e.g., binary search, merge sort, quicksort, depth-first search, breadth-first search, and many other fundamental algorithms) as well as canonical data structures (e.g., arrays, matrices, hash tables, binary search trees, heaps) were built exclusively for small datasets?

The answer to this question is neither short nor simple, but if it had to be short and simple, it would be "yes." The notion of what constitutes a massive dataset is relative and depends on many factors, but the fact of the matter is that most bread-and-butter algorithms and data structures that we know about and work with on a daily basis have been developed with an implicit assumption that all data fits in the main memory, or *random-access memory* (RAM) of a computer. So, once you load all your data into RAM, it is relatively fast and easy to access any element of it, at which point the ultimate goal, from the efficiency point of view, becomes achieving the greatest productivity in the fewest number of CPU cycles. This is what the good old Big-O analysis ($O(.)$) teaches us about: it commonly expresses the worst-case number of basic operations the algorithm has to perform in order to solve a problem. These unit operations can be comparisons, arithmetic, bit operations, memory cell read/write/copy, or anything that directly translates into a small number of CPU cycles.

However, if you are a data scientist, a developer, or a backend engineer working for a company that collects data from its users, storing all data into the working memory of your computer is often infeasible. Many applications today, such as banking, e-commerce, scientific applications, and the Internet of Things (IoT), routinely manipulate datasets of terabyte (TB) or petabyte (PB) sizes (i.e., you don't have to work for Facebook or Google to encounter massive data at work).

You might be asking yourself how large the dataset has to be for someone to benefit from the techniques shown in this book. We deliberately avoid putting a number on what constitutes a massive dataset or what a "big-data company" is, as it depends on the problem being solved, the computational resources available to the engineer, system requirements, and so forth. Some companies with enormous datasets also have copious resources and can afford to delay thinking creatively about scalability issues by investing in the infrastructure (e.g., by buying tons of RAM). A developer working with moderately large datasets, but with a limited budget for the infrastructure, and extremely high system performance requirements from their client, can benefit from the techniques shown in this book as much as anyone else. Yet, as we will see, even the companies with virtually infinite resources choose to fill that extra RAM with clever space-efficient data structures.

The problem of massive data has been around for much longer than social networks and the internet. One of the first papers [1] to introduce *external-memory algorithms* (a class of algorithms that neglect the computational cost of the program in favor of optimizing far more time-consuming data-transfer cost) appeared back in 1988. As the practical motivation for the research, the authors use the example of large banks having to sort 2 million checks daily, about 800 MB worth of checks to be sorted overnight before the next business day, using the working memories of that time (~2–4 MB). Figuring out how to sort all the checks while being able to sort only 4 MB worth of checks at one time, and figuring out how to do so with the smallest number of trips to disk, was a relevant problem back then, and it has only grown in relevance since. Data has grown tremendously since then, but more importantly, it has grown at a much faster rate than the average size of RAM memory.

The main consequence of the rapid growth of data, and the main idea motivating algorithms in this book, is that most applications today are *data intensive*. Data intensive (in contrast to CPU intensive) means that the bottleneck of the application comes from transferring data back and forth and accessing data, rather than doing computations on that data once it's available. This fact is central to designing algorithms for large datasets, and it is from there that ideas of succinct data structures and external memory–oriented algorithms stem from. In section 1.4, we will delve into more details as to why data access in a computer is much slower than the computation.

The picture only gets more complex as we zoom out of the view of a single computer. Most applications today are distributed and complex data pipelines, with thousands of computers exchanging data over networks. Databases and caches are distributed, and many users simultaneously add and query large amounts of content. Data formats have become diverse, multidimensional, and dynamic. In order to be effective, the applications need to respond to changes very quickly.

In streaming applications [2], data effectively flies by without ever being stored, and the application needs to capture the relevant features of the data with a degree of accuracy that renders it relevant and useful, without scanning it again. This new context calls for a new generation of algorithms and data structures, a new application builder's toolbox that is optimized to address many challenges specific to massive data systems. The intention of this book is to teach you exactly that—the fundamental algorithmic techniques and data structures for developing scalable applications.

1.1   An example

To illustrate the main themes of this book, consider the following example: you are working for a media company on a project related to news article comments. You are given a large repository of comments with the following associated basic metadata information:

```
{
    comment-id: 2833908010
    article-id: 779284
    user-id: 9153647
    text: this recipe needs more butter
    views: 14375
    likes: 43
}
```

You are looking at approximately 3 billion user comments totaling 600 GB in data size. Some of the questions you would like to answer about the dataset include determining the most popular comments and articles, classifying articles according to themes and common keywords occurring in the comments, and so on. But first we need to address the issue of duplicates that accrued over multiple instances of scraping and ascertain the total number of distinct comments in the dataset.

1.1.1   *An example: How to solve it*

A common way to store unique elements in a data structure is to create a key-value dictionary where each distinct element's unique ID is mapped to its frequency. There are many libraries that implement key-value dictionaries, such as map in C++, HashMap in Java, dict in Python, and so on. Key-value dictionaries are commonly implemented either as a balanced binary tree (e.g., a red-black tree in C++'s map), or, alternatively, as hash tables (e.g., Python's dict.)

> **Red-black-tree vs. hash-table implementations**
> The tree dictionary implementations, apart from lookup/insert/delete that run in fast logarithmic time, offer equally fast predecessor/successor operations, that is, the ability to explore data back and forth efficiently using lexicographical ordering. Most hash table implementations lack the ability to efficiently traverse the items in the lexicographical order; however, the hash table implementations offer fast constant-time performance on most common operations of lookup/insert/delete.

For simplicity of our example, let's assume we are working with Python's dict, a hash table. Using comment-id as the key and the number of occurrences of that comment-id as the value will help us effectively eliminate duplicates (see the (comment-id -> frequency) dictionary on the left side of figure 1.1).

However, we might need up to 24 GB in order to store <comment-id, frequency> pairs for 3 billion comments, using 8 bytes per pair (4 bytes for comment-id and 4 bytes for frequency). Depending on the method used to implement the underlying hash table, the data structure will need 1.5 or 2 times the space taken for elements for the bookkeeping (empty slots, pointers, etc.), bringing us close to 40 GB.

If we are also to classify articles according to certain topics of interest, we can again employ dictionaries (other methods are possible as well) by constructing a separate dictionary for each topic (e.g., sports, politics, science, etc.), as shown on the right side of figure 1.1. The role of the (article-id -> keyword_frequency) dictionaries here is to count the number of occurrences of topic-related keywords in all the comments; for example, the article with the article-id 745 has 23 politics-related keywords in its associated comments. We pre-filter each comment-id using the large (comment-id -> frequency) dictionary to only account for distinct comments. A single table of this sort can contain dozens of millions of entries, totaling close to 1 GB, and maintaining such hash tables for, say, 30 topics can cost up to 30 GB for data only, and approximately 50 GB in total.

We hope this small example demonstrates that we can start from a fairly common and naïve problem, and before we know it, catch ourselves with a number of clunky data structures that we can't fit into memory.

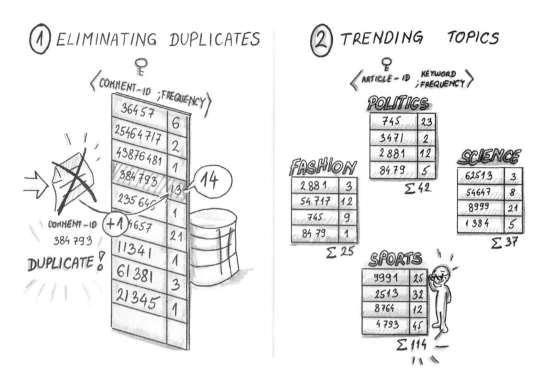

Figure 1.1 In this example, we build a (comment-id, frequency) hash table to help us store distinct comment-ids with their frequency count. An incoming comment-id 384793 is already contained in the table, and its frequency count is incremented. We also build topic-related hash tables, where for each article, we count the number of times associated keywords appeared in its comments (e.g., in the sports theme, keywords might be "soccer," "player," "goal," etc.). For a large dataset of 3 billion comments, these data structures may require from dozens to a hundred gigabytes of RAM memory.

You might think to yourself, can't we multiply a couple of numbers beforehand and easily predict how large the data structures are going to become? Well, in real life it often does not work like that. Rarely do people start designing their systems from scratch having massive data in mind. Companies often start out by trying to create a system that works, and can later become victims of their own success, where the user base grows rapidly in a short amount of time, and the old system, designed by developers who have left, needs to grapple with this new demanding workload. Most often, parts of the system get redesigned as the need arises.

When the number of items in a dataset becomes large, then every additional bit per item contributes to the burden on the system. Common data structures that are the bread and butter of every software developer can become too large to efficiently work with, and we need more succinct alternatives (see figure 1.2).

Figure 1.2   **Most common data structures, including hash tables, become difficult to store and manage with large amounts of data.**

1.1.2   *How to solve it, take two: A book walkthrough*

With daunting dataset sizes, we are faced with a number of choices. It turns out that if we settle for a small margin of error, we can build a data structure similar to a hash table in functionality, only more compact. There is a family of *succinct data structures* that comprise part 1 of the book. These are the data structures that use a tiny amount of space to approximate the answers to these common questions:

- *Membership*—Does a comment/user X exist?
- *Frequency*—How many times did user X comment? What is the most popular keyword?
- *Cardinality*—How many truly distinct comments/users do we have?

These data structures use much less space to process a dataset of *n* items than a hash table (think 1 byte per item or less, versus 8–16 bytes per item in a hash table).

A *Bloom filter,* which we will discuss in chapter 3, will use eight times less space than the (comment-id -> frequency) hash table and will answer membership queries with about a 2% false positive rate. In this introductory chapter, we avoid getting into the gritty mathematical details of how we arrive at these numbers, but the difference between Bloom filters and hash tables that is worth emphasizing is that Bloom filters do not store the keys (e.g., comment-id) themselves. Bloom filters compute hashes of keys and use them to modify the data structure. Thus, the size of the Bloom filter mainly depends on the number of keys inserted, not their size (or whether it's a string or a small or a large integer).

Another data structure that we will learn about in chapter 4, *Count-min sketch*, will use more than 24 times less space than the `(comment-id -> frequency)` hash table to estimate the frequency of each `comment-id`, exhibiting a small overestimate in the frequency in over 99% of the cases. We can also use Count-min sketch to replace the `(article-id -> keyword_frequency)` hash tables and use about 3 MB per topic hash table, which costs about 20 times less than the original scheme.

Lastly, the data structure *HyperLogLog* from chapter 5 can estimate the cardinality of the set with only 12 KB, exhibiting the error to less than 1% of the true cardinality.

If we further relax the requirements on accuracy for each of these data structures, we can get away with even less space. Because the original dataset still resides on disk, there is also a way to control for an occasional error so that we are not stuck with the false positives; we just need a little extra effort to verify those.

COMMENT DATA AS A STREAM

Quite likely, we will encounter the problem of news comments and articles in the context of a fast-moving *event stream* rather than as a static dataset. Assume that the event here constitutes any modification to the dataset, such as clicking Like or inserting/deleting a comment or an article, and the events arrive in real time as streaming data to our system. You will learn more about this streaming data context in chapter 6.

Note that in this setup we can also encounter duplicates of `comment-id`, but for a different reason: every time someone clicks Like on a particular comment, we receive the event with the same `comment-id` but with an amended count on the `likes` attribute. Given that events arrive rapidly and on a 24/7 basis and that we cannot afford to store all of them, for many problems of interest we can only provide approximate solutions. Mainly, we are interested in computing basic statistics on data in real time (e.g., the average number of likes per comment in the past week), and without the ability to store the like count for each comment, we can resort to random sampling.

We could draw a random sample from the data stream as it arrives using the *Bernoulli sampling algorithm* that we cover in chapter 7. To illustrate, if you have ever plucked flower petals in the love-fortune game "(S)he loves me, (s)he loves me not" in a random manner, you could say that you probably ended up with "Bernoulli-sampled" petals in your hand (do not use this on a date). This sampling scheme offers itself conveniently to the one-passover data context.

Answering some more granular questions about the comments data, such as how many likes a comment needs to be in the top 10% of liked comments, will also trade accuracy for space. We can maintain a type of a dynamic histogram (see chapter 8) of the complete viewed data within a limited, realistic, fast-memory space. This sketch, or a summary of the data, can then be used to answer queries about any quantiles of our complete data with some error.

COMMENT DATA IN A DATABASE

Lastly, we might want to store all comment data in a persistent format (e.g., a database on disk/cloud), and build a system on top that would enable the fast insertion, retrieval, and modification of live data over time. In this kind of setup, we favor accuracy over speed, so we are comfortable storing tons of data on disk and retrieving it in a slower manner, as long as we can guarantee queries will have 100% accuracy.

Storing data on remote storage and organizing it so that it lends itself to efficient retrieval is a topic of the algorithmic paradigm called *external-memory algorithms*, which we will begin to explore in chapter 9. External-memory algorithms address some of the most relevant problems of modern applications, such as the design and implementation of database engines and their indices. In our particular comments data example, we need to ask whether we are building a system with mostly static data, but that is constantly queried by users (i.e., *read optimized*), or a system where users frequently add new data and modify it, but query it only occasionally (i.e., *write optimized*). Or, perhaps, it is a combination, where both fast inserts and fast queries are equally important (i.e., *read-write optimized*).

Very few engineers implement their own storage engines, but almost all of them use them. To knowledgeably choose between different alternatives, we need to understand what data structures power them underneath. The insert/lookup tradeoff is inherent in databases, and it is reflected in the design of data structures that run underneath MySQL, TokuDB, LevelDB, and many other storage engines out there. Some of the most popular data structures to build databases include B-trees, B^ε-trees, and LSM-trees, and each serves a different sort of a workload. We will discuss these different types of performance and the tradeoffs in chapter 10. Also, we may be interested in solving other problems with data sitting on disk, such as ordering comments lexicographically or by a number of occurrences. To do that, we need a sorting algorithm that will efficiently sort data in a database or in a file on disk. You will learn how to do that in the last chapter of our book, chapter 11.

1.2   *The structure of this book*

As the earlier section outlines, this book revolves around three main themes, divided into three parts.

Part 1 (chapters 2–5) deals with *hash-based* sketching data structures. This part begins with a review of hash tables and specific hashing techniques developed for massive data setting. Even though the hashing chapter is planned as a review chapter, we suggest you use it as a refresher on hashing, and also use the opportunity to learn about modern hash techniques devised to deal with large datasets. Chapter 2 also serves as good preparation for chapters 3–5 considering that the sketches are hash based. The data structures we present in chapters 3–5, such as Bloom filters, Count-min sketch, Hyperloglog, and their alternatives, have found numerous applications in databases, networking, and so on.

Part 2 (chapters 6–8) introduces data streams. From classical techniques, such as Bernoulli and reservoir sampling, to more sophisticated methods, such as sampling from a moving window, we introduce a number of sampling algorithms suitable for different streaming data models. The created samples are then used to calculate estimates of the total sums or averages, and so on. We also introduce algorithms for calculating (ensemble of) ε-approximate quantiles such as q-digest and t-digest.

Part 3 (chapters 9–11) covers algorithmic techniques for scenarios when data resides on SSD/disk. First we introduce the external-memory model and then present optimal algorithms for fundamental problems such as searching and sorting, illuminating key algorithmic tricks in this model. This part of the book also covers data structures that power modern databases such as B-trees, B^ε-trees, and LSM-trees.

1.3   What makes this book different and whom it is for

There are a number of great books on classical algorithms and data structures, including *The Algorithm Design Manual* (3rd ed.) by Skiena (Springer, 2020); *Introduction to Algorithms* (3rd ed.) by Cormen, Leiserson, Rivest, and Stein (The MIT Press, 2022); *Algorithms* (4th ed.) by Sedgewick and Wayne (Addison-Wesley, 2011); and, for a more introductory and friendly take on the subject, *Grokking Algorithms* by Bhargava (Manning, 2016). The algorithms and data structures for massive datasets are slowly making their way into mainstream textbooks, but the world is moving fast, and our hope is that our book can provide a compendium of the state-of-the-art algorithms and data structures that can help a data scientist or a developer handling large datasets at work.

The book is intended to offer a good balance of theoretical intuition, practical use cases, and code snippets in Python. We assume that a reader has some fundamental knowledge of algorithms and data structures, so if you have not studied the basic algorithms and data structures, you should cover that material before embarking on this subject. Massive data algorithms are a very broad subject, and this book is meant to serve as a gentle introduction.

The majority of the books on massive data focus on a particular technology, system, or infrastructure. This book does not focus on the specific technology; neither does it assume familiarity with any particular technology. Instead, it covers underlying algorithms and data structures that play a major role in making these systems scalable.

Often, the books that do cover algorithmic aspects of massive data focus on machine learning. However, an important aspect of handling large data that does not specifically deal with inferring meaning from data, but rather has to do with handling the size of the data and processing it efficiently, whatever the data is, has often been neglected in the literature. This book aims to fill that gap.

There are some excellent books that address specialized aspects of massive datasets [3]. With this book, we intend to present these different themes in one place, often citing the cutting-edge research and technical papers on relevant subjects. Lastly, our hope is that this book will teach a more advanced algorithmic material in a down-to-earth manner, providing mathematical intuition instead of the technical proofs that characterize most resources on this subject. Illustrations play an important role in communicating some of the more advanced technical concepts, and we hope you enjoy them (and learn from them).

Now that the introductory remarks are out of the way, let's discuss the central issue that motivates topics from this book.

1.4   *Why is massive data so challenging for today's systems?*

There are many parameters in computers and distributed systems architecture that can shape the performance of a given application. Some of the main challenges that computers face in processing large amounts of data stem from hardware and general computer architecture. Now, this book is not about hardware, but in order to design efficient algorithms for massive data, it is important to understand some physical constraints that are making data transfer such a big challenge. Some of the main issues we discuss in this chapter include the large asymmetry between the CPU and the memory speed, different levels of memory and the tradeoffs between the speed and size for each level, and the issue of latency versus bandwidth.

1.4.1   *The CPU memory performance gap*

The first important asymmetry that we will discuss is between the speeds of CPU operations and memory access operations in a computer, also known as the CPU memory performance gap [4]. Figure 1.3 shows, starting from 1980, the average gap between

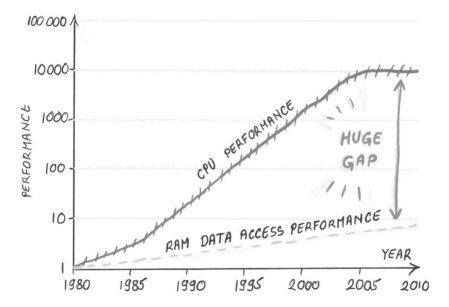

Figure 1.3   CPU memory performance gap graph, adopted from Hennessy & Patterson's computer architecture. The graph shows the widening gap between the speeds of memory accesses to CPU and RAM main memory (the average number of memory accesses per second over time.) The vertical axis is on the log scale. Processors show an improvement of about 1.5 times per year up to year 2005, while the improvement of access to main memory has been only about 1.1 times per year. Processor speed-up has somewhat flattened since 2005, but this is being alleviated by using multiple cores and parallelism.

the speeds of processor memory access and main memory access (DRAM memory), expressed in the number of memory requests per second (the inverse of latency).

Intuitively, this gap shows that performing computations is much faster than accessing data. If we are stuck with the mindset that only cares about optimizing CPU computation, then in many cases our analyses will not jive well with reality.

1.4.2   Memory hierarchy

Aside from the CPU memory gap, there is a hierarchy of different types of memory built into a computer that have different characteristics. The overarching tradeoff has been that the memory that is fast is also small (and expensive), and the memory that is large is also slow (but cheap). As shown in figure 1.4, starting from the smallest and

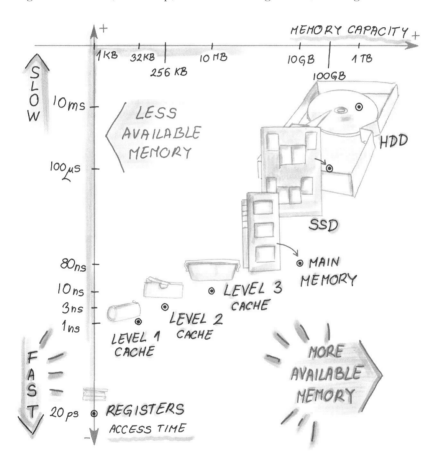

Figure 1.4   Different types of memories in the computer. Starting from registers in the bottom left corner, which are blindingly fast but also very small, we move up (getting slower) and right (getting larger) with level 1 cache, level 2 cache, level 3 cache, and main memory, all the way to SSD and/or HDD. Mixing up different memories in the same computer allows for the illusion of having both the speed and the storage capacity by having each level serve as a cache for the next larger one.

the fastest, the computer hierarchy usually contains the following levels: registers, level 1 cache, level 2 cache, level 3 cache, main memory, solid state drive (SSD), and/or the hard disk (HDD). The last two are persistent (nonvolatile) memories, meaning the data is saved if we turn off the computer, and as such are suitable for storage.

In figure 1.4, we can see the access times and capacities for each level of the memory in a sample architecture [5]. The numbers vary across architectures and are more useful when observed in terms of ratios between different access times rather than the specific values. For example, pulling a piece of data from cache is roughly 1 million times faster than doing so from the disk.

The hard disk and the needle, some of the few remaining mechanical parts of a computer, work a lot like a record player. Placing the mechanical needle on the right track is the time-consuming part of accessing disk data. Once the needle is on the right track, the data transfer can be very fast, depending on how fast the disk spins.

1.4.3   Latency vs. bandwidth

A similar phenomenon is where "latency lags bandwidth" [6] and holds for different types of memory. The bandwidth in various systems, ranging from microprocessors to main memory, hard disk, and network, has tremendously improved over the past few decades, but latency hasn't improved at the same rate, even though latency is the important measurement in many scenarios where common user behavior involves many small random accesses as opposed to one large sequential one.

To offset the cost of the expensive initial call, data transfer between different levels of memory is done in chunks of multiple items. Those chunks are called cache lines, pages, or blocks, depending on the memory level we are working with, and their size is proportionate to the size of the corresponding level of memory; for cache they are in the range 8–64 bytes, and for disk blocks they can be up to 1 MB [7]. Due to the concept known as *spatial locality*, where we expect the program to access memory locations that are in the vicinity of each other and close in time, transferring data in sequential blocks effectively pre-fetches the items we will likely need in the near future.

1.4.4   What about distributed systems?

Most applications today run on multiple computers, and having data sent from one computer to another adds yet another level of delay. Data transfer between computers can be from hundreds of milliseconds to a couple of seconds long, depending on the system load (e.g., number of users accessing the same application), number of hops to destination, and other details of the architecture (see figure 1.5).

1.5   Designing algorithms with hardware in mind

After looking at some crucial aspects of modern computer architecture, the first important takeaway is that, although technology improves constantly (e.g., SSDs are a relatively new development and they do not share many of the issues of hard disks), some of the issues, such as the tradeoff between the speed and the size of memories,

Figure 1.5   Cloud access times can be high due to the network load and complex infrastructure. Accessing the cloud can take hundreds of milliseconds or even seconds. We can observe this as another level of memory that is even larger and slower than the hard disk. Improving the performance in cloud applications can also be hard because times to access or write data on a cloud are unpredictable.

are not going away any time soon. Part of the reason for this is purely physical: to store a lot of data, we need a lot of space, and the speed of light sets the physical limit as to how fast data can travel from one part of the computer to the other, or one part of the network to the other. To extend this to a network of computers, we will cite an example [8] showing that, for two computers 300 meters away from each other, the lower physical limit of data exchange is 1 microsecond.

Hence, we need to design algorithms that can work around hardware limitations. Designing succinct data structures (or taking data samples) that can fit into small and fast levels of memory helps because we avoid expensive disk seeks. In other words, *reducing space saves time.*

Yet, in many applications we still need to work with data on disk. Here, designing algorithms with optimized patterns of disk access and caching mechanisms that enable the smallest number of memory transfers is important, and this is further linked to how we lay out and organize data on a disk (say, in a relational database). Disk-based algorithms prefer smooth scanning over the disk over random hopping; this way, we get to make use of good bandwidth and avoid poor latency, so one meaningful direction is transforming an algorithm that does many random reads/writes into one that does sequential reads/writes. Throughout this book, we will see how classical algorithms can be transformed and new ones designed, with space-related concerns in mind.

However, it is also important to keep in mind that modern systems have many performance metrics other than scalability: security, availability, maintainability, and so on. Real production systems need an efficient data structure and an algorithm running under the hood, but with a lot of bells and whistles on top to make all the other stuff work for their customers (see figure 1.6). However, with ever-increasing amounts of data, designing efficient data structures and algorithms has become more important than ever before, and we hope that in the coming pages you will learn how to do exactly that.

Figure 1.6   An efficient data structure with bells and whistles

Summary

- Applications today generate and process large amounts of data at a rapid rate. Traditional data structures, such as key-value dictionaries, can grow too big to fit in RAM memory, which can lead to an application choking due to the I/O bottleneck.

- To process large datasets efficiently, we can design space-efficient hash-based sketches, do real-time analytics with the help of random sampling and approximate statistics, or deal with data on disk and other remote storage more efficiently.

- This book serves as a natural continuation of the basic algorithms and data structures book/course because it teaches you how to transform the fundamental algorithms and data structures into algorithms and data structures that scale well to large datasets.

- The key reasons why large data is a major issue for today's computers and systems are that CPU (and multiprocessor) speeds improve at a much faster rate than memory speeds, and the tradeoff between the speed and size for different types of memory in the computer, as well as the latency versus bandwidth phenomenon, leads to applications processing data at a slower rate than performing computations. These trends are not likely to change soon, so the algorithms and data structure that address the I/O cost and issues of space are only going to increase in importance over time.

- In data-intensive applications, optimizing for space means optimizing for time.

Part 1

Hash-based sketches

In the next few chapters, we will explore probabilistic succinct data structures. We will see how bread-and-butter problems in the world of regular algorithms, such as frequency estimation, membership queries, and the count-distinct problem, become harder to tackle as the amount of data grows and classical data structures start to spill out of RAM. We turn our attention to a collection of data structures that help solve the same problems, only with much less space. What's the catch? These data structures will not always give you 100% accuracy. The good news is that the error rates are often low and are greatly compensated for by major wins in data structure storage. The data structures exhibited in part 1 include Bloom filters, quotient filters, count-min sketch, HyperLogLog, and some compact variants of hash tables. These data structures are highly configurable to the desired error rate and are, in that sense, highly versatile. The next few chapters will be all about squeezing in the most functionality in the least amount of RAM space, and every bit will count. But first we begin with a review of hash tables and hashing, which serve as the building blocks of the many data structures to come.

Review of hash tables and modern hashing

This chapter covers

- Reviewing dictionaries and why hashing is ubiquitous in modern systems
- Refreshing the basic collision-resolution techniques
- Exploring cache efficiency in hash tables
- Using hash tables for distributed systems and consistent hashing
- Learning how consistent hashing works in P2P networks

We begin with the topic of hashing for a number of reasons. First, classical hash tables have proved irreplaceable in modern systems, making it harder to find a system that does not use them than one that does. Second, recently there has been a lot of innovative work addressing algorithmic issues that arise as hash tables grow to fit massive data, such as efficient resizing, compact representation, and space-saving tricks. In a similar vein, hashing has over time been adapted to serve in massive peer-to-peer systems where the hash table is split among servers; here, the key challenge is the assignment of resources to servers and the load balancing of resources as servers dynamically join and leave the network. Lastly, we begin with hashing because it forms the backbone of all the succinct data structures we present in part 1 of the book.

Aside from the basics of how hash tables work, in this chapter we show examples of hashing in modern applications such as deduplication and plagiarism detection. We touch on how Python implements dictionaries as a part of our discussion on hash table design tradeoffs. Section 2.8 discusses consistent hashing, the method used to implement distributed hash tables. This section features code samples in Python that you can try out and play with to gain a better understanding of how hash tables are implemented in a distributed and dynamic multiserver environment. The last part of the section on consistent hashing contains coding exercises for a reader who likes to be challenged. If you feel comfortable with all things related to classical hashing, skip to section 2.8, or, if you are familiar with consistent hashing, skip to chapter 3.

2.1 *Ubiquitous hashing*

Hashing is one of those subjects that, no matter how much attention they got in your programming, data structures, and algorithms courses, it probably was not enough. Hash tables and hash functions are virtually everywhere. To illustrate this, consider the process of writing an email (see figures 2.1–2.4). First, when logging into your email account, the password you typed in gets hashed, and the hash is checked against the database to verify a match.

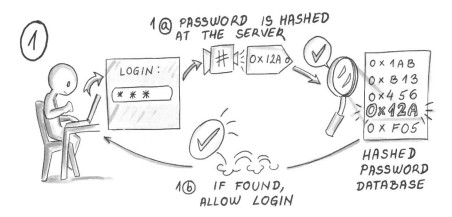

Figure 2.1 Logging into email and hashing

While writing an email, the spell-checker uses hashing to check whether a given word exists in the dictionary.

When the email is sent, often source-destination IP address pairs are hashed to determine to which intermediate server the packet should go in order to effectively load balance the traffic.

Figure 2.2 **Spell-checking and hashing**

Figure 2.3 **Network packets and hashing**

Lastly, when the email arrives at the destination, the spam filters sometimes hash email contents to find spam-like words and filter likely spam.

Figure 2.4 **Spam filters and hashing**

We bet that in all the places where security is important, and in all the places where the lookup speed is important, you're bound to find stuff being hashed.

This chapter discusses both hashing and hash tables, and sometimes it switches unexpectedly back and forth. They are clearly not the same thing, but we will observe hashing less in the context of cryptography and more in the context of being utilized in a hash table—or, in the future chapters, in some other data structures. Hash tables are as ubiquitous as hashing, and programmers use them every day (e.g., when building key-value maps), often without knowing that there is a hash table sitting underneath.

To find out why hash tables are so widely used, we need to compare them to other data structures and see how well different data structures implement what we call a *dictionary*—an abstract data type that can do lookup, insert, and delete operations.

2.2 A crash course on data structures

Many data structures can perform the role of a dictionary, but different data structures exhibit different performance tradeoffs and thus lend themselves to different usage scenarios. For example, consider a plain *unsorted array*; this rather simple data structure offers ideal constant-time performance on inserts ($O(1)$) as new elements are appended to a log. However, the lookup in the worst case requires a full linear scan of data ($O(n)$). An unsorted array can serve well as a dictionary implementation for applications where we want extremely fast inserts and where lookups are extremely rare.[1]

Sorted arrays allow fast logarithmic time lookups using binary search ($O(\log n)$), which, for many array sizes, is effectively as good as constant time (logarithm with base 2 of 1 billion is less than 30). However, we pay the price in the maintenance of the sorted order when we insert or delete and have to move over a linear number of items in the worst case ($O(n)$). Linear time operations mean that we need to visit roughly every element during a single operation, a forbidding cost in most scenarios.

Linked lists, unlike sorted arrays, can insert works in constant time by simply inserting at the head of the list. Deletion is possible from anywhere in the list in constant time ($O(1)$) by relinking a few pointers, provided we located where to insert/delete. More care is needed in the case of a singly linked list, where with a deletion we would need to provide the pointer to the position before the element to be deleted. The only way to find that position is to traverse the linked list by following pointers, even if the linked list were sorted, which brings us back to linear time. Whichever way you look at it, with simple linear structures such as arrays and linked lists, there is at least one operation that costs $O(n)$, and to avoid it we need to break out from this linear structure.

Balanced binary search trees have dictionary operations dependent on the depth of the tree, and *balanced binary trees* use different balancing mechanisms (AVL, red-black, etc.) that keep the tree depth at $O(\log n)$. Hence, all insert, lookup, and delete operations take logarithmic time in the worst case. Just like with binary search, for many tree sizes, there is little difference in the performance between constant time and logarithmic time. Logarithmic time is much closer to constant than to linear when it

---

[1] If we are guaranteed to never need a lookup, there is even a better way to "implement" inserts: do nothing.

comes to speed, so being able to do all dictionary operations in this guaranteed amount of time should make us happy.

In addition, balanced binary search trees maintain the sorted order of elements, which makes them an excellent choice for performing fast-range, predecessor, and successor queries. Balanced binary trees are provably your best choice for a dictionary if we compare all data structures that work based on element comparisons ($<$, $>$, $=$).

However, we are not limited to building data structures with only comparisons; computers are capable of many other operations, including bit shifts, arithmetic operations, and other operations, and all of those are very cleverly used by hash functions to break out from the logarithmic bound.

The ultimate benefit of hash tables and hashing is that they cut the dictionary operation costs to $O(1)$ on all operations. If you are thinking this is too good to be true, to some extent you are right: unlike the bounds mentioned thus far, where the runtime is guaranteed (i.e., worst case), the constant-time runtime in hash tables is expected. The worst case can still be as bad as linear time $O(n)$, but with a good hash table design, we can almost always avoid such instances.

So, even though the worst case on a lookup for a hash table is the same as that on an unsorted array, in the case of the hash table, $O(n)$ will almost never happen, while in the case of an array, it will quite consistently happen.

The reason is the following: in a hash table, a good hash function will scramble the input item and, based on that scrambled result, send the item to some bucket in a hash table where it can be found later. The word *hash* comes from the French *hachis*, often used to describe a type of dish where meat is chopped and minced into many little pieces (also related to *hatchet*). Because, on average, different items will be minced into different results, they are usually scattered to different buckets in a hash table. This enables fast lookup because no particular bucket will hold too many items. The lookup operation will mince the query element and directly look it up in the corresponding bucket. However, it is possible that the hash function minces very different input items into the same number and sends them all to the same bucket. In that case, mincing did not help our case, and we need to scan through all the items in the bucket to see if our query item is present. This is an extremely rare case, and when it happens we can decide to use a different hash function for that particular input.

Hash tables, on the other hand, are poorly suited for all applications where having your data ordered is important. The natural consequence of mincing data is that the order of items is not preserved. The issue comes in focus in databases where answering a range query requires navigating the sorted order of elements; for instance, listing all employee ages between 35 and 56, or finding all points on a coordinate x between 3 and 45 in a spatial database. Hash tables are most useful when looking for an exact match in the database. However, it is possible to use hashing to answer queries about similarity (e.g., in plagiarism detection), as we will see in the scenarios in the next section. Table 2.1 compares the most common data structures.

Table 2.1 Summary of comparison of different data structure performance for dictionary operations. Unsorted arrays work well as data logs. Sorted arrays work well for the retrieval in a static dataset. Linked lists are good for fast deletions when the right position in the list is provided. Balanced binary search trees are both fast and versatile when it comes to various operations and guarantee fast worst-case performance. Predecessor/successor in balanced binary search trees runs in constant time when provided the location of the element whose predecessor/successor we are looking for; otherwise, it is logarithmic. Hash tables are the fastest in the expected sense. However, their ability to traverse the sorted order is not as good as that of balanced binary search trees.

	Lookup	Insert	Delete	Predecessor/ successor
Unsorted array	$O(n)$	$O(1)$	$O(n)$	$O(n)$
Sorted array	$O(\log n)$	$O(n)$	$O(n)$	$O(1)$
Linked list	$O(n)$	$O(1)$	$O(1)*$	$O(n)$
Balanced binary search tree	$O(\log n)$	$O(\log n)$	$O(\log n)$	$O(1)$
Hash table	$O(1)$ (expected)	$O(1)$ (expected)	$O(1)$ (expected)	$O(n)$

2.3 *Usage scenarios in modern systems*

There are many applications of hashing everywhere you look. Here are two that we particularly like.

2.3.1 *Deduplication in backup/storage solutions*

Many companies, such as Dropbox and Dell EMC Data Domain storage systems, deal with storing large amounts of user data by taking frequent snapshots and backups. Clients for these companies are often large corporations that hold enormous amounts of data, and if the snapshots are taken frequently enough (say, every 24 hours), the majority of the data between the consecutive snapshots will remain unchanged. In this scenario, it's important to quickly find the parts that have changed and store only them, thereby saving time and space in storing a new copy. To do that, we need to be able to efficiently identify duplicate content.

Deduplication is the process of eliminating duplicates, and the majority of its modern implementations use hashing. For example, consider *ChunkStash* [1], a deduplication system specifically designed to provide fast throughput using flash. In ChunkStash, files are split into small chunks that are fixed in size (say, 8 KB), and every chunk content is hashed to a 20-byte SHA-1 fingerprint; if the fingerprint is already present, we only point to the existing fingerprint. If the fingerprint is new, we can assume the chunk is also new, and we both store the chunk to the data store and store the fingerprint in the hash table, with the pointer to the location of the corresponding chunk in the data store (see figure 2.5).

Chunking the files helps identify near-duplicates, where small edits have been made to a large file.

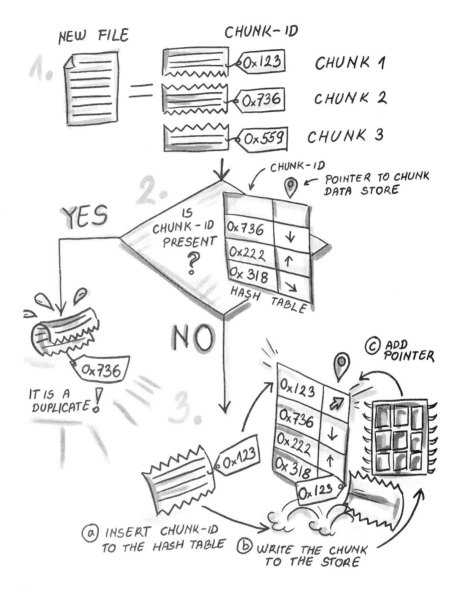

Figure 2.5 Deduplication process in backup/storage solutions. When a new file arrives, it is split into small chunks. In our example, the file is split into three chunks, and each chunk is hashed (e.g., chunk 1 has chunk-id 0x123, and chunk 2 has chunk-id 0x736). Chunk-id 0x123 is not found in the hash table. A new entry is created for this particular chunk-id, and the chunk itself is stored. chunk-id 0x736, having been found in the hash table, is deemed a duplicate and isn't stored.

There are more intricacies to this process than what we show. For example, when writing the new chunk to the flash store, the chunks are first accumulated into an in-memory write buffer, and, once full, the buffer is flushed to flash in one fell swoop. This is done to avoid repeated small edits to the same page, a particularly expensive operation in flash. But let's stay in the in-memory lane for now; buffering and writing efficiently to disk will be given more attention in part 3.

2.3.2 *Plagiarism detection with MOSS and Rabin–Karp fingerprinting*

Measure of Software Similarity (MOSS) is a plagiarism-detection service, mainly used to detect plagiarism in programming assignments. One of the main algorithmic ideas in MOSS [2] is a variant of the Rabin–Karp string-matching algorithm [3] that relies on k-gram fingerprinting (k-gram is a contiguous substring of length k). Let's first review the algorithm.

Given a string t that represents a large text, and a string p that represents a smaller pattern, a string-matching problem asks whether there exists an occurrence of p in t. There is rich literature on string-matching algorithms, most of which perform substring comparisons between p and t, but the Rabin–Karp algorithm performs comparisons of the hashes of substrings, and does so in a clever way. It works extremely well in practice, and the fast performance (which should not surprise you at this point) is partly due to hashing.

Namely, the algorithm checks whether the substrings match character by character (only when the hashes of substrings match). In the worst case, we will get many false matches due to *hash collisions*, when two different substrings have the same hash but substrings differ. In this case, the total runtime is $O(|t||p|)$, like that of a brute-force string-matching algorithm. But in most situations when there are not many true matches, and with a good hash function, the algorithm zips through t (i.e., it works in linear time). False matches might contribute to the worst-case performance, but, as discussed earlier, good hash function will make sure it does not happen as often. See figure 2.6 for an example of how the algorithm works.

The time to compute the hash depends on the size of the substring (a good hash function should take all characters into account), so by itself, hashing does not make the algorithm faster. However, Rabin–Karp uses *rolling hashes* where, given the hash of a k-gram $t[j, \ldots, j + k - 1]$, computing the hash for the k-gram shifted one position to the right, $t[j + 1, \ldots, j + k]$, takes only constant time (see figure 2.7). This can be done if the rolling hash function is such that it allows us to, in some way "subtract" the first character of the first k-gram, and "add" the last character of the second k-gram (a very simple example of such a rolling hash is a function that is a sum of ASCII values of characters in the string.)

The Rabin–Karp algorithm could be used in a straightforward manner to compare two assignments for plagiarism by splitting files into smaller chunks and fingerprinting them. However, in MOSS, we are interested in a large group of submitted assignments and all potential instances of plagiarism. This means all-to-all comparisons and an impractical quadratic-time algorithm. To battle the quadratic time, MOSS selects a small number of fingerprints as representative of each file to be compared. The application builds an *inverted index*, a way to map the fingerprint to its position in

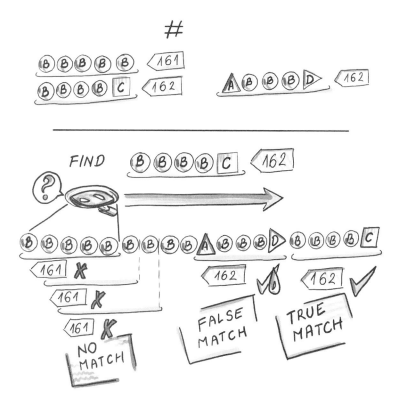

Figure 2.6   Example of a Rabin–Karp fingerprinting algorithm. We are looking for a pattern `p=BBBBC` in the larger string `t=BBBBBBBBBABBBDBBBBC`. The hash `BBBBC` is equal to **162** and is a mismatch for the hash `161` of `BBBBB` that occurs at the beginning of the long string. As we shift right, we repeatedly encounter hash mismatches until the substring `ABBBD`, with the hash of `162`. Then we check the substrings and establish a false match. At the very end of the string, we again encounter the hash match at `BBBBC`, and upon checking the substrings, we report a true match.

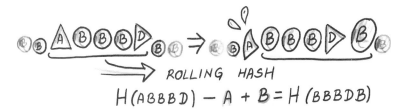

$$H(ABBBD) - A + B = H(BBBDB)$$

Figure 2.7   Rolling hash. Computing the hash for all but the first substring of *t* is a constant-time operation. For example, for `BBBDB`, we needed to "subtract" A and "add" B to `ABBBD`.

the documents where it occurs. From this mapping, we can further compute a list of similar documents. Note that the list will only have documents that have matches, so we are avoiding the blind all-to-all comparison.

There are many different techniques for how to choose the set of representative fingerprints for a document. The one MOSS employs is having each *window* of consecutive characters in a file (e.g., a window can be 50 characters in length) select a minimum hash of the *k*-grams belonging to that window. Having one fingerprint per window is helpful because it helps us avoid missing large consecutive matches, among other things.

2.4   *O(1)—What's the big deal?*

After seeing some use cases of hashing, let's peel another layer of the onion for dictionaries. Now that you've read about all the tradeoffs between different aspects of performance in section 2.2, you might be asking yourself why it is so hard to design a perfect data structure—one that does lookups, inserts, and deletes all in $O(1)$ in the worst case. And, more specifically, you may want to know if we can design a hash table that can guarantee constant-time operations. It's the "Why can't we just have it all?" question of the data structures. While in general this is not possible, there are special situations that enable it.

For example, let's say you have a set of data; to make it simple, let's say you have a set of 100 numbers and an equally sized hash table. Because you have a static dataset, you could conjure a custom hash function that would make sure each item goes to a different bucket of the hash table, a hash function customized to this particular dataset. This would enable the perfect performance.

Another such scenario is if you have a set of numbers that are positive integers and you know what the maximum is (call it M). If M is not too large, we can design a hash table of size M and have each number go to the bucket numbered by its value. Again, provided there are no duplicates, we get one element per bucket, resulting in constant-time performance on inserts, lookups, and deletes.

But these are special situations, and, generally speaking, knowing our data beforehand or having a very specific sort of input is more than we can expect most of the time.

The main challenge of hashing well is that hash functions need to provide a mapping of every potential item to a corresponding hash table bucket. The set that represents all potential items, regardless of the type of data we are dealing with, is likely extremely large, much larger than the size of our actual dataset and, consequently, the number of hash table buckets. We will refer to this set of all potential items as the universe U, the size of our dataset as n, and the hash table size as m.

The values of n and m are roughly proportional. In other words, if you have 1 million elements to store, you would probably want to plan to have a hash table similar in size. Depending on what hash table design we want to use, we might use 0.5 million buckets, or 2 million buckets, or something else; either way, we need a constant factor close to n. But both of those values are considerably smaller than U. This is why the hash function that maps the elements of U to m buckets will inevitably end up with a fairly large subset of U mapping to the same bucket of the hash table. Even if the hash function perfectly evenly distributes the items from the universe, there is at least one bucket to which at least $|U|/m$ items get mapped. We do not know what items will be contained in our dataset, and if $|U|/m \geq n$, it is feasible that all items in our dataset hash to the same bucket. It is not very likely that we will get such a dataset, but it is possible.

For example, consider the universe of all potential phone numbers of the format *ddd-dd-ddd-dddd*, where d is a digit zero–nine. Because each of the 12 digits can take on 10 different values, this means that $|U| = 10^{12}$, and if $n = 10^5$ (the dataset size) and $m = 10^6$ (the size of the table), even if the hash function perfectly distributes items from the universe, we can still end up with all the items in one bucket. Consider the case of perfectly even distribution of the universe into buckets; then each bucket has $10^{12}/10^6 = 10^6$ elements assigned to it. Because our dataset size is smaller than 10^6, it is possible to find such a dataset where all elements go to the same bucket. It would also be bad if some constant fraction of our dataset (i.e., one-half or one-third) went into the same bucket.

The fact that this is possible should not discourage us. In most practical applications, even simple hash functions are good enough for this to very rarely happen, but collisions will happen in common cases, and we need to know how to deal with them.

2.5   *Collision resolution: Theory vs. practice*

We will devote this section to two common collision-resolution mechanisms: linear probing and chaining. There are many others, but we will cover these two, as they are the most popular choices in the hash tables running underneath your code. As you probably know, *chaining* associates with each bucket of the hash table of an additional data structure (e.g., a linked list or a binary search tree), where the items hashed to the corresponding bucket get stored. New items get inserted up front ($O(1)$), but search and delete require advancing through the pointers of the appropriate list, the operation whose runtime is highly dependent on how evenly items are distributed across the buckets. To refresh your memory on how chaining works, see figure 2.8.

Linear probing is a particular instance of *open addressing*, a hashing scheme where we store items inside the actual hash table slots. In linear probing, to insert an item, we hash it to a corresponding bucket, and if the slot determined by the bucket is empty, we store the item into it. If it is occupied, we look for the first available position by scanning downward in the table and wrapping around the end of the table, if needed. An alternative variant of open addressing, quadratic probing, advances in quadratic-sized steps when looking for the next position to insert.

The search in linear probing, just like the insert, begins from the position of the slot determined by the bucket we hashed to, and we scan downward until we either find the element searched for or encounter an empty slot. Deletion is a bit more

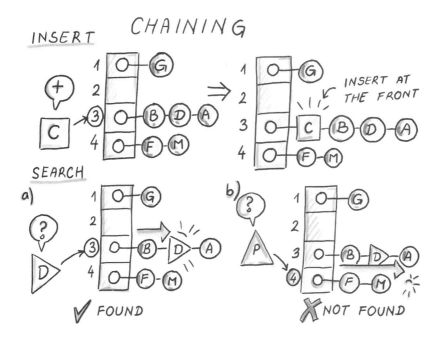

Figure 2.8   An example of insert and search with chaining

involved, as it cannot simply remove an item from its slot—it might break a chain, which would lead to an incorrect result of a future search. There are many ways to address this; a simple way is placing a tombstone flag at the position of the deleted element. See figure 2.9 for an example of linear probing.

First let's see what theory tells us about pros and cons of these two collision-resolution techniques. Theoretically speaking, in studying hash functions and collision-resolution techniques, computer scientists will often use the assumption of hash functions being ideally random. This allows us to analyze the process of hashing using probability and the analogy of throwing n balls into n bins uniformly and randomly.

With high probability, the fullest bin will have $O(\log n/\log \log n)$ balls (http://mng.bz/QWjm); hence the longest chain in the chaining method is no longer than $O(\log n/\log \log n)$, giving an upper bound on the lookup and delete performance.

The high-probability bounds are stronger than the expectation bounds we discussed earlier. The expression "with high probability" means that, if our input is of size n, then the high-probability event happens with the probability of at least $1 - 1/n^c$, where $c \leq 1$ is some constant. In our case, the high probability event will be a chain or a consecutive run in a hash table with an upper logarithmic limit on its size. In other words, we are upper bounding the probability of the chain/run growing longer than logarithmic length. So, the higher the constant and the input size, the less likely it is that the high-probability event will not occur, but at $c = 1$, we're already good.

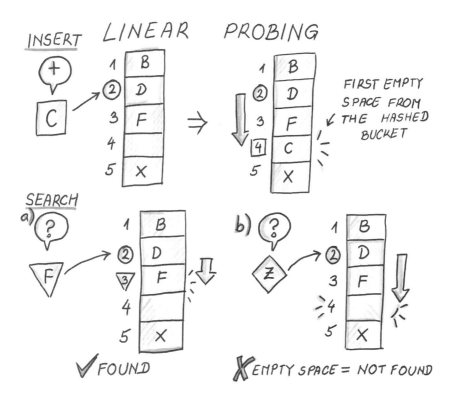

Figure 2.9 An example of insert and search with linear probing

What this means, practically, is that many other failures will happen before the high-probability event fails us.

The logarithmic lookup time is not bad, but if all lookups were like this, then the hash table would not offer significant advantages over, say, a binary search tree. In most cases, though, we expect a lookup to be a constant (assuming the number of items is proportional to the number of buckets in the chaining table).

Using pairwise independent hashing, one can show that the worst-case lookups in linear probing are close to $O(\log n)$ [4]. Families of k-wise independent hash functions are the closest we have gotten to mimicking the random behavior well thus far. At runtime, one of the hash functions from the family is selected uniformly and randomly to be used throughout the program. This protects us from the adversary who can see our code: by choosing one among many hash functions randomly at runtime, we make it harder to produce a pathological dataset, and even if it happens, it will not be our fault. Decisions like this can also affect the security of our application.

It makes intuitive sense that the worst-case lookup cost in linear probing is slightly higher than that of chaining, as the elements hashing to different buckets can contribute to the length of the same linear probing run. But does the fancy theory translate into real-world performance differences?

We are, in fact, missing an important detail. The linear probing runs are laid out sequentially in memory, and most runs are shorter than a single cache line, which has to be fetched anyway, no matter the length of the run. The same cannot be said about the elements of the chaining list, for which the memory is allocated in a nonsequential fashion. Hence, chaining might need more access to memory, which significantly impacts the actual runtime. A similar case is with another clever collision-resolution technique called *cuckoo hashing* that promises that an item contained in the table will be found in one of the two locations determined by two hash functions, deeming the lookup cost constant in the worst case. However, the probes are often in very different areas of the table, so we might need two memory points of access.

Considering the gap in the amount of time required to access memory versus CPU that we discussed in chapter 1, it makes sense that linear probing is often the collision-resolution method of choice in many practical implementations. Next, we explore an example of a modern programming language implementing its key-value dictionary with hash tables.

2.6   *Usage scenario: How Python's dict does it*

Key-value dictionaries are ubiquitous across different languages. For standard libraries of C++ and Java, for example, they are implemented as map, unordered_map (C++), and HashMap (Java); map is a red-black tree that keeps items ordered, and unordered_map and HashMap are unordered and are running hash tables underneath. Both use chaining for collision resolution. In Python, the key-value dictionary is dict. Here is a simple example of how to create, modify, and access keys and values in dict:

```
d = {'turmeric': 7, 'cardamom': 5, 'oregano': 12}
print(d.keys())
print(d.values())
print(d.items())
d.update({'saffron': 11})
print(d.items())
```

The output is as follows:

```
dict_keys(['turmeric', 'cardamom', 'oregano'])
dict_values([7, 5, 12])
dict_items([('turmeric', 7), ('cardamom', 5), ('oregano', 12)])
dict_items([('turmeric', 7), ('cardamom', 5), ('oregano', 12), ('saffron', 11)])
```

The authors of Python's default implementation, CPython, explain in its documentation [5] how dict is implemented (here, we focus only on the case when keys are integers): for the table size $m = 2^i$, the hash function is $h(x) = x \bmod 2^i$ (i.e., the bucket number is determined by the last i bits of the binary representation of x.) This works well in a number of common cases, such as the sequence of consecutive numbers, where it does not create collisions; it is also easy to find cases where it works extremely poorly, such as a set of all numbers with identical last i bits. Moreover, if used in combination with linear probing, this hash function can lead to clustering and long runs of consecutive items. To avoid long runs, Python employs the following probing mechanism

```
j = ((5*j) + 1) mod 2**i
```

where j is the index of a bucket where we will attempt to insert next. If the slot is taken, we will repeat the process using the new j. This sequence makes sure that all m buckets in the hash table are visited over time, and it makes sufficient skips to avoid clustering in the common case. To make sure higher bits of the key are used in hashing, the variable perturb that is originally initialized to the $h(x)$ and a constant PERTURB_SHIFT set to 5 is used:

```
perturb >>= PERTURB_SHIFT
j = (5*j) + 1 + perturb
```

⟵ **j % 2^i is the next bucket we will attempt.**

If the insertions match our $(5 * j) + 1$ pattern, then we are in trouble, but Python, and most practical implementations of hash tables, focus on what seems to be a very important practical algorithm design principle: making the common case simple and fast and not worrying about an occasional glitch when a rare bad case occurs.

2.7 *MurmurHash*

In this book, we are interested in fast, good, and simple hash functions. To that end, we make a brief mention of MurmurHash, which was invented by Austin Appleby and is a fast noncryptographic hash function employed by many implementations of the data structures we introduce in our future chapters. The name *Murmur* comes from the basic operations multiply and rotate that are used to mince the keys. One Python wrapper for MurmurHash is mmh3 (https://pypi.org/project/mmh3/), which we can install in the console using

```
pip install mmh3
```

The package mmh3 gives a number of ways to do hashing. A basic hash function gives a way to produce signed and unsigned 32-bit integers with different seeds

```
import mmh3
print(mmh3.hash("Hello"))
print(mmh3.hash(key = "Hello", seed = 5, signed = True))
print(mmh3.hash(key = "Hello", seed = 20, signed = True))
print(mmh3.hash(key = "Hello", seed = 20, signed = False))
```

which produces a different hash for different choices of seed and signed parameters:

```
316307400
-196410714
-1705059936
2589907360
```

To produce 64-bit and 128-bit hashes, we use `hash64` and `hash128` functions, where `hash64` uses the 128-bit hash function and produces a pair of 64-bit signed or unsigned hashes. Both 64-bit and 128-bit hash functions allow us to specify the architecture (x64 or x86) in order to optimize the function on the given architecture

```
print(mmh3.hash64("Hello"))
print(mmh3.hash64(key = "Hello", seed = 0, x64arch= True, signed = True))
print(mmh3.hash64(key = "Hello", seed = 0, x64arch= False, signed = True))
print(mmh3.hash128("Hello"))
```

which produces the following (pairs of) hashes:

```
(3871253994707141660, -6917270852172884668)
(3871253994707141660, -6917270852172884668)
(6801340086884544070, -5961160668294564876)
212681241822374483350353521234914329628
```

2.8 Hash tables for distributed systems: Consistent hashing

The first time consistent hashing was spotlighted was in the context of web caching [6]. Caches are fundamental in computer science and have improved systems across many domains. On the web, for example, caches relieve the hotspots that occur when many clients request the same webpage from a server. Servers host webpages, clients request them via browsers, and caches sit in between and host copies of frequently accessed webpages. In most situations, caches are able to satisfy the request faster than the home servers and distribute the load between themselves so that no cache is overwhelmed. Once a cache miss occurs (i.e., the webpage is not found in the cache), the cache fetches the website from the originating server. An important problem to solve in this setup is assigning web pages (in future text, `resources`) to caches (in future text, `nodes`), considering the following constraints:

- The mapping from a resource to a node should be fast and easy. The client and the server should be able to quickly compute the node responsible for a given resource.
- The resource load among different nodes should be fairly equal in order to avoid the hotspots.
- The mapping should be flexible in the face of frequent node arrivals and departures. As soon as the node leaves (i.e., a spontaneous failure occurs), its resources should be efficiently reassigned to other node(s), and when a new node is added, it should receive an equal portion of the total network load. All this should happen seamlessly, without too many other nodes/resources being affected.

2.8.1 A typical hashing problem

From the first two requirements, it looks like we have a hashing problem on our hands: nodes are the buckets to which resources get hashed, and a good hash function can ensure a fair load balance. Holding a hash table can help us figure out which node holds which resource. So, when a query occurs, we hash the resource and see what bucket (node) should contain it (figure 2.10, left). This would be fine if we were not in a highly dynamic distributed environment, where nodes join and leave (fail) all the time (figure 2.10, right.) The challenge lies in satisfying the requirement: how to reassign nodes' resources when they leave the network, or how to assign some resources to a newly arriving node, keeping in mind that load balance remains fairly equal, and without disturbing the network too much.

Figure 2.10 Using a hash table, we can map resources to nodes and help locate the appropriate node for a queried resource (left). The problem arises when nodes join/leave the network (right.)

As we know, classical hash tables can be resized by rehashing using a new hash function with a different range and copying the items over to a new table. This is a very expensive operation, and it typically pays off because it is only done once in a while and is amortized against a large number of inexpensive operations. For our dynamic web caching scenario, where node arrivals and departures happen constantly, changing resource-to-node mappings every time a minor change to the network occurs is highly impractical (figure 2.11).

In the following sections, we will show how consistent hashing helps satisfy all three requirements of our problem. We begin by introducing the concept of a hashring.

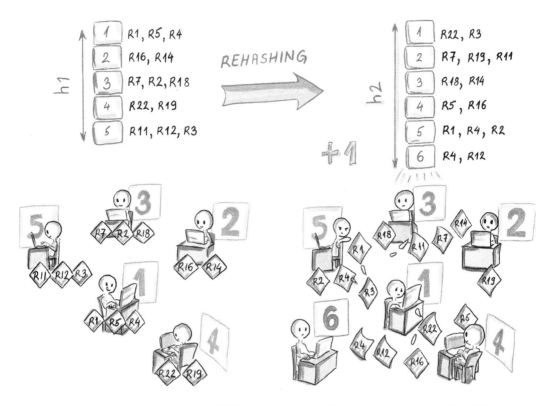

Figure 2.11 Rehashing is not feasible in a highly dynamic context because one node join/failure triggers reassignment of all resource-node allocations. In this example, changing the hash table size from 5 to 6 changed node allocations for most resources. The bottom right illustration shows the "in-between" moment when nodes hold some out-of-date and some new resources.

2.8.2   Hashring

The main idea of consistent hashing is to hash *both* resources and nodes to a fixed range $R = [0, 2^k - 1]$. It is helpful to visually imagine R spread out around a circle, with the northmost point being 0 and the rest of the range spread out clockwise in increasing order uniformly around the circle. We call this circle the *hashring*.

Each resource and node have a position on the hashring defined by their hashes. Given this setup, each resource is assigned to the first node encountered clockwise on the hashring. A good hash function should ensure that each node receives a fairly equal load of resources. See an example in figure 2.12.

To illustrate how consistent hashing works, along with node arrivals and departures, we show a simple Python implementation of the class HashRing step by step. Our implementation, shown in a sequence of small snippets, is only a simulation of the algorithm (the actual implementation of consistent hashing involves network calls

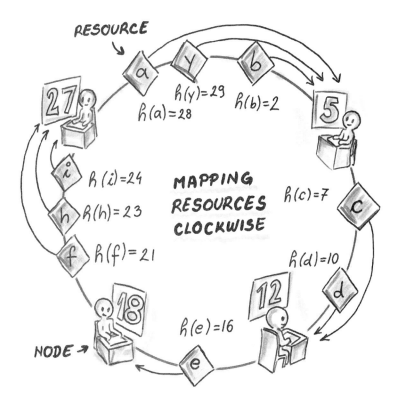

Figure 2.12 Mapping resources to nodes in the hashring. The example shows the hashring R = [0,31] and nodes whose hashes are 5, 12, 18, and 27. Resources a, y, and b are assigned to node 5, c and d are assigned to node 12, e is assigned to node 18, and f, h, and i are assigned to node 27.

between nodes, etc.). HashRing is implemented using a circular doubly linked list of nodes where each node stores its resources in a local dictionary:

```
class Node:
    def __init__(self, hashValue):
        self.hashValue = hashValue
        self.resources = {}
        self.next = None
        self.previous = None

class HashRing:
    def __init__(self, k):
        self.head = None
        self.k = k
        self.min = 0
        self.max = 2**k - 1
```

The constructor of the HashRing class uses the parameter k, which initializes the range to $[0, 2^k - 1]$. The Node class has an attribute hashValue that denotes its position on the ring and a dictionary `resources` that holds its resources. The rest of the code is highly reminiscent of a typical, circular, doubly linked list implementation.

The first basic method describes the legal range of resource and node hash values that we allow on the hashring:

```
def legalRange(self, hashValue):
    return self.min <= hashValue <= self.max
```

To assign the resources to their closest nodes, we define the notion of closest on the hashring using the following `distance` method:

```
def distance(self, a, b):
    if a == b:
        return 0
    elif a < b:
        return b - a
    else:
        return (2**self.k) + (b - a)
```

For example, if we initialize an empty hashring with k=5

```
hr = HashRing(5)
print(hr.distance(29,5))
print(hr.distance(29,12))
print(hr.distance(5,29))
```

we obtain the following output:

```
8
15
24
```

The ring distance from resource 29 to node 5 is 8, shorter than the distance from 29 to 12 (and, in fact, shorter than to any other node from our example from figure 2.6, which makes node 5 the assigned node of resource 29). Keep in mind that the order of arguments in this function matters.

2.8.3 Lookup

The first functionality to implement with respect to `HashRing` is the lookup of the appropriate node given a hash value of the resource. We march along the hashring, starting from the first node (with the smallest hash value) and following the forward links as long as the current and the next node are on the same side of the resource. The loop condition is broken when we are about to skip over the resource; that is, the current node precedes the resource, and the next node comes immediately after the resource, and that is the node we need to return. If the resource is present, then that is the node containing the resource. This functionality is contained in the look-upNode method:

```
def lookupNode(self, hashValue):
    if self.legalRange(hashValue):
        temp = self.head
        if temp is None:
            return None
        else:
            while(self.distance(temp.hashValue, hashValue) >
        self.distance(temp.next.hashValue, hashValue)):
                temp = temp.next
            if temp.hashValue == hashValue:
                return temp
            return temp.next
```

In this implementation, we assume no hash collisions: no two distinct nodes (and no two distinct resources) will have the same hash value. However, it can happen that a resource and a node land on the same position on the hashring, in which case the resource with hash value i is assigned to node i.

2.8.4   Adding a new node/resource

When a new node A is added to the hashring, some of the resources previously belonging to what is now A's successor might need to be reassigned to A. These are the resources that now have a smaller distance to A than to their previously assigned node (i.e., A is on their clockwise path to their currently assigned node). See figure 2.13 for an example of inserting a node with a hash value of 30.

Notice that this manner of adding a node is congruent with the last constraint from the beginning of the section: when a new node is added, only resources of one other node have potentially changed their mappings, and all other mappings remain untouched.

First, let's see how the functionality of moving resources is implemented in a helper method, moveResources, that will also be used later for node deletions:

```
def moveResources(self, dest, orig, deleteTrue):          ◁    Move some resources
    delete_list = []                                            from orig to dest.
    for i, j in orig.resources.items():
        if (self.distance(i, dest.hashValue) < self.distance(i, orig.hashValue)
    or deleteTrue):
            dest.resources[i] = j
            delete_list.append(i)
            print("\tMoving a resource " + str(i) + " from " +
        str(orig.hashValue) + " to " + str(dest.hashValue))
    for i in delete_list:              ◁
        del orig.resources[i]               Delete the reassigned
                                            resources from orig.
```

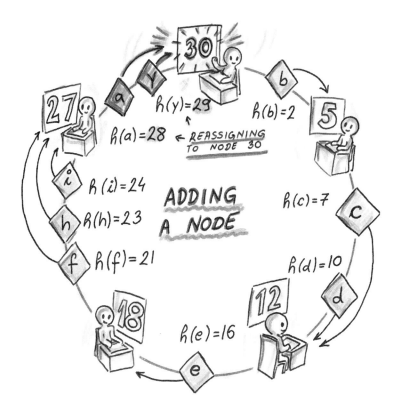

Figure 2.13   New node arrival. The resources a and y, with respective hash values 28 and 29, are now being reassigned to the newly inserted node with the hash value 30.

Special cases for node addition are involved when the newly added node becomes the head node or when the existing list is empty. For the common case, we use the lookup function from earlier to locate the correct place for a new node and then do the needed rewiring of the hashring:

```
def addNode(self, hashValue):
    if self.legalRange(hashValue):
        newNode = Node(hashValue)
        if self.head is None:                    Empty
            newNode.next = newNode            ⟵   hashring
            newNode.previous = newNode
            self.head = newNode
            print("Adding a head node " + str(newNode.hashValue) + "...")
        else:
            temp = self.lookupNode(hashValue)    ⟵——— Successor
            newNode.next = temp
            newNode.previous = temp.previous
            newNode.previous.next = newNode
            newNode.next.previous = newNode
```

```
        print("Adding a node " + str(newNode.hashValue) +
        ". Its prev is " + str(newNode.previous.hashValue) +
        ", and its next is " + str(newNode.next.hashValue) + ".")
        self.moveResources(newNode, newNode.next, False)
        if hashValue < self.head.hashValue:
            self.head = newNode
```

Changes the
head pointer

Now that we know how to add nodes, we can also add some resources. To add a new resource, we naturally employ the `lookupNode` method and update the `resources` dictionary of the appropriate node with the new resource. To add a new resource, we have to have at least one node on the hashring:

```
def addResource(self, hashValueResource):
    if self.legalRange(hashValueResource):
        print("Adding a resource " + str(hashValueResource) + "...")
        targetNode = self.lookupNode(hashValueResource)
        if targetNode is not None:
            value = "Dummy resource value of " + str(hashValueResource)
            targetNode.resources[hashValueResource] = value
        else:
            print("Can't add a resource to an empty hashring")
```

2.8.5   Removing a node

Removal of a node in the hashring works in the following manner: when node B leaves the hashring, which often corresponds to a spontaneous failure of a node, then the resources previously belonging to B should be assigned to what was B's successor on the hashring (see figure 2.14). Again, only a small fraction of resources are affected by this change.

   The implementation needs to take into account the cases of empty and one-item hashrings and attempt to remove a nonexistent node or remove the head item where the head pointer needs to be amended:

```
def removeNode(self, hashValue):
    temp = self.lookupNode(hashValue)
    if temp.hashValue == hashValue:
        print("Removing the node " + str(hashValue) + ": ")
        self.moveResources(temp.next, temp, True)
        temp.previous.next = temp.next
        temp.next.previous = temp.previous
        if self.head.hashValue == hashValue:
            self.head = temp.next
            if self.head == self.head.next:
                self.head = None
        return temp.next
    else:
        print("Nothing to remove.")
```

Removes the
head item

If removing from
one-item hashring

No such
node

Lastly, in order to be able to show the contents of the hashring, we implement a simple print method that shows the current state of the hashring, with nodes printed out

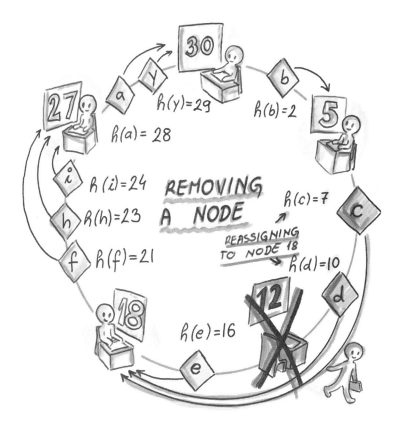

Figure 2.14 Node removal. In this example, the node with the hash value 12 leaves the network, and its resources c and d, with hash values 7 and 10, respectively, are reassigned to the node with the hash value 18, the previous successor of 12.

in increasing (clockwise) order, starting from the northmost point of the ring, along with each node's local resources stored in a local hash table:

```
def printHashRing(self):
    print("*****")
    print("Printing the hashring in clockwise order:")
    temp = self.head
    if self.head is None:
        print("Empty hashring")
    else:
        while(True):
            print("Node: " + str(temp.hashValue) + ", ", end=" ")

            print("Resources: ", end=" ")
            if not bool(temp.resources):
                print("Empty", end="")
            else:
                for i in temp.resources.keys():
                    print(str(i), end=" ")
```

```
                    temp = temp.next
                    print(" ")
                    if (temp == self.head):
                        break
        print("*****")
```

With all this functionality under our belt, we are now ready to show an example.

AN EXAMPLE

Let's start by running the process shown in figures 2.12 and 2.13. First, we add a number of nodes and resources in the arbitrary order and watch how resource reassignments take place as nodes 5, 27, and 30 get added. Note that any order of additions of nodes and resources (as long as the first object added is a node, not a resource) should result in the same hashring

```
hr = HashRing(5)
hr.addNode(12)
hr.addNode(18)
hr.addResource(24)
hr.addResource(21)
hr.addResource(16)
hr.addResource(23)
hr.addResource(2)
hr.addResource(29)
hr.addResource(28)
hr.addResource(7)
hr.addResource(10)
hr.printHashRing()
```

which gives us the following output:

```
Adding a head node 12...
Adding a node 18. Its prev is 12, and its next is 12.
Adding a resource 24...
Adding a resource 21...
Adding a resource 16...
Adding a resource 23...
Adding a resource 2...
Adding a resource 29...
Adding a resource 28...
Adding a resource 7...
Adding a resource 10...
*****
Printing the hashring in the clockwise order:
Node: 12, Resources:  24 21 23 2 29 28 7 10
Node: 18, Resources:  16
*****
```

Now we add two remaining nodes from figure 2.12 and see how resource reassignments take place:

```
hr.addNode(5)
hr.addNode(27)
```

```
hr.addNode(30)
hr.printHashRing()
```

The output is as follows:

```
Adding a node 5. Its prev is 18, and its next is 12.
    Moving a resource 24 from 12 to 5
    Moving a resource 21 from 12 to 5
    Moving a resource 23 from 12 to 5
    Moving a resource 2 from 12 to 5
    Moving a resource 29 from 12 to 5
    Moving a resource 28 from 12 to 5
Adding a node 27. Its prev is 18, and its next is 5.
    Moving a resource 24 from 5 to 27
    Moving a resource 21 from 5 to 27
    Moving a resource 23 from 5 to 27
Adding a node 30. Its prev is 27, and its next is 5.
    Moving a resource 29 from 5 to 30
    Moving a resource 28 from 5 to 30
*****
Printing the hashring in the clockwise order:
Node: 5, Resources:  2
Node: 12, Resources:  7 10
Node: 18, Resources:  16
Node: 27, Resources:  24 21 23
Node: 30, Resources:  29 28
*****
```

This output reflects the state of the hashring in figure 2.13. Now let's remove a node:

```
hr.removeNode(12)
hr.printHashRing()
```

The final hashring, as shown in figure 2.14, looks as follows:

```
Removing the node 12:
    Moving a resource 7 from 12 to 18
    Moving a resource 10 from 12 to 18
*****
Printing the hashring in the clockwise order:
Node: 5, Resources:  2
Node: 18, Resources:  16 7 10
Node: 27, Resources:  24 21 23
Node: 30, Resources:  29 28
*****
```

2.8.6   *Consistent hashing scenario: Chord*

Chord [7] is the distributed lookup protocol for peer-to-peer networks that uses consistent hashing. The scheme from Chord, aside from being used in a number of peer-to-peer networks, has also been repurposed for Amazon's Dynamo, a highly scalable data store that stores various core services of Amazon's e-commerce platform [8].

The simplistic linked-list protocol we implemented leaves a lot to be desired in terms of efficiency for a real production system. To route a request from a resource, we expect to follow a linear number of forward pointers, and each such pointer translates into a network call between two machines. The time required to route the call will not scale in big systems. Also, to route the request, each machine needs to maintain a copy of the hashring, thus consuming a nontrivial amount of local memory.

Chord improves on the basic algorithm by having each node store only the information on other $O(\log n)$ nodes. Each node x maintains a so-called *finger* table that stores the key-value mapping of points on the hashring at exponentially increasing distances from x (we call these *keys fingers*) to their successor nodes. This helps the lookup algorithm find the right node in a logarithmic number of steps.

Specifically, for the hashring with interval $R = [0, 2^k - 1]$, the finger table of a node x contains all fingers `f_i` such that `distance(x, f_i)` = 2^{i-1} for all $i \leq k$. The fingers' successors can be computed using the `lookupNode` method we implemented earlier. For an example, see figure 2.15 and the finger table for node x=5.

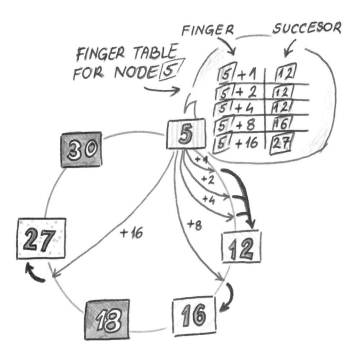

Figure 2.15   Example finger table for node 5 on the hashring where R = [0,31]. Node 5 has five entries stored in its finger table, for the successors of the points 5 + 1 = 6, 5 + 2 = 7, 5 + 4 = 9, 5 + 8 = 13, and 5 + 16 = 21. The respective successors are 12, 12, 12, 16, and 27.

How can we use finger tables to speed up the lookup? The lookup operation in this scheme works in such a way that, if the finger table of a node where the request originates does not contain the resource y, then the node forwards the request to the successor determined by the finger with the smallest distance to the resource. The example is shown in figure 2.16, with the lookup of the resource with hash value 29 starting at node 5.

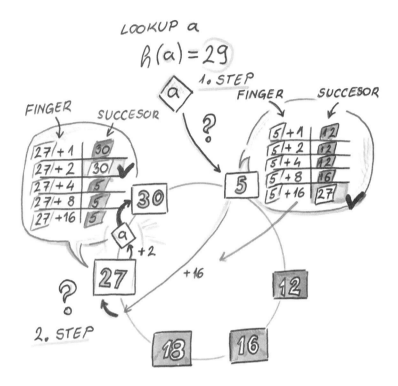

Figure 2.16   Lookup procedure with a finger tables. To locate resource 29 starting from node 5, we first follow the finger (21 = 5 + 16), as it is the finger with smallest distance to 29. Its successor is 27, so the request is forwarded to 27. In the finger table of node 27, we take the finger 2, which gives us exactly 29. Its successor is 30, where the request is finally routed (i.e., if the resource exists, it will be found at node 30).

Here are a couple of coding exercises to test your understanding of Chord and finger tables.

2.8.7   *Consistent hashing: Programming exercises*

EXERCISE 1

Given the code for HashRing class, add a new attribute fingerTable of type dict to the Node class definition. Now implement a buildFingerTables(self) method in the HashRing class that builds a finger table for each node in the hashring using the methods we already implemented. Along with the pair containing a finger and a successor, your finger table should also store the direct pointer to the given node (to allow direct access to the node from the finger table).

EXERCISE 2

Now that each node contains its own finger table, implement a more efficient lookup in a chordLookup(self,hashValue) method. Then create a large hashring with dozens of thousands of nodes and resources, and measure the average number of hops required by the new lookup method. Compare that to the naïve linear-time lookup we implemented.

EXERCISE 3

With node additions and removal, finger tables can become out of date and need to be rebuilt. Modify the implementation of HashRing such that finger tables always remain up-to-date.

Summary

- Hash tables are irreplaceable in modern systems, such as networks, databases, storage solutions, text-processing applications, and so on. Depending on an application and the workload, hash tables can be designed to suit different needs, such as speed versus space, simplicity versus optimizing the worst case, and so on.

- There are a large number of collision-resolution techniques, but the most frequently used ones are chaining and linear probing (section 2.5). Linear probing has benefits when it comes to cache efficiency. The bigger the hash table, the larger the effect of cache efficiency than the effect of the number of probes on the performance.

- Most production-quality hash tables, such as Python's dict (section 2.6), are about optimizing the common case and do not worry about solving rare pathological cases if they will complicate the common case.

- MurmurHash (section 2.7) is an example of a widely used fast and simple non-cryptographic hash function, often employed by hash-based data structures we will learn about in this book.

- Consistent hashing (section 2.8) solves the problem of hash tables that are distributed among many machines, as is the case in peer-to-peer environments. Consistent hashing has been implemented in many peer-to-peer products such as BitTorrent and also in data store systems such as Amazon's Dynamo.

Approximate membership: Bloom and quotient filters

3

Bloom filters have become a standard in systems that process large datasets. Their widespread use, especially in networks and distributed databases, comes from the effectiveness they exhibit in situations where we need a hash table functionality but do not have the luxury of space. They were invented in the 1970s by Burton Bloom [1], but they only really "bloomed" in the last few decades due to an increasing need to tame and compress big datasets. Bloom filters have also piqued the interest of the computer science research community, which developed many variants on top of the basic data structure in order to address some of the filters' shortcomings and adapt them to different contexts.

One simple way to think about Bloom filters is that they support insert and lookup in the same way that hash tables do, but using very little space (i.e., 1 byte per item or less). This is a significant savings when keys take up 4–8 bytes. Bloom filters do not store the items themselves, and they use less space than the lower theoretical limit required to store the data correctly; therefore, they exhibit an error rate. They have false positives, but they do not have false negatives, and the one-sidedness of the error can be used to our benefit. When the Bloom filter reports the item as Found/Present, there is a small chance it is not telling the truth, but when it reports the item as Not Found/Not Present, we know it's telling the truth. In situations where the query answer is expected to be Not Present most of the time, Bloom filters offer great accuracy plus space-saving benefits.

For instance, Bloom filters are used in Google's WebTable [2] and Apache Cassandra [3], which are among the most widely used distributed storage systems for handling massive data. Namely, these systems organize their data into a number of tables called *sorted string tables* (SSTs) that reside on disk and are structured as key-value maps (e.g., a key might be a URL, and a value might be website attributes or contents). WebTable and Cassandra simultaneously handle adding new content into tables and answering queries, and when a query arrives, it is important to locate the SST containing the queried content without explicitly querying each table. To that end, dedicated Bloom filters in RAM are maintained, one per SST, to route the query to the correct table.

In the example shown in figure 3.1, we are given 50 SSTs on disk and 50 associated Bloom filters in RAM. As soon as the Bloom filter reports Not Present on a lookup, the query is routed to the next Bloom filter. The first time a Bloom filter reports the item as Present (in this example, SST3's Bloom filter), we go to disk to check if the item is present in the table. In the case of a false alarm, we continue routing the query until a Bloom filter reports Present and the data is also found on disk and returned to the user, as with SST50.

Bloom filters are most useful when placed strategically in high-ingestion systems. For example, having an application perform an SSD/disk read/write can easily bring down the throughput of an application from hundreds of thousands of ops per second to only a couple of thousand or even a couple of hundred ops/sec. If we place a Bloom filter in RAM to serve the lookups instead, we can avoid this performance slump and maintain consistently high throughput across different components of an application. More details on how Bloom filters are integrated in the bigger picture of streaming systems will be given in chapter 6.

In this chapter, you will learn how Bloom filters work and when to use them, with various practical scenarios as examples. You will also learn how to configure the parameters of the Bloom filter for your particular application. There is an interesting interplay between the space (m), number of elements (n), number of hash functions (k), and the false positive rate (f). For readers who are more mathematically inclined, we will spend some time understanding where the formulas relating important Bloom filter parameters come from and whether one can do better than the Bloom filter.

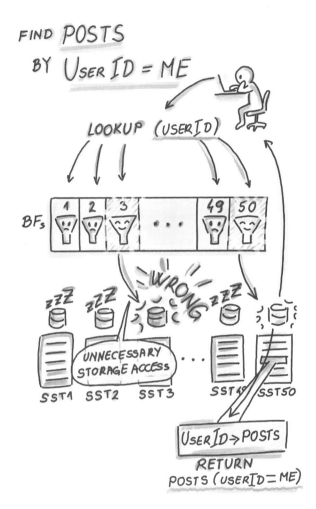

Figure 3.1   Bloom filters in distributed storage systems. In this example, we have 50 SSTs on disk, and each table has a dedicated Bloom filter that can fit into RAM due to its much smaller size. When a user does a lookup, the lookup first checks the Bloom filters, thus avoiding expensive disk seeks.

In section 3.7, we will explore a very different data structure that is functionally similar to Bloom filters. A *quotient filter* [4] is a compact hash table that offers space-saving benefits at the cost of false positives, but also offers other advantages. If you are confident in your knowledge of Bloom filters, skip to section 3.7.

3.1   *How it works*

Bloom filters have two main components:

- A bit array `A[0..m-1]`, with all slots initially set to 0
- k independent hash functions h_1, h_2, …, h_k, each mapping keys uniformly randomly onto a range $[0, m-1]$

3.1.1   *Insert*

To insert an item x into the Bloom filter, we first compute the k hash functions on x, and for each resulting hash, set the corresponding slot of A to 1 (see pseudocode and figure 3.2):

```
Bloom_insert(x):
    for i ← 1 to k
        A[h_i(x)] ← 1
```

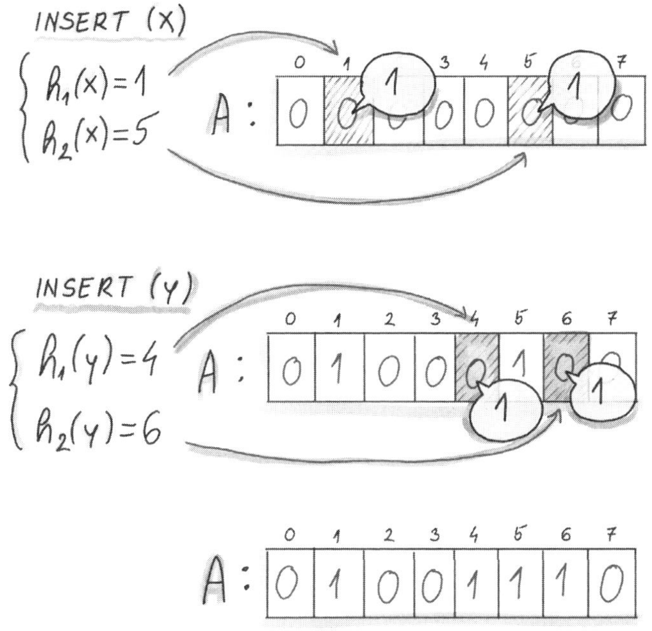

Figure 3.2   Example of an insert into a Bloom filter. In this example, an initially empty Bloom filter has m = 8 and k = 2 (two hash functions). To insert an element x, we first compute the two hashes on x, the first of which generates 1 and the second 5. We proceed to set A[1] and A[5] to 1. To insert y, we also compute the hashes and similarly set positions A[4] and A[6] to 1.

3.1.2   *Lookup*

Similar to insert, lookup computes k hash functions on x, and the first time one of the corresponding slots of A equals 0, the lookup reports the item as Not Present; otherwise it reports the item as Present:

```
Bloom_lookup(x):
    for i ← 1 to k
        if(A[h_i(x)] = 0)
            return NOT PRESENT
    return PRESENT
```

Figure 3.3 shows an example of a lookup on the resulting Bloom filter from figure 3.2 and how it can generate true positives (on element x that was actually inserted) and false positives (on element z that was never inserted).

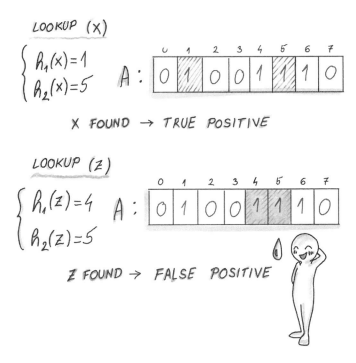

Figure 3.3 Example of a lookup on a Bloom filter. To do a lookup on *x*, we compute the hashes (which are the same as in the case of an insert), and we return `Found/Present`, as both bits in corresponding locations equal 1. Then we do a lookup of an element *z*, which we never inserted, and its hashes are respectively 4 and 5, and bits at locations `A[4]` and `A[5]` equal 1; thus, we again return `Found/Present`.

As seen in figure 3.3, false positives can occur when some other elements together set the bits of some other element to 1 (in this example, two previous items, x and y, have set z's bit locations to 1).

Asymptotically, the insert operation on the Bloom filter costs $O(k)$. Considering that the number of hash functions rarely goes above 12, this is a *constant-time operation*. The lookup might also need $O(k)$ in case the operation has to check all the bits, but most unsuccessful lookups will give up way before then; we will see that, on average, an unsuccessful lookup in a well-configured Bloom filter takes about one to two probes before giving up. This makes for an incredibly fast lookup operation.

3.2   Use cases

In the chapter introduction, we saw the application of Bloom filters to distributed storage systems. In this section, we will see more applications of Bloom filters to distributed networks: the Squid network proxy and the Bitcoin mobile app.

3.2.1   Bloom filters in networks: Squid

Squid is a web proxy cache. Web proxies use caches to reduce web traffic by maintaining a local copy of recently accessed links from which they can serve clients' requests for webpages, files, and so on. One of the protocols [5] suggests that each proxy also keeps a summary of the neighboring proxies' cache contents and checks the summaries before forwarding any queries to neighbor proxies. Squid implements this functionality using Bloom filters called *cache digests* (https://wiki.squid-cache.org/SquidFaq/AboutSquid) (see figure 3.4).

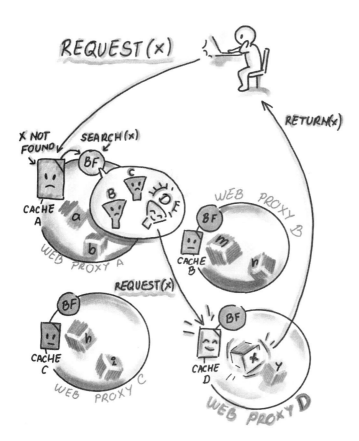

Figure 3.4   Bloom filter in Squid web proxy. A user requests a web page *x*, and a web proxy *A* cannot find it in its own cache, so it locally queries the Bloom filters of *B*, *C*, and *D*. The Bloom filter for *D* reports `Present`, so the request is forwarded to *D*. The resource is found at *D* and returned to the user.

Cache contents frequently go out of date, and Bloom filters are occasionally broadcasted between the neighbors. Because Bloom filters are not always up to date, false negatives can arise when a Bloom filter claims the element is present in a proxy but the proxy no longer contains the resource.

3.2.2 *Bitcoin mobile app*

Peer-to-peer networks use Bloom filters to communicate data, and a well-known example of this is Bitcoin. An important feature of Bitcoin is ensuring transparency between clients, which is ensured by having each node be aware of everyone's transactions. However, for nodes that are operating from a smartphone or a similar device of limited memory and bandwidth, keeping a copy of all transactions is highly impractical, so Bitcoin offers the option of *simplified payment verification* (SPV), where a node can choose to be a *light node* by advertising a list of transactions it is interested in. This is in contrast to full nodes that contain all the data (figure 3.5).

Figure 3.5   In Bitcoin, light clients can broadcast what transactions they are interested in and thereby block the deluge of updates from the network.

Light nodes compute and transmit a Bloom filter of the list of transactions they are interested in to the full nodes. This way, before a full node sends information about a transaction to the light node, it first checks its Bloom filter to see whether a node is interested in it. If a false positive occurs, the light node can discard the information upon its arrival [6].

More recently, Bitcoin has also offered other methods of transaction filtering with improved security and privacy properties.

3.3 A simple implementation

A basic Bloom filter is fairly straightforward to implement. We show a simple implementation that uses a Python wrapper for MurmurHash, mmh3, which we discussed in chapter 2. By setting k different seeds, we are able to obtain k different hash functions. The implementation also uses bitarray, a library that allows space-efficient encoding of the filter you need to install to run the code:

```python
import math
import mmh3
from bitarray import bitarray

class BloomFilter:
    def __init__(self, n, f):           # Provide the number of elements and the desired false positive rate.
        self.n = n
        self.f = f
        self.m = self.calculateM()
        self.k = self.calculateK()

        self.bit_array = bitarray(self.m)
        self.bit_array.setall(0)
        self.printParameters()

    def calculateM(self):
        return int(-math.log(self.f)*self.n/(math.log(2)**2))

    def calculateK(self):
        return int(self.m*math.log(2)/self.n)

    def printParameters(self):
        print("Init parameters:")
        print(f"n = {self.n}, f = {self.f}, m = {self.m}, k = {self.k}")

    def insert(self, item):
        for i in range(self.k):
            index = mmh3.hash(item, i) % self.m
            self.bit_array[index] = 1

    def lookup(self, item):
        for i in range(self.k):
            index = mmh3.hash(item, i) % self.m
            if self.bit_array[index] == 0:
                return False

        return True
```

You can try out the implementation by inserting a couple of items of type string:

```python
bf = BloomFilter(10, 0.01)
bf.insert("1")
bf.insert("2")
bf.insert("42")
print("1 {}".format(bf.lookup("1")))
print("2 {}".format(bf.lookup("2")))
print("3 {}".format(bf.lookup("3")))
```

```
print("42 {}".format(bf.lookup("42")))
print("43 {}".format(bf.lookup("43")))
```

The constructor of this sample implementation lets the user set the maximum number of elements (n) and the desired false positive rate (f), while the constructor does the job of setting two other parameters (m and k). This is a common choice, as we often know how large of a dataset we're dealing with and how high of a false positive rate we are willing to admit. To understand how the remaining parameters are set in this implementation and how to configure a Bloom filter to get the most bang for your buck, read on.

3.4   Configuring a Bloom filter

First, we outline main formulas relating important parameters of the Bloom filter. We use the following notation for the four parameters of the Bloom filter:

- n = number of elements to insert
- f = the false positive rate
- m = number of bits in a Bloom filter
- k = number of hash functions

The formula that determines the false positive rate as a function of the other three parameters is as follows (equation 3.1):

$$f \approx \left(1 - e^{-\frac{nk}{m}}\right)^k \qquad \text{(Equation 3.1)}$$

If you would like to understand how this formula is derived, there are more details in section 3.5. Right now, we are more interested in visually reasoning about this formula.

Figure 3.6 shows the plot of f as a function of k for different choices of m/n (bits per element). In many real-life applications, fixing the bits-per-element ratio is meaningful. Common values for the bits-per-element ratio are between 6 and 14, and such ratios allow us fairly low false positive rates, as shown in figure 3.6.

Starting from the top to the bottom curve, we have 6, 8, 10, 12, and 14, respectively, as choices for the bit-per-element ratio. As the ratio increases, the false positive rate drops, given the same number of hash functions. Also, the curves show the trend that increasing k up until some point (going from left to right), for a fixed m/n reduces the error, but after some point, increasing k increases the error. This two-fold effect occurs because having more hash functions allows a lookup more chances to find a 0, but sets more bits to 1 during an insert. Thus, the shape of the curves indicates that it is better to err on the larger side.

The curves are fairly smooth, and when $m/n = 8$ (i.e., we are willing to spend 1 byte per element), for example, if we use anywhere between 4 and 8 hash functions, the false positive rate will not go above 3%, even though the optimal choice of k is between 5 and 6.

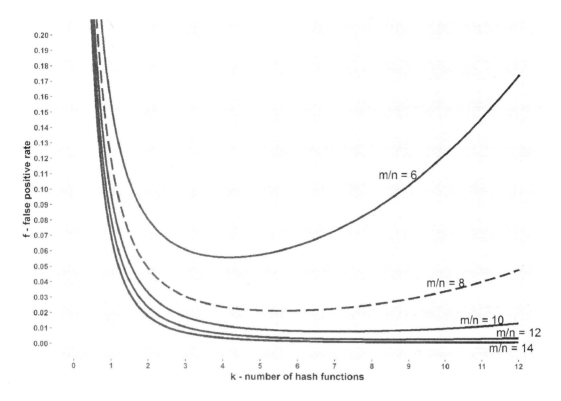

Figure 3.6   The plot relating the number of hash functions (k) and the false positive rate (f) in a Bloom filter. The graph shows the false positive rate for a fixed bits-per-element ratio (m/n), different curves corresponding to different ratios.

The minimum false positive rate for each curve gives us the optimal k for a particular bits-per-element ratio (which we get by doing a derivative on equation 3.1 with respect to k; see equation 3.2):

$$k_{opt} = \frac{m}{n}\ln 2 \qquad\qquad \textbf{(Equation 3.2)}$$

For example, when $m/n = 8$, $k_{opt} = 5.545$. We can use this formula to optimally config-ure the Bloom filter, and an interesting consequence of choosing parameters this way is that in such a Bloom filter, the false positive rate is (equation 3.3.)

$$f_{opt} = \left(\frac{1}{2}\right)^{k} \qquad\qquad \textbf{(Equation 3.3)}$$

Equation 3.3 is obtained by plugging equation 3.2 into equation 3.1. The constructor in our implementation takes in n and f and uses them to compute m and k, using equations 3.2 and 3.3, while making sure that k and m have to be integers. If equation

3.2 produces a noninteger, and we need to round up or down, then equation 3.3 is no longer an absolutely exact false positive rate. The only correct formula to plug into, to obtain the exact false positive rate, is equation 3.1, but even with equation 3.3, the difference produced by rounding up or down is minor. Often, it is better to choose the smaller of the two possible values of k to reduce the amount of computation.

One might find the expression $(1/2)^k$ in equation 3.3 interesting in connection with the fact that a false positive occurs when a lookup encounters k 1s in a row. Indeed, an optimally filled Bloom filter has about a 50% probability that a random bit is 1. This is another way of saying that if your Bloom filter has too many 0s or 1s, the chances are that it is not well configured.

There are different ways to write constructors for the Bloom filter depending on what initial parameters have been provided. Usually, k is a synthetic parameter that is calculated from other, more organic requirements, such as space, number of elements, and the false positive rate. Either way, if you ever have to write different Bloom filter constructors, here are a couple of examples that show how to compute the remaining parameters.

Example 1: Calculating f from m, n, and k

You are trying to analyze the false positive rate of an already existing Bloom filter that was initially built to store 10^6 elements but ended up storing 10 times more. The Bloom filter has been giving very poor performance, and we are interested in its false positive rate. The filter capacity is 3 MB, and it uses two hash functions.

ANSWER

Using equation 3.1, we obtain the following:

$$f = \left(1 - e^{-\frac{nk}{m}}\right)^k = \left(1 - e^{-\frac{2 \times 10^7}{3 \times 8 \times 10^6}}\right)^2 = \left(1 - \left(\frac{1}{e}\right)^{\frac{5}{6}}\right)^2 \approx 32\%$$

Example 2: Calculating f and k from n and m

Say that you wish to build a Bloom filter for $n = 10^6$ elements, and you have about 1 MB available for it ($m = 8 * 10^6$ bits). Find the optimal false positive rate and determine the number of hash functions.

ANSWER

From equation 3.2, the ideal number of hash functions should be $k = \ln2 * 8 * 10^6 / 10^6 = 5.544$. Equation 3.3 tells us that the false positive rate is $f \approx (1/2)^{5.544} \approx 0.0214$, but we need a legal value of k. In this situation, we might choose $k = 5$ or $k = 6$. In both cases, we will still obtain a 2% false positive rate.

3.4.1   *Playing with Bloom filters: Mini experiments*

Now that we have a basic understanding of how Bloom filters work, here are a couple of mini experiments to take our understanding to the next level.

EXERCISE 1

Use the provided Python implementation to create a Bloom filter where $n = 10^7$ and $f = 0.02$. For elements, use uniform random integers (without repetition) from the range $= [0,10^{12}]$ and convert them into strings (insert them as strings). Save the inserted elements into a separate file.

Perform 10^6 lookups that are uniformly randomly selected elements from U. Keep track of the false positive rate and verify whether it is ~2%. Measure the time required to perform the lookups. Make sure not to include the time required for the random number generation involving selecting the keys in your measurements.

Now perform 10^6 successful lookups by uniformly randomly (without repetition) choosing from the file of inserted elements, and measure the time required to perform the lookups. Make sure you do not include the time required to read from the file or generate random numbers. What takes more time—uniform random lookups or successful lookups?

EXERCISE 2

Using the provided implementation, create a Bloom filter such as the one in Example 2. Now create two other filters, one in which the dataset is 100 times larger than the original one, and another one in which the dataset is 100 times smaller, leaving the same false positive rate. What do you notice about the size of the filter as the dataset size changes?

EXERCISE 3

In some literature, a variant of a Bloom filter is described where different hash functions have the "jurisdiction" over different parts of the Bloom filter. In other words, k hash functions split the Bloom filter into k equal-sized consecutive chunks of m/k bits, and during an insert, the ith hash function sets bits in the ith chunk. Implement this variant of the Bloom filter and check if and how this change might affect the false positive rate in comparison to the original Bloom filter.

Next, we give some instruction on how the formula for the false positive rate of the Bloom filter is derived, and how lower bounds for the space-error tradeoff in data structures work.

The next section is theoretical and intended for mathematically inclined readers. If you are more practically inclined, feel free to skip to section 3.6.

3.5   *A bit of theory*

First, let's see where the main formula for the Bloom filter false positive rate (equation 3.1) comes from. For this analysis, we assume that hash functions are independent (the results of one hash function do not affect the results of any other hash function) and that each hash function maps keys uniformly randomly over the range $[0 \ldots m-1]$.

If t is the fraction of bits in the Bloom filter that are still 0 after all n inserts took place, and k is the number of hash functions, then the probability f of a false positive is

$$f = (1-t)^k$$

because we need to get k 1s in order to report `Present`. Obtaining k 1s can also be a result of a successful lookup of an actually inserted element; however, if we consider queries to be uniformly randomly selected from a universe much larger than the dataset, then the probability of a true positive is a negligible fraction of this quantity.

The value of t is impossible to know before all inserts take place because it depends on the outcome of hashing, but we can work with *probability* p of a bit being equal to 0 after all inserts took place (i.e., $p = \Pr$; a fixed bit equals 0 after n inserts).

The value of p will, in the probabilistic sense, translate to the percentage of 0s in the filter (t). We derive the value of p to be equal to the following expression:

$$p = \left(1 - \frac{1}{m}\right)^{nk} \approx e^{-\frac{nk}{m}}$$

To understand why this is true, let's start from the empty Bloom filter. Right after the first hash function h_1 has set one bit to 1, the probability that a fixed bit in the Bloom filter equals 1 is $1/m$, and the probability that it equals 0 is accordingly $1 - 1/m$.

After all the hashes of the first insert finished setting bits to 1, the probability that the fixed bit still equals 0 is $(1-1/m)^k$, and after we finished inserting the entire dataset of size n, this probability is $(1-1/m)^{nk}$. The approximation $(1+1/x)^x \approx e$ then further gives $p \approx e^{-nk/m}$.

It is tempting to just replace t in the expression for the false positive rate with p, and this will give us equation 3.1. After all, p describes the expected value of a random variable denoting the percentage of 0s in the filter, but what if the actual percentage of 0s can substantially vary from its expectation?

Using *Chernoff bounds*—a theorem curtailing the probability of a random variable deviating substantially from its mean—we can show that the fraction of 0s in the Bloom filter is highly concentrated around its mean. The general statement of Chernoff bounds holds for random variables X that are a sum of mutually independent indicator random variables. We define a random variable X that denotes the total number of 0s in a Bloom filter $X = \sum_{i=1}^{m} X_i$, where $X_i = 0$ if the ith bit in the Bloom filter equals 1, and $X_i = 1$ otherwise.

Using Chernoff bounds, we will show that the value X does not significantly deviate from its mean. In our case, X_is is not independent, however, it is slightly negatively correlated (even better!). One bit being set to 1 slightly lowers the chance of other bits being set to 1.

The general statement of the Chernoff upper bound (we can do something similar for the lower bound), where μ is the mean of the random variable X, is as follows:

$$Pr[X > (1 + \delta)\mu] < \left(\frac{e^{\delta}}{(1 + \delta)^{1+\delta}} \right)^{\mu}$$

Applied to our case, $\mu = E[X] = mp = me^{-nk/m}$. If we choose $\delta = 1$ and plug into the Chernoff bound, we obtain the probability that X will deviate from its mean by more than a factor of 2:

$$Pr[X > 2pm] < \left(\frac{e}{4} \right)^{me^{-\frac{nk}{m}}}$$

We can safely assume that $nk = \theta(m)$, which further tells us that the probability that X deviates from the mean by more than a factor of 2 is exponentially small ($< (\frac{3}{4})^{\theta(m)}$). Hence, p is a good approximation for t, the percentage of 0s in the Bloom filter, which justifies replacing t in the formula from the beginning of this section. This finalizes our derivation of equation 3.1.

3.5.1   Can we do better?

Bloom filters pack the space really well, but are there, or can there be, better data structures? In other words, for the same amount of space, can we achieve a better false positive rate? To answer this question, we need to derive a *lower bound* that relates the amount of space the data structure uses in bits (m) with the maximum false positive rate the data structure allows (f). Note that the lower bound is independent of any particular data structure design and tells us about the theoretical limits of *any* data structure—even one that has not been invented yet.

A data structure is an m-bit string and has a total of 2^m distinct encodings. Each individual encoding of a data structure, in addition to reporting Present for some n elements, will also admit $f(U - n)$ false positives, a fraction f of the rest of the universe. Of the total $n + f(U - n)$ elements for which the data structure reports Present, we do not know which are the true positives and which are the false positives, so one encoding of the data structure serves to represent every n-sized subset we grab. There are $(n + f(U - n)$ *choose* $n)$ such sets.

In total, the data structure needs to be able to "cover" all $(U$ *choose* $n)$ n-sized subsets in the universe U. Together, these facts give us the inequality shown in figure 3.7, which describes our lower bound.

Taking the logarithm on both sides, along with the fact that $U \gg n$, and some additional algebraic manipulation, the inequality from figure 3.7 will give us

$$m \geq n \log_2 \left(\frac{1}{f} \right)$$

How does that compare to the false positive rate of the Bloom filter?

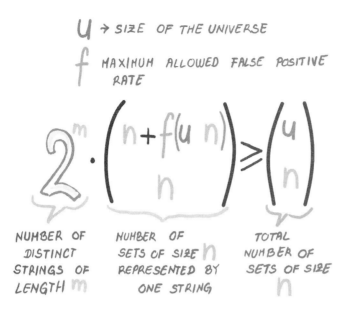

NUMBER OF   NUMBER OF   TOTAL
  DISTINCT   SETS OF SIZE n NUMBER OF
STRINGS OF   REPRESENTED BY   SETS OF SIZE
LENGTH m ONE STRING n

Figure 3.7   The inequality describing the space-error lower bound

From equations 3.2 and 3.3, we can derive the relationship between m and the false positive rate of the Bloom filter (here we will refer to it as f_{BF}). We have that $f_{BF} = (1/2)^k \geq (1/2)^{ln\ 2(m/n)}$. Again, taking the logarithm and doing some algebraic simplifications, we get that

$$m \geq n \log_2 \left(\frac{1}{f_{BF}} \right) \log_2 e.$$

Comparing that to the lower bound, we obtain that the Bloom filter space is $\log_2 e \approx 1.44$ factors away from optimal. There exist data structures that are closer to the lower bound than the Bloom filter, but some of them are very complex to understand and implement.

3.6   *Bloom filter adaptations and alternatives*

The basic Bloom filter data structure has been widely used in a number of systems, but Bloom filters also leave a lot to be desired, and computer scientists have developed various modified versions of Bloom filters that address some of these drawbacks. For example, the standard Bloom filter does not handle deletions. There is a version of the Bloom filter called *counting Bloom filter* [7] that uses counters instead of individual bits in the cells. The `insert` operation in the counting Bloom filter increments the respective counters, and the `delete` operation decrements the corresponding counters. Counting Bloom filters use more space (about four times more) and can also lead to false negatives; for example, when we repeatedly delete the same element, thereby bringing down some other element's counters to zero.

Another issue with Bloom filters is their inability to efficiently resize. In the Bloom filter, we do not store the items or the fingerprints, so the original keys need to be brought back from the persistent storage in order to build a new Bloom filter.

Also, Bloom filters are vulnerable when the queries are not drawn uniformly randomly. Queries in real-life scenarios are rarely uniform random. Instead, many queries follow the Zipfian distribution, where a small number of elements is queried a large number of times, and a large number of elements is queried only once or twice. This pattern of queries can increase our effective false positive rate if one of our "hot" elements (i.e., the elements queried often) results in a false positive. A modification to the Bloom filter called a *weighted Bloom filter* [8] addresses this issue by devoting more hashes to the "hot" elements, thus reducing the chance of a false positive on those elements. There are also new adaptations of Bloom filters that are *adaptive* (i.e., upon the discovery of a false positive, they attempt to correct it) [9].

Another vein of research has focused on designing data structures functionally similar to the Bloom filter, but their design has been based on particular types of compact hash tables. In the next section, we cover one such interesting data structure: the *quotient filter*. Some of the methods employed in the next section are closely tied to designing hash tables for massive datasets, the topic of the previous chapter, but we cover it here because the main applications of quotient filters are functionally equivalent to Bloom filters, and we find uses in similar contexts.

3.7   Quotient filter

A quotient filter [10], at its simplest, is a cleverly designed hash table that uses linear probing. The difference between a quotient filter and a common hash table is that instead of storing keys into slots, as in a classic linear probing hash table, the quotient filter stores the hashes (the term *fingerprint* will be used interchangeably for *hash*). More precisely, the quotient filter stores a piece of each hash, but as we will see, it is able to reliably restore an entire hash.

On the "fidelity spectrum," a quotient filter is somewhere between a hash table and a Bloom filter. If two distinct keys hash to the same fingerprint, the quotient filter will not be able to differentiate them the way a hash table would. But if two keys hash to different fingerprints, a quotient filter will be able to tell them apart; this is not the case with Bloom filters, where the query on a key with a unique set of k hashes might generate a false positive.

A quotient filter has similar functionality to a Bloom filter, but it has a very different design. Using longer fingerprints, quotient filters can reduce the false positive rate, but longer fingerprints might also consumes too much space.

In this section, we will see different tricks that the quotient filter employs to compactly store fingerprints. The ability to restore the full fingerprint comes in handy when we want to delete elements; yes, quotient filters can efficiently delete.

In addition, a quotient filter can resize itself, and merging two quotient filters into a larger quotient filter is a seamless, fast operation. Efficient merging, resizing, and deletions are all features that might make you want to consider using a quotient filter instead of a Bloom filter in some applications; these features are especially handy in dynamic distributed systems. Truth be told, quotient filters are a tad more complex to understand and implement than Bloom filters, but learning about them, in our opinion, is well worth your time.

In the coming sections, we will explore the design of a quotient filter, first by learning what quotienting is, then by describing how a quotient filter uses metadata bits with quotienting to save space. The best way to view a quotient filter is as a game of saving a bit here or there and employing various tricks to that end. A quotient filter is not the only data structure of this sort, but some of the tricks that you learn here can be generally useful in understanding similar data structures based on compact hash tables.

3.7.1   Quotienting

Quotienting [11] divides a hash of each item into a *quotient* and a *remainder*: in the quotient filter, the quotient is used to index into the corresponding bucket of the hash table, and the remainder is what gets stored in the corresponding slot. For example, given the h-bit hash, and table size $m = 2^q$, the quotient is the value determined by the leftmost q bits of the hash, and the remainder represents the remaining $r = h - q$ bits. The example in figure 3.8 shows the fingerprint partition on a small example where $m = 32$ (so, $q = 5$) and $h = 11$.

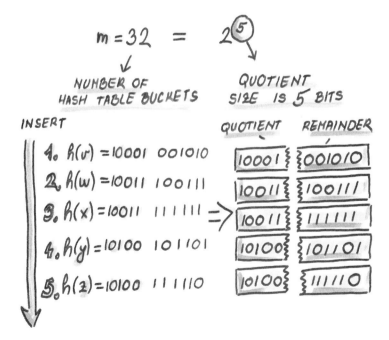

Figure 3.8   **Quotienting in a hash table. The item y has the hash** `10100` `101101`; **therefore, the remainder,** `101101` (`35`), **will be stored in the slot determined by a quotient, at bucket** `10100` (`20`).

The following snippet of code shows how, once the key is hashed and the hash is stored into the variable `fingerprint`, the insert into the quotient filter (`filter`) proceeds:

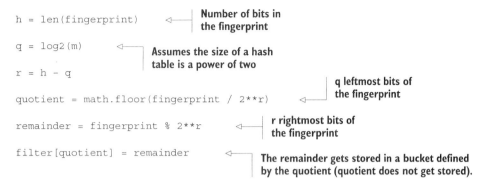

So far, so good. If no collisions occur (i.e., no two fingerprints ever have the same quotient), every remainder occupies its own bucket *b*. It is easy to reconstruct a full fingerprint by concatenating the binary representation of the bucket number *b* with the binary representation of the remainder stored at bucket *b*. Even in this small example, we managed to save *q* = 5 bits per slot due to quotienting.

It is important to keep in mind that in a quotient filter we can reconstruct the fingerprints, which helps with resizing and merging, but we cannot reconstruct the original elements. Again, we are somewhere between hash tables, which hold actual keys, and Bloom filters, which cannot reconstruct which element had which hashes.

However, collisions in hash tables are quite common, and quotient filters resolve collisions using a variant of linear probing. We smell trouble already because, as a consequence of linear probing, some remainders will be pushed down from their original bucket, thus losing the quotient-remainder association. To reconstruct the full fingerprint, a quotient filter uses three extra metadata bits per slot. Three bits are a small price to pay for saving ~20–30 bits per slot on a quotient in larger hash tables. In the next section we explain how metadata bits facilitate operations in the quotient filter.

3.7.2 *Understanding metadata bits*

Before we introduce what metadata bits stand for, a bit of terminology is needed. If you get confused by terms in this section, do not worry too much, as things should become clearer as we work on examples, see what runs and clusters are for, and see what role each metadata bit plays when resolving collisions during an insert or a lookup.

A *run* is a consecutive sequence of quotient filter slots occupied with remainders (i.e., fingerprints) with the same quotient (all fingerprints that collided on one particular bucket). All remainders with the same quotient are stored consecutively in the filter and in the sorted order of remainders. Due to collisions and pushing remainders down when collisions occur, a run can begin arbitrarily far from its corresponding bucket.

A *cluster* is a sequence of one or more runs. It is a consecutive sequence of quotient filter slots occupied by remainders, where the first remainder is stored in its originally hashed slot (we call this the *anchor* slot). The end of a cluster is denoted either by an empty slot or by the beginning of a new cluster.

When performing a lookup on the quotient filter, we need to decode remainders along with relevant metadata bits to retrieve the full fingerprints. The decoding always begins at the start of a containing cluster (i.e., at the anchor slot) and works downward. The three metadata bits at each slot help decode the cluster in the following manner:

- `bucket_occupied`—This tells us whether any key has ever hashed to the given bucket. It is 1 if some key hashed to the bucket, and 0 otherwise. This bit tells us what all the possible quotients are in the cluster.
- `run_continued`—This tells us whether the remainder currently stored in this slot has the same quotient as the remainder right above it. In other words, this bit is 0 if the remainder is first in its run, and 1 otherwise. This bit tells us where each run in the cluster begins and ends.
- `is_shifted`—This tells us whether the remainder currently stored in the slot is in its originally intended position or if it has been shifted. This bit helps us locate the beginning of the cluster. It is set to 0 only at an anchor slot, and set to 1 otherwise.

3.7.3   *Inserting into a quotient filter: An example*

Now, let's work through the insertion of the elements v, w, and x, which you can see in figure 3.9. We begin with an initially empty quotient filter of $32 = 2^5$ slots, where each slot, as well as all three metadata bits, are initially set to 0:

1. Insert v: $h(v) = 10001001010$. The bucket determined by the quotient `10001` is previously unoccupied. We set the `bucket_occupied` bit to 1 and store the remainder into the slot determined by its quotient. Note that we do not need any additional action on other bits, as this item is currently both the beginning of a run and of a cluster.

2. Insert w: $h(w) = 10011100111$. Again, we set the `bucket_occupied` bit to 1 at `10011` and store the remainder into the corresponding slot as it is available, and do not modify any other bits.

3. Insert x: $h(x) = 10011111111$. The bucket `10011` is already occupied when we try to set the bucket to 1, so wherever we store the remainder, we will need to set `run_continued` of that slot to 1. The slot at the hashed bucket is taken, so wherever we store the remainder, we will need to set the `is_shifted` bit of that slot to 1 as well. Given that we are at the start of the cluster that has only one run (whose quotient is equal to the quotient of x), we scan downward to find the first available slot within the run at bucket `10100`. We store the remainder and set the `run_continued` and `is_shifted` bits to 1.

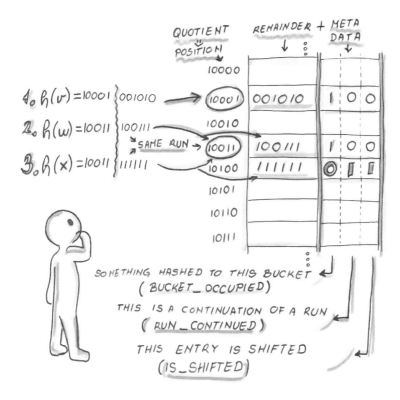

Figure 3.9 Insertion into quotient filter and metadata bits

Currently, the quotient filter has two clusters, each of which has one run. Now we insert a few more elements (follow along in figure 3.10):

1. Insert y: $h(x) = 10100101101$. The `bucket_occupied` bit at `10100` was 0, and we set it to 1 (`run_continued` at the final remainder's slot will be set to 0), and the slot at the hashed bucket is taken (`is_shifted` at the final remainder's slot will be set to 1). Starting from the beginning of the cluster, we look for the first place to store our new run. The first available slot is at bucket `10101`, so we store the remainder and set the metadata bits accordingly.

2. Insert z: $h(x) = 10100111110$. The `bucket_occupied` bit of z's bucket is already set to 1 (`run_continued` at the final slot will be 1), and the original slot is taken (`is_shifted` at the final slot will be 1). Starting from the start of the cluster, we decode and find where our appropriate run is. We scan down the run to the bucket `10110` to store z's remainder and set bits accordingly.

Our insert sequence is rather simplified because the insertions arrive in the sorted order of fingerprint values. A sorted order of inserts into a quotient filter is a common scenario due to the way quotient filters are merged and resized, similar to merging

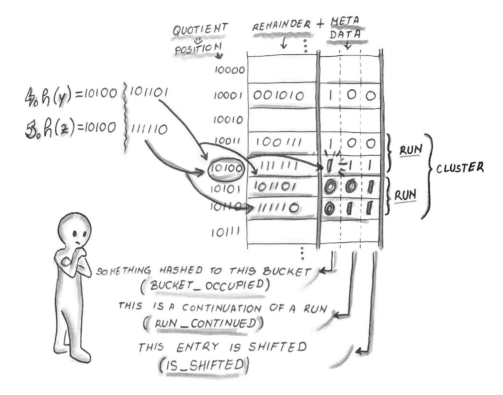

Figure 3.10   Insertion of *y* and *z* into the quotient filter.

sorted lists in a merge-sort, but we also need to be able to handle scenarios when inserted fingerprints arrive in the arbitrary order.

When elements are inserted out of the sorted fingerprint order, then once the correct run is found for the remainder to be inserted into it, it might push down multiple items of that run and other elements in that cluster. Consider the example of inserting an element, a, $h(a) = 10100000000$, into our resulting quotient filter from figure 3.10. The element would belong to the second run of the second cluster that currently occupies slots determined by buckets `10101` and `10110`. An element a would move the entire run one slot below in order to get stored at slot `10101` because its remainder is the first in the ascending sorted order in that run, thus also triggering the changes in metadata bits.

Why do we need to have remainders sorted within a run (and runs among clusters)? The answer to that question will come when we talk about efficient resizing and merging.

Another important hash table–related note is that having to potentially move an entire cluster of items while inserting/deleting and decoding a whole cluster while performing lookup underlines the importance of small cluster sizes. The more empty space we leave, the smaller the probability of getting large clusters that insert, and lookup operations need to scan through and decode. Just like with common hash tables with linear probing, quotient filters work faster when the load factor is kept at 75–90% than when it is higher.

3.7.4   *Python code for lookup*

Now that we conceptually understand insert, let's see how lookup works using code in Python. For the purposes of understanding the underlying logic, we will, for a moment, set aside the mechanics of compactly storing the data structure, which involves a lot of bit unpacking and shifting. Our implementation for the class `Slot` and the class `QuotientFilter` is "sparse" in that a metadata bit is an entire Boolean variable, so it takes up more than one bit of memory. Our Python code is based on the pseudocode from the original paper:

```python
import math

class Slot:
    def __init__(self):
        self.remainder = 0
        self.bucket_occupied = False
        self.run_continued = False
        self.is_shifted = False


class QuotientFilter:
    def __init__(self, q, r):
        self.q = q
        self.r = r
        self.size = 2**q                    ◁──┘ Filter size
        self.filter = [Slot() for _ in range(self.size)]

    def lookup(self, fingerprint):
        quotient = math.floor(fingerprint / 2**self.r)
        remainder = fingerprint % 2**self.r
        if not self.filter[quotient].bucket_occupied:
            return False                    ◁──  No element has ever
        b = quotient                             hashed to this bucket.
        while(self.filter[b].is_shifted):
            b = b - 1
        s = b
        while b != quotient:                ◁──  b tracks occupied buckets, and
            s = s + 1                            s tracks corresponding runs.
            while self.filter[s].run_continued:  ◁──  Go down the run and
                s = s + 1                             advance the bucket number.
            b = b + 1
            while not self.filter[b].bucket_occupied:
                b = b + 1
        while self.filter[s].remainder != remainder:   ◁──  Now s points to the
            s = s + 1                                       start of the run where
            if not self.filter[s].run_continued:            our element might be
                return False                                contained.
        return True
```

Go up to the start of the cluster.

Skip empty buckets.

The lookup begins by searching for the beginning of the cluster where the item we are searching for might be contained. In other words, to find out whether an element is present, we need to decode a whole cluster.

After we find the beginning of a cluster that contains the fingerprint's bucket, for each occupied bucket we locate its corresponding run and skip through that run until encountering the bucket that equals the quotient of our fingerprint and the start of its run (if that never happens, we return `False`.) Once the appropriate run is found, the lookup procedure searches inside the run for the fingerprint's remainder.

Insertion code would also use a modified version of the lookup procedure that returns the position of the queried element, not a Boolean value. It would start by marking the appropriate bucket as occupied. Then it would use the lookup algorithm to find the appropriate location to insert the remainder, which might require shifting other remainders down until an empty slot is reached. Deletes work in a similar fashion, where they might need to move elements up to fill the hole created by the deletion, or sometimes deletes are implemented by placing a tombstone element in the said position, thereby eliminating the need for moving remainders around. If the deleted element is the only element in its run, then we also need to unmark the `bucket_occupied` bit. All operations in the quotient filter wrap around the table if the end of the table is reached, just like in common hash tables with linear probing.

STORING A QUOTIENT FILTER

An important detail in the implementation of the quotient filter, as well as many other types of compact hash tables, is how data is laid out in memory. Specifically, the slot size generally does not equal the unit sizes of addressable memory (e.g., bytes), so the byte and slot boundaries often do not align. For example, say we have a quotient filter with the remainder of length $r = 7$ bits, as well as three metadata bits (10 bits per slot in total). Figure 3.11 shows the memory layout of the quotient filter slots.

For example, to read slot 3's `run_continued` bit, we need to access the fifth bit of byte 4. To decode a cluster, we need to do a lot of bit-shifting and bit-unpacking

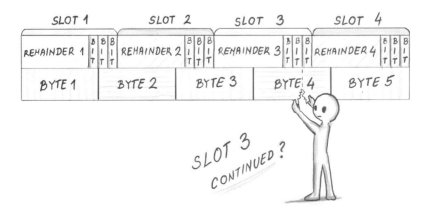

Figure 3.11   The memory layout of quotient filter slots

operations, so the quotient filter implementations (most often written in C) pay the price of small space with extra CPU cost, which, as we will see in section 3.8, impacts the in-RAM insert and lookup performance for high-load factors in a quotient filter. Unlike a Bloom filter insert that elegantly hops around setting bits to 1, a quotient filter can be very CPU-intensive. This, however, can be a good kind of a problem, as quotient filter operations move sequentially through the table, while the Bloom filter pays the price in weak spatial locality.

3.7.5 Resizing and merging

If we want to double the size of the quotient filter, it is sufficient to retrieve the fingerprint, readjust the quotient and remainder size by stealing one bit from remainder and giving it to the quotient, and insert the new fingerprint into a twice-as-large quotient filter. Generally, resizing works by traversing the quotient filter in the sorted order, decoding fingerprints as we go, and inserting them in that sorted order into the new quotient filter. The fast append operation lets us zip through the quotient filter, as inserting in the sorted order does not require a great deal of decoding and moving remainders around. A simple example of resizing a small quotient filter of size 4 is shown in figure 3.12.

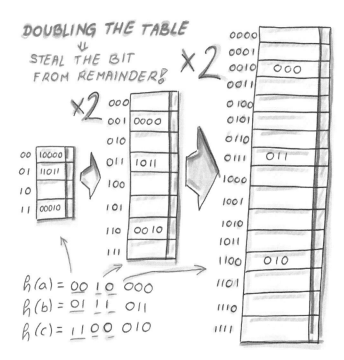

Figure 3.12 Resizing a quotient filter of size 4 that contains three elements. For the sake of simplicity, we assume that no collisions occurred between those three elements and every remainder is stored in its original bucket. A fingerprint 110010 that hashed to bucket 11 (with remainder 0010) in the original quotient filter gets stored at bucket 110 of the second quotient filter (with remainder 0010), and in a 1100 bucket of the final quotient filter (with remainder 010).

Similar to how resizing is performed, we can merge two quotient filters in a fast linear-time fashion, as we would with two sorted lists in merge-sort, again enabling a fast append into a larger quotient filter.

Recall that in a Bloom filter, we cannot simply merge or resize, as we do not preserve the original elements or fingerprints. To resize a Bloom filter, we need to save the original set of keys and reload it into memory to build a new Bloom filter, which is infeasible in fast-moving streams and high-ingestion databases.

3.7.6   *False positive rate and space considerations*

In a quotient filter, false positives occur as a result of two distinct keys generating the same fingerprint. The analysis [12] shows that, given the table of 2^q slots and fingerprint length $p = q + r$, the probability of a false positive is comparable to $\frac{1}{2_r}$. The amount of space required by the quotient filter hash table is $2^q(r + 3)$ bits. The number of items inserted into a quotient filter is $n = \alpha 2^q$ where the load factor α has a significant effect on the performance of insert, lookup, and delete operations.

There also exists a variant of quotient filter that only uses two metadata bits and uses $2^q(r + 2)$ bits for storage, without compromising the false positive rate, but this variant substantially complicates the decoding step, making common operations too CPU-intensive on longer clusters.

Practically speaking, due to the extra space required for a linear probing table, quotient filters tend to take up slightly more space than Bloom filters for common false positive rates. For extremely low false positive rates, quotient filters are more space efficient than Bloom filters.

There are other succinct membership query data structures based on hash tables that we will not study in this chapter (e.g., the cuckoo filter [13], based on cuckoo hashing). However, we hope that the ideas you learn by studying Bloom filters and getting a taste of quotient filters, as well as their performance comparison in the next section, give you the right lens to learn about similar data structures that are out there.

3.8   *Comparison between Bloom filters and quotient filters*

In this section, we will summarize performance differences between Bloom filters and quotient filters. Spoiler: differences in the performance are not dramatic in either direction. However, what is more interesting are the behavioral differences between the two data structures, which stem from the way they have been designed, and that might help us understand the nature of these data structures better. Our analysis relies on the experiments previously performed in the original quotient filter paper; figure 3.13 is a rough sketch of some of their findings.

In all three graphs, the x axis represents the fraction of the data structure fullness, and the y axis represents the cumulative throughput as the data structure fills up. In this particular experiment, both data structures were given the same amount of space (2 GB) and were filled up with as many elements as possible without deteriorating the false positive rate, which was set to 1/64 for both data structures. In the case of

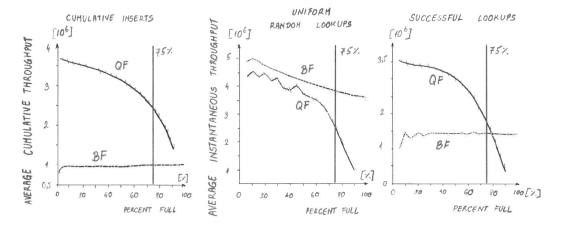

Figure 3.13 Performance comparison of Bloom filters and quotient filters on inserts, uniform random lookups, and successful lookups, respectively.

quotient filters, performance becomes very poor after 90% occupancy, so quotient filters are only filled up until 90% full.

UNIFORM RANDOM INSERTS

As seen in figure 3.13 (left), inserts are significantly faster in quotient filters than in Bloom filters. While quotient filters at 75% occupancy have the cumulative throughput of ~3 million inserts per second, Bloom filters have the cumulative throughput of ~1.5 million inserts per second. Bloom filters need k random writes for each insert, while quotient filters usually need only 1 random write, and that is the main cause for the difference in the performance. For higher false positive rates, Bloom filters might require more hash functions, which can further degrade the insert performance. For Bloom filters, the insert performance is a flat line as the data structure fills up, while inserts slow down for the quotient filter as it fills up, as it has to decode larger clusters and drops significantly after $\alpha = 0.8$.

UNIFORM RANDOM LOOKUPS

Uniform random lookups are slightly faster in Bloom filters than in quotient filters (figure 3.13, center); the difference becomes more striking after data structures reach 70% occupancy, and quotient filters start decoding larger clusters. Generally, uniform random lookups are faster than inserts in Bloom filters. Given a large enough universe, most uniform random lookups are unsuccessful, and when optimally filled Bloom filters reject an unsuccessful lookup after one to two probes on average; reading just one to two bits is hard to beat performance-wise.

Recall our Google WebTable query-routing example at the beginning of the chapter: unsuccessful lookup is common, so having this operation run very fast is quite favorable for Bloom filters. The uniform random lookup performance only slightly drops as the Bloom filter gets fuller, because the proportion of one bit increases, and with it, the number of bits the lookup has to check before it gives up. Quotient filters need to do a bit more work than Bloom filters by decoding a containing cluster, but this still amounts to one random read plus additional bit unpacking.

SUCCESSFUL LOOKUPS

Successful lookups exhibit similar performance trends to inserts (figure 3.13, right), and quotient filters again outperform Bloom filters unless for very high load factors. A Bloom filter has to check k random bits on a successful lookup (its performance is independent of how full the data structure is), while the quotient filter performance degrades with higher occupancy and larger clusters.

The experimental results do not point to a clear winner between Bloom filters and quotient filters, but their other features may point to better suitability in particular settings: a Bloom filter is simpler to implement and creates less of a burden on the CPU. A quotient filter supports deletions and works very well in distributed settings where efficient merging and resizing is important. Quotient filter variants adapted for SSD/disk also outperform Bloom filter variants intended for SSD/disk due to fast sequential merging and a small number of random reads/writes in quotient filters. To learn more about SSD/disk-adapted versions of Bloom filters and quotient filters, see a related review [14].

Summary

- Bloom filters have been widely applied in the context of distributed databases, networks, bioinformatics, and other domains where regular hash tables are too space consuming.
- Bloom filters trade accuracy for the savings in space, and there is a relationship between the space, false positive rate, number of elements, and number of hash functions in the Bloom filter.
- Bloom filters do not meet the space versus accuracy lower bound, but they are simpler to implement than more space-efficient alternatives and have been adapted over time to deal with deletes, different query distributions, and so on.
- Quotient filters are based on compact hash tables with linear probing and are functionally equivalent to Bloom filters, with the benefit of spatial locality: the ability to delete, merge, and resize efficiently.
- Quotient filters are based on the space-saving method of quotienting and extra metadata bits that allow the full fingerprint reconstruction.
- Quotient filters offer better performance than Bloom filters on uniform random inserts and successful lookups, while Bloom filters win on uniform random (unsuccessful) lookups. The performance of quotient filters is dependent on a load factor (a lower load factor is better), and the performance of Bloom filters is dependent on the number of hash functions (fewer hash functions are better).

Frequency estimation
and count-min sketch

4

This chapter covers

- Exploring practical use cases where frequency estimates arise and how count-min sketch can help
- Learning how count-min sketch works
- Exploring use cases of a sensor and an NLP app
- Learning about the error versus space tradeoff in count-min sketch
- Understanding dyadic ranges and how range queries can be solved with count-min sketch

Popularity analysis, such as producing a bestseller list on an e-commerce site, computing top-k trending queries on a search engine, or reporting frequent source-destination IP address pairs on a network, is a common problem in today's data-intensive applications. Anomaly detection (i.e., monitoring changes in systems that are awake 24/7, such as sensor networks or surveillance cameras) falls under the same algorithmic umbrella as measuring popularity. Anomaly detection is often observed through a sudden spike in the value of a certain parameter, such as the temperature or location change in a sensor, an object appearance in the frame, or the number of units by which a company's stock rose or fell in a given time interval.

In essence, both problems translate into measuring frequency: for each unique item key, build a data structure that can tell me how many times we encountered it. This is a problem where key-value dictionaries fit like a glove, and the amount of space taken by the dictionary is proportional not to the total sum of frequencies encountered (N), but to the total number of distinct items whose frequencies we would like to measure (n). That number, however, might be very large. This chapter deals with alternative solutions to the element-wise frequency problem when the number of distinct items is too large.

When do we encounter a large number of distinct elements? Let's say we want to count the number of times different products were sold on an e-commerce site. If we look at the distribution of sales across products, what often happens is that there is a small number of distinct products that make up the majority of sales, and a large number of products that are sold a small number of times. This sort of distribution (also known as Zipf's law) has been observed in many different domains. What's tricky about measuring frequency with this type of distribution is that there is both a legitimate need to solve this problem due to large variations in frequency and a scalability issue lurking just around the corner due to many low-frequency items.

Another practical situation in which scalability issues can occur is when keys are pairs of elements, for instance, source-destination IP address pairs, or word pairs in a piece of text, where n can grow quadratically with respect to the total number of distinct IP addresses (or words), which itself might be quite high.

Also, these issues are about more than limitations on space. In this chapter, we will be interested in measuring frequency in rapid-moving streams that pose a number of difficult constraints on our choice of a data structure and an algorithm. For instance, our algorithm will be able to see each element just once (or a small, constant number of times), before we discard it and move to the next one. Solving problems such as top-k queries and heavy hitters is often impossible in this highly constrained setup. Thus, we need to resort to approximate solutions.

We will learn how a probabilistic succinct data structure, count-min sketch, can help us approximately measure frequency and solve related problems while achieving enormous space savings. We begin with the problem of heavy hitters and discuss why linear space is essential for the correct solution to this problem if we are to solve it in one pass. Then we introduce count-min sketch and its design, and we use case scenarios in the context of sensors and NLP. Toward the end of the chapter, we also discuss the error versus space tradeoff in count-min sketch and how count-min sketch can be used to answer approximate range queries.

4.1   *Majority element*

Let's start with a simple problem: given an array of N elements, and provided that the array contains an element that occurs at least $\lfloor N/2 \rfloor + 1$ times (i.e., majority element), the task is to output that element.

EXERCISE 1

Before moving on, try to design and implement a linear-time algorithm with constant space (other than the storage for the array) for the majority problem.

This problem can be solved using a one-pass-over-the-array algorithm [1] (also known as Boyer–More majority vote algorithm) that uses only two extra variables, as shown in the following Python code:

```python
def majority(A):
    index = 0
    count = 1
    for i in range(len(A)):
        if A[i] == A[index]:
            count += 1
        else:
            count -= 1
        if count == 0:
            index = i
            count = 1
    return A[index]
```

> If there is a majority element in A, this function returns it.

The `majority` function tracks the current frontrunner for the title of majority element and resets the frontrunner once the number of occurrences (one or more) of other elements cancel it out. Assuming the provided list has a majority element, the algorithm shown will output it; otherwise, it might output an arbitrary element. If we are uncertain about whether the array has a majority element, we can perform one more sweep over the array to make sure that the returned value is indeed a majority. We show how the algorithm works on two examples—a list with a majority element and a list with an element that is almost a majority:

```python
A = [4, 5, 5, 4, 6, 4, 4]
print(majority(A))

C = [3, 3, 4, 4, 4, 5]
print(majority(C))
```

The output is

```
4
5
```

There is also a more visual way of thinking about this problem: grab an arbitrary pair of adjacent numbers in the array that are not equal to each other, throw them out, and contract the hole created by removing the two elements. Continue grabbing pairs of different elements anywhere in the array until you are left with one distinct element, potentially its multiple copies; this element is the majority. Figure 4.1 illustrates the algorithm by showing goats vying for their position on the bridge, with the type 2 goat winning as the "majority goat."

Figure 4.1 We find a majority element in an array by having different neighboring elements throw each other out. In this example, after we throw out (1,2), (2,5), (3,2), and then (3,2) and (4,2), we are left with the majority element 2.

Both algorithms illustrate that this problem can be solved simply in linear time with a constant memory overhead. But does this approach extend to the case of general heavy hitters?

4.1.1 *General heavy hitters*

The general heavy-hitters problem with a parameter k asks that the algorithm outputs all elements in the array of N items that occur more than N/k times (the majority element is the simple instance where $k = 2$.) There can be at most $k - 1$ heavy hitters, but there could also be fewer or none.

Since there can many heavy hitters, the simple application of our frontrunner algorithm implies that we should maintain many heavy-hitter candidates concurrently.

To illustrate the difficulty arising from this setup, consider the following extreme case observed [2] when $k = N$: say we are witnessing a long data stream in which all elements discovered thus far have been distinct, and a single repetition of an element would term that element a heavy hitter. To identify a potential heavy hitter, we need to be saving each new incoming distinct element, as we do not know which one will have a repetition.

This toy example is a bit sneaky; its purpose is not to illustrate the practically occurring problem instance as much as to convince you that with larger k, the memory consumption and algorithmic complexity for solving heavy hitters grows if we want to solve the problem exactly, and that we need to turn to solving this problem approximately.

What will be approximated in heavy hitters? The (ε, k) heavy hitters ask to report all elements that occur at least $N/k - \varepsilon N$ times, that is, all the heavy hitters, and all the elements that are at most εN short of being heavy hitters for some previously set value of ε. In other words, the data structure that will store frequencies will overestimate the frequencies for some elements by the fraction ε of the total sum of frequencies N.

The data structure recording approximate frequencies that we will focus on in this chapter is count-min sketch (CMS), devised by Cormode and Muthukrishnan in 2005 [3]. Count-min sketch is like a young, up-and-coming cousin of a Bloom filter. Similar to how a Bloom filter answers membership queries approximately with less space than hash tables, the count-min sketch estimates *frequencies* of items in less space than a hash table or any linear-space key-value dictionary. Another important similarity is that the count-min sketch is hashing-based, so we continue in the vein of using hashing to create compact and approximate sketches of data. Next we explore how count-min sketch works.

4.2   Count-min sketch: How it works

CMS supports two main operations: `update`, the equivalent of an insert, and `estimate`, the equivalent of a lookup. For the input pair (a_t, c_t) at timeslot t, `update` increases the frequency of an item a_t by the quantity c_t (if, in a particular application, $c_t = 1$, that is, the counts do not make particular sense, we can override update to only use a_t as an argument). The `estimate` operation returns the frequency estimate of a_t. The returned estimate can be an overestimate of the actual frequency, but never an underestimate (and that is not an accidental similarity with the Bloom filter false positives.)

Count-min sketch is represented as a matrix of integer counters with d rows and w columns (`CMS[1..d][1..w]`), with all counters initially set to 0 and d independent hash functions, $(h_1, h_2, ..., h_d)$. Each hash function has the range $[1..w]$, and the jth hash function is dedicated to the ith row of the CMS matrix, $1 \leq j \leq d$.

4.2.1   *Update*

The update operation adds another instance (or c_t instances) of an item to the dataset. Using d hash functions, update computes d hashes on a_t, and for each hash value $h_j(a_t)$, $1 \le j \le d$, the respective position in the jth row is incremented by c_t:

```
CMS_UPDATE(aₜ,cₜ):
    for j ← 1 to d
        CMS[j][hⱼ(aₜ)] += cₜ
```

An example of how update works is shown in figure 4.2, where we begin with an empty count-min sketch and perform updates of elements x, y, and z, with quantities/frequencies 2, 1, and 3, respectively.

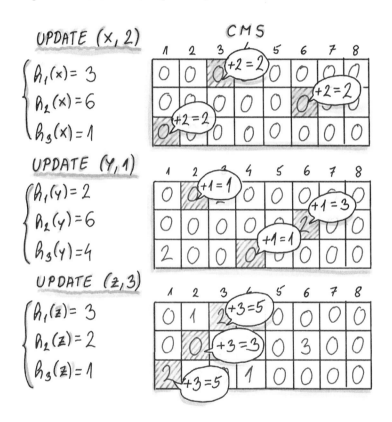

Figure 4.2   Three update operations of *x*, *y*, and *z* performed on an initially empty 3 x 8 CMS. Computed hashes indicate which columns in the respective rows of count-min sketch need to be updated.

4.2.2   *Estimate*

The estimate operation reports the approximate frequency of the queried item. Just like update, estimate also computes d hashes, and it returns the minimum among d

counters in d different rows, where the counter location in the jth row is specified by hash $h_j(a_t)$, $1 \leq j \leq d$:

```
CMS_ESTIMATE(a_t):
    min = CMS[1][h_1(a_t)]
    for j ← 2 to d
        if(CMS[j][h_j(a_t)] < min)
            min = CMS[j][h_j(a_t)]
    return min
```

An example of how `estimate` works is shown in figure 4.3, where the `estimate` of element y returns the correct answer, whereas the `estimate` of x returns an overestimate. As we can see from the example, count-min sketch can overestimate the actual frequency due to hashes of different items colliding and contributing to counts of other elements; however, the overestimate happens only if there was a collision in each row.

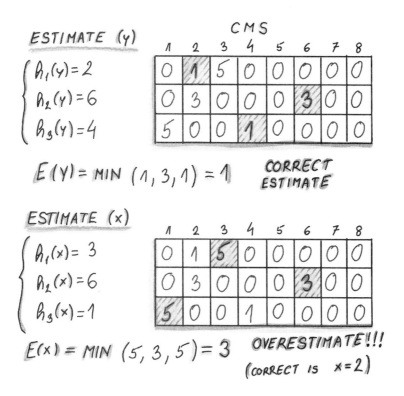

Figure 4.3   Example of the `estimate` operation on the count-min sketch from figure 4.2. In the case of element y, whose true frequency is 1, count-min sketch reports the correct answer of 1 (the minimum of 1, 3, and 1). However, in the case of the element x, whose true frequency is 2, count-min sketch reports 3 (the minimum of 5, 3, and 5). Refer to figure 4.2 to convince yourself that during earlier update operations, y and z together incremented all the counters that are used by x, thus resulting in an overestimate for x.

4.3 Use cases

Now we move onto practical applications of count-min sketch in two different domains: a sensor smart-bed application and a natural language–processing (NLP) application.

4.3.1 Top-k restless sleepers

The quality of sleep has for a long time been linked to outcomes in an individual's mental and physical health. However, it is only recently, with the wide access to new technologies and the ability to process enormous datasets, that we have been able to capture very detailed sleep-related data for a large number of individuals. Smart beds, for example, that come equipped with hundreds of sensors capable of recording different parameters during sleep, such as movement, pressure, temperature, and so on, can help us gain new insights into people's sleep patterns. Based on sensor data, different bed components can adapt and modify in real time—parts of the bed can be pulled up, warmed up, cooled down, and so on.

Consider a smart-bed company that collects data from its users and stores it in one central database. There are millions of users and sensors that send out data every second; hence the amount of data is quickly becoming too large to process and analyze in a straightforward manner. Let's assume that one smart bed features 100 sensors and that there are 10^8 customers using this type of smart bed; then our hypothetical company collects a total of 10^8 (customers) × 3,600 (seconds per hour) × 24 (hours per day) × 100 (sensors) = 8.6×10^{14} tuples of data daily, resulting in terabytes of storage on a daily basis. Our specific example is hypothetical, but the size of the collected data and the related problem we study are not.

With every purchase of a smart bed comes the SleepQuality mobile app that allows the beds' users to monitor their sleep over time. One of the new app features monitors restlessness in sleepers and notifies the most restless sleepers that their sleeping patterns are out of whack in comparison to the rest of the smart sleepers. To implement this feature, the app takes into account different sensor readings and collects its findings into one point on the quality-of-sleep scale. Due to the sheer amount of data coming in, the company engineers decided to try count-min sketch to store the quantities received from users' sensors.

As shown in figure 4.4, data arrives at a frequent rate, and at each timestep, the (user-id, amount) pair updates the count-min sketch by a given amount. In our simplified example, the keys in count-min sketch correspond to individual users; for a more refined analysis of how particular sensor readings change, the key should be a (user-id, sensor-id) pair instead.

After updating count-min sketch in this manner, we will be able to produce the approximate frequency estimate for any queried user. But in order to maintain the list of top-k restless sleepers, we will have to do a bit more than maintain the count-min sketch. Remember that the count-min sketch is just a matrix of counters, and it does not save any information on different user IDs or the ordering of relevant frequencies.

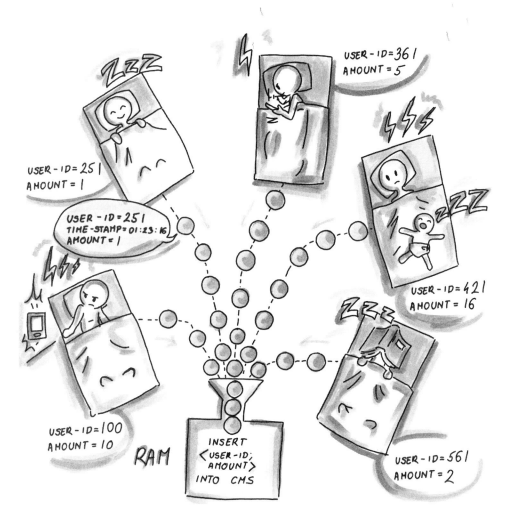

Figure 4.4   All sleep data is sent to a central archive, but before that, it is input into count-min sketch in RAM for later analysis. The (user-id, amount) **pair is used as the input for the data structure, where the frequency of** user-id **increases by amount. The key that is hashed is** user-id.

EXERCISE 2

Before moving onto the solution, think about what the right data structure could be to use alongside count-min sketch to store the top-k restless sleepers at each point of time, using only $O(k)$ extra space.

One solution uses a *min-heap*, as shown in figure 4.5. Min-heap maintains the current k "winners" of the restlessness contest, with the possibility for updates each time a new update to the count-min sketch is received. Namely, when a new element arrives to update count-min sketch, after the update, we perform the estimate operation on this particular item. If the reported frequency is higher than the minimum item in the

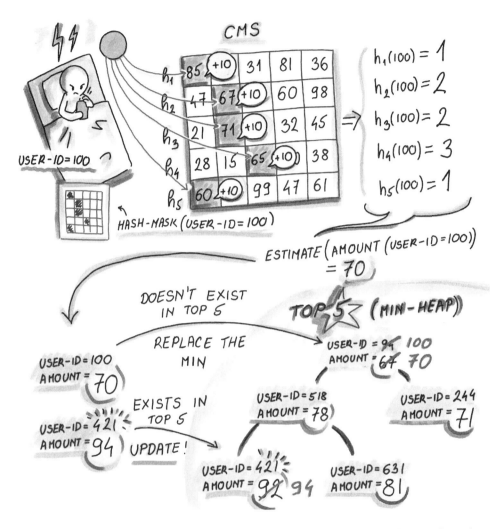

Figure 4.5   Using min-heap and count-min sketch together to find top-k restless sleepers. Every time the count-min sketch is updated with a (user-id, amount) pair, (100, 10) in this example, to maintain a correct list of top-k restless sleepers, we do an estimate on the frequency of the recently updated user-id. In our case, the estimate for user-id 100 will be 70. Then, if user-id is not present in the min-heap and has a higher value than the min (as it does in our example), we will extract the min and insert the new (user-id, amount) pair into the min-heap. If the pair was already present, its amount needs to be updated by deleting and reinserting the pair with the new, updated (higher) amount.

min-heap (easily accessible in $O(1)$), then the minimum of the heap is deleted and the new item is inserted. Also note that each time an update occurs for an element already in the heap, the updated frequency count needs to be reflected in the element's position in the heap.

In this example, we showed that count-min sketch can be used instead of a typical key-value dictionary to preserve information on frequencies for the SleepQuality app, thereby saving a lot of space (though we have not yet analyzed the space requirements). At the same time, we used a min-heap of size $O(k)$ to store the information on top-k restless sleepers. Min-heap maintains up-to-date estimates at each point in time, so whenever we wish to send the notification to such users, we have the information at our disposal.

4.3.2   *Scaling the distributional similarity of words*

The *distributional similarity* problem asks that, given a large text corpus, we find pairs of words that might be similar in meaning based on the contexts in which they appear (or, as the linguist John R. Firth put it, "You will know a word by a company it keeps"). For example, the words *kayak* and *canoe* will be surrounded by similar words such as *water, sport, weather, river*, and so on. As context for a given word, we choose the window of size k (e.g., $k = 3$), which includes k words before and k words after the given word in the text, or less, if we are crossing the boundary of a sentence.

One way to measure distributional similarity for a given word-context pair is using *pointwise mutual information (PMI)* [4]. The formula for PMI for words A and B is as follows

$$PMI(A, B) = \log_2 \frac{Prob(A \cap B)}{Prob(A)Prob(B)}$$

where $Prob(A)$ denotes the probability of occurrence of A, that is, the number of occurrences of A in corpus divided by the total number of words in the corpus. It's a fancy way of saying that PMI measures how likely A and B are to co-occur in our corpus in comparison to how often they would co-occur if they were independent. The higher the PMI, the more similar the words. Typically, to compute the PMIs for all word-context pairs or the specific word-context pairs of interest, we preprocess the corpus to produce the type of matrix shown in figure 4.6, which contains all word-context pair frequencies.

For better association scores between words, the more text we use, the better, but with the larger corpus, even if the number of distinct words is fairly reasonable in size, the number of word-context pairs quickly gets out of hand.

For example, a research paper that measured distributional similarity using sketching techniques [5] used the Gigaword data set—a dataset obtained from English text news sources containing 9.8 GB of text and about 56 million sentences. This results in 3.35 billion word-context pair tokens and 215 million unique word-context pairs; just storing those pairs with their counts takes 4.6 GB. The solution is to transform the matrix such that the word-context pair frequencies are stored in the count-min sketch, and because the number of distinct words is not too large, we can afford to store words with their counts in their own hash table (see the last column of the matrix)

Figure 4.6   **Creating a matrix M where the entry** `M[A][B]` **contains the number of times the word** *A*
appears in the context *B* **is one way to preprocess the text corpus for computing PMI. For example,**
kayak **appears three times in the context of** *water* **and zero times in the context of** *furniture*. **We also**
produce the additional count for each word (the last column of the matrix) and count for each context
(the last row in the matrix), as well as for the total number of words (lower right corner).

and the contexts with their counts in their own hash table (see the last row of the
matrix). The transformation can be seen in figure 4.7.

The space savings achieved using count-min sketch in this example were over a factor of 100. The authors of this research report that a 40 MB sketch gives results comparable to other methods that compute distributional similarity using much more
space. Producing this count-min sketch and the two hash tables takes just one pass
over preprocessed and cleaned data, which is a big boon for the streaming datasets.
We could produce top-*k* PMIs with an additional sweep of the data.

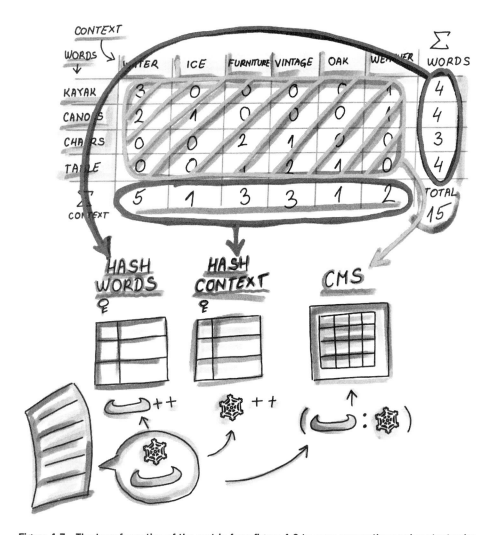

Figure 4.7 The transformation of the matrix from figure 4.6 to save space: the word-context pairs stored in the main body of the matrix are replaced by a count-min sketch that stores frequencies of word-context pairs. Because the number of distinct words (and contexts) is not that large, we can store each in their own hash table with the appropriate counts. In other words, when we encounter a new pair (`word, context`), we increment the count of the pair in the CMS and increment respective counts in the word hash table and the context hash table. To calculate the PMI for a word-context pair, we do an `estimate` query on the count-min sketch and find the appropriate counts of the word and the context in the respective hash tables.

You might be wondering how we can configure count-min sketch (i.e., how we set its dimensions) and what the relationship is between frequency overestimate and the size of count-min sketch. Count-min sketch has two error parameters, ε and δ, and their values are used to determine the dimensions of the sketch. In the next section, we will delve into more detail about the relationship between the errors and space requirements.

4.4   *Error vs. space in count-min sketch*

Count-min sketch exhibits two types of errors: ε (epsilon), which regulates the band of the overestimate, and δ (delta), the failure probability. For a stream S that has come up to the timeslot t, $S = (a_1, c_1), (a_2, c_2), \ldots, (a_t, c_t)$, if we define N as the total sum of frequencies observed in the stream $N = \sum_i^t = 1 C_t$, then the overestimate error ε can be expressed as the percentage of N by which we can overshoot the actual frequency of any item. In other words, for an element x and its true frequency f_x, count-min sketch estimates the frequency as f_{est}

$$f_x \leq f_{est} \leq f_x + \varepsilon N$$

with a probability at least $1 - \delta$. Usually δ is set to be small (e.g., 0.01) so that we can count on the overestimate error to stay in the promised band with high probability. There is a small probability, δ, that the overestimate in CMS can be unbounded.

Just like with the Bloom filter, we can tune CMS to be more accurate, but that will cost us space. Whatever the (ε, δ) values are that we desire for our application, to achieve the bounds stated, we need to configure the dimensions of count-min sketch to be $w = e/\varepsilon$ and $d = \ln(1/\delta)$. Hence, the space required by count-min sketch, expressed in the number of integer counters, will be (equation 4.1)

$$O\left(\frac{e \ln \left(\frac{1}{\sigma} \right)}{\varepsilon} \right) \qquad \text{(Equation 4.1)}$$

Note that CMS tends to be small, even when used on large datasets. Count-min sketch is often hailed for its space requirements—they do not depend on the dataset size—but this is only true if you desire the error to be a fixed percentage of the dataset size. For example, keeping the allowed band of error fixed at 0.3% of N will not require increasing the size of count-min sketch even if we double the value of N, but the actual absolute overestimate band will double. One could argue that with twice as large N, the application should be able to afford an overestimate error that is twice as large.

However, what leaves us wanting when it comes to count-min sketch error properties is that the overestimate error is only sensitive to the total sum of frequencies N, not to the individual element frequency. Therefore, the band of error can wildly vary if we observe it with respect to the element's individual frequency: if the maximum overestimate is $\varepsilon N = 200$, then we can equally expect that to be the overestimate for an element with frequency 10,000 and for an item whose frequency is 10. In the latter case, the estimate can overshoot the truth by 20 times the true frequency.

4.5   *A simple implementation of count-min sketch*

Now we are ready to see a bare implementation of count-min sketch. As with Bloom filters, we use the mmh3 MurmurHash wrapper for d hash functions:

```
import numpy as np
import mmh3
from math import log, e, ceil

class CountMinSketch:
    def __init__(self, eps, delta):
        self.eps = eps
        self.delta = delta
        self.w = int(ceil(e/eps))          | Sets width
        self.d = int(ceil(log(1. / delta)))  ◁——— Sets depth
        self.sketch = np.zeros((self.d, self.w))

    def update(self, item, freq=1):
        for i in range(self.d):
            index = mmh3.hash(item, i) % self.w
            self.sketch[i][index] += freq

    def estimate(self, item):
        return min(self.sketch[i][mmh3.hash(item, i) % self.w] for i
 in range(self.d))
```

Try the code that shows the usage of the CountMinSketch class. Play with the updates and see how estimates change:

```
cms = CountMinSketch(0.0001, 0.01)
for i in range(100000):
    cms.update(f'{i}', 1)
print(cms.estimate('0'))
```

In section 4.5.1, we provide a few exercises to test your understanding of configuring count-min sketch. Section 4.5.2 discusses the intuition behind deriving error rates in count-min sketch and is more theoretical in nature. As such, it is primarily intended for readers with an interest in the mathematical underpinnings of the data structure, and otherwise can be skipped.

4.5.1 Exercises

The following exercises are intended to check your understanding of count-min sketch, how it is configured, and how its shape and size affect the error rate.

EXERCISE 3

Given $N = 10^8$, $\varepsilon = 10^{-6}$, and $\delta = 0.1$, determine the error properties of the count-min sketch.

EXERCISE 4

Calculate the space requirements for the count-min sketch from exercise 3.

EXERCISE 5

Consider what happens with the size (and, more specifically, the shape) of count-min sketch if we desire a fixed absolute error (εN) while N increases. For example, say we want to keep the overestimate at 100 or less, like in exercise 3, but for an N that is twice as big.

EXERCISE 6

Can you design two count-min sketches that consume the same amount of space but have very different performance characteristics (with respect to their errors)? What is the practical constraint limiting the depth of the count-min sketch to low values (<30)?

EXERCISE 7

How would you solve the problem of the approximate k-heavy hitters mentioned in the beginning of the chapter with the help of count-min sketch? Specifically, how would you set ε to facilitate solving this problem? Recall that in approximate k-heavy hitters, we would like to report all heavy hitters and potentially those that are εN short of being heavy hitters.

4.5.2   Intuition behind the formula: Math bit

As we have observed in our simple count-min sketch implementation, to achieve the overestimate of at most εN with a probability of at least $1 - \delta$, the width of the count-min sketch w should be set to e/ε, and the depth of the count-min sketch d should be set to $\ln(1/\delta)$. Why is w related to ε and d related to δ?

To understand why, let us consider the process of performing updates to count-min sketch, and let us specifically focus our attention on the first row. By the time we have performed all updates to count-min sketch, the sum of the counters in the first row (and any single row) will be equal to N. Assuming that hash functions distribute updates uniformly randomly across cells, then the random variable X describing the value stored at any one fixed cell C in the first row, after all updates have been performed, has an average (or expected) value of $E[X] = N/w$.

This also means that when we perform an estimate for a particular item whose counter in the first row is found at cell C, other elements could contribute to its counter by no more than N/w on average. To obtain the average overestimate in one row to be no more than εN, we can set $w = 1/\varepsilon$. Clearly, the overestimate amount is related to the width of the data structure.

$E[X]$ tells us about average behavior, but X can significantly deviate from its expectation: in some cells, values can be much higher than in others. We can somewhat mildly bound an overestimate in one row using Markov's inequality, which tells us that if X is a nonnegative random variable, and $c > 1$, then

$$Pr\left(X \geq c \times E[X]\right) \leq \frac{1}{c}$$

Applying Markov's inequality to our case, we get the following:

$$Pr\left(X \geq \frac{eN}{w}\right) \leq \frac{1}{e}$$

In other words, the probability of a particular cell in the first row having the value of eN/w or larger is no greater than $1/e$. But this is not good enough: to bound the probability of overestimates higher than εN, we consider all d rows. Recall that to report an overestimate of q in count-min sketch, the corresponding cells in *each* row need to have an overestimate of at least q. If we apply the probability arising from Markov's inequality across all levels (note that outcomes of hash functions to different levels are mutually independent), we find that

$$Pr\left(\text{the overestimate in each row is at least } \frac{eN}{w}\right) \leq \left(\frac{1}{e}\right)^{d}$$

By setting $w = e/\varepsilon$ and $d = \ln(1/\delta)$, we find that the probability that the overestimate is more than εN is at most δ.

4.6   Range queries with count-min sketch

As the final application of count-min sketch in this chapter, we'll discuss how to report frequency estimates for ranges as opposed to single points. Range reporting has tremendous importance in databases, where the queries are often posed to reveal properties of groups and categories rather than single data points; queries such as "Give me all employees who have worked for the company between a and b years or who have salaries between x and y" naturally translate into range queries. Time series are another example of ranges; for example, "How many books were sold on Amazon.com between December 20th and January 10th of this year?"

Balanced binary search trees are good data structures for navigating ranges, as the items are in lexicographical order, so the cost of the range query, after the initial point search, is proportional to the mere cost of outputting the range query results; this is in contrast to hash tables that scatter data all over the table and where querying for a range might require a full scan of the table, even if zero items are reported. As you might imagine, that does not paint a promising picture for exploring ranges using our hash-based sketch.

The straightforward employment of count-min sketch to answer frequency estimates on ranges—by turning the range query for the range $[x, y]$ into $y - x + 1$ point queries for each point along the query interval—does not give desired results. In addition to the query time growing linearly with the size of the range, the error also increases linearly with the size of the range, so instead of promising the overestimate of at most εN with a probability of at least $1 - \delta$, we can promise at most $(y - x + 1)\varepsilon N$, which, for large ranges, will deem the data structure futile. For example, if we built a count-min sketch with a maximum overestimate of $\varepsilon N = 7$, a range query of interval size 10,000 could produce an overestimate of up to 70,000.

4.6.1   Dyadic intervals

To avoid the linearly growing error, we need to find a way to decompose an arbitrary range into a small number of subranges. This way, we can obtain tighter frequency estimates by summing up frequency estimates of the smaller ranges without accumulating substantial errors [6].

The main idea is to divide a range into a small number of so-called *dyadic ranges*. Given a complete universe interval as $U = [1, n]$, we define a collection of dyadic ranges at $\log_2 n + 1$ different levels: dyadic ranges of level i, $0 \leq i \leq \log_2 n$ are of length 2^i and can be expressed as $[j2^i + 1, (j+1)2^i]$, where $0 \leq j \leq n/2^i - 1$ (see figure 4.8 for a set of dyadic ranges for universe interval $U = [1,16]$).

The interesting property of dyadic ranges is that any arbitrary range can be decomposed into at most $2\log U$ dyadic ranges. Later in this section, we will show the Python code that can decompose an arbitrary range into a set of dyadic ranges, but first, as an example, consider our small universe from figure 4.8, and see a few examples of separating ranges into the smallest set of dyadic ranges:

- Range [5,14] can be separated into three dyadic ranges: [5,8], [9,12], [13,14]
- Range [2,16] can be separated into four dyadic ranges: [2,2], [3,4], [5,8], [9,16]
- Range [9,13] can be separated into two dyadic ranges: [9,13], [13,13]

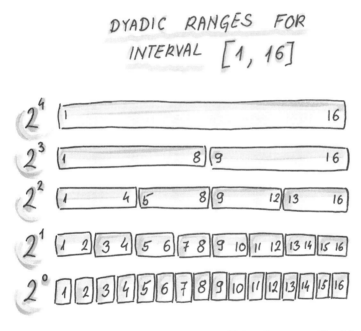

Figure 4.8 Dyadic ranges for the interval [1, 16]. Dyadic ranges of level 0 are the bottom, with ranges of size 1; then the ranges of level 1 are the level above, with the ranges of size 2; and general dyadic ranges at level *i* are of size 2^i. Dyadic ranges across different levels are mutually aligned.

To report the range frequency as the sum of frequencies of dyadic ranges, as updates take place, we need to maintain the frequency information for each dyadic range. To that end, we can use one count-min sketch to serve all updates for dyadic ranges of one level (dyadic ranges of the same size) for a total of $O(\log n)$ count-min sketches. Next, we describe this scheme in more detail.

4.6.2   *Update phase*

Considering that our unit elements are now dyadic ranges, we need to convert an update of a single element arriving to our system to an update of each dyadic range the element is contained in. For example, when updating the frequency of element 5 in our example universe [1,16], we will update the frequency of the following dyadic ranges: [5], [5,6], [5,8], [1,8], and [1,16]. Ranges can be hashed just like regular elements, so there is no obstacle in a dyadic range of the format [*l,r*] being treated as one element.

We accomplish this using $O(\log n)$ count-min sketches by building one count-min sketch for each level of dyadic range; the elements to be updated/estimated in the count-min sketch on the level i will be the dyadic ranges of that level. Figure 4.9 shows

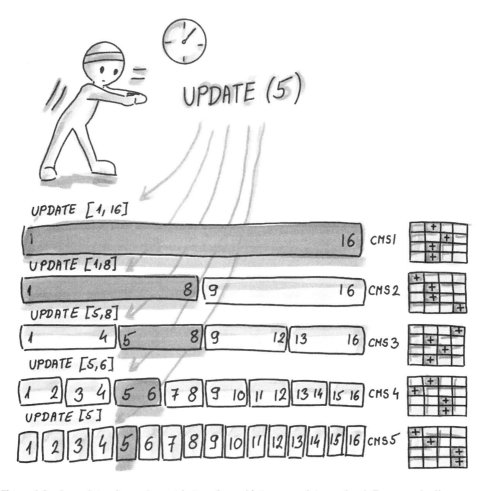

Figure 4.9   An update of one element is transformed into one update per level. For example, if we update 5, we effectively update [1,16] in CMS1, [1,8] in CMS2, [5,8] in CMS3, [5,6] in CMS4, and [5] in CMS5. Instead of updating an element, we are updating a corresponding range to which the element belongs in the relevant CMS.

how the update of a new element takes place: an arriving new element will be updated in each count-min sketch by updating its containing range in the respective CMS.

4.6.3 *Estimate phase*

Now we are ready to perform an estimate on a particular range using dyadic ranges. First we divide the query range into its own set of dyadic ranges. For each dyadic range, we perform an estimate in the CMS that resides on its level (there can be at most two dyadic ranges on the same level per query.) The final result comes from summing up all the estimates. Figure 4.10 shows how we can do the range estimate for [3,13], whose frequency estimate we obtain by estimating the following dyadic ranges in the respective CMSs and summing them: [3,4], [5,8], [9,12], and [13].

Figure 4.10 In this example, the query range [3,13] is separated into [3,4]∪[5,8]∪[9,12]∪[13], and we will obtain the frequency estimate for [3,13] by obtaining the frequency estimates for the mentioned ranges and summing them.

It helps to know that every range can be partitioned into at most 2log n dyadic ranges (at most two per level). Both for the update and for the estimate, the runtime is logarithmic and the error grows only logarithmically. We can make the error the same as in the original single-count min sketch by making the individual CMSs in this scheme, by a logarithmic factor, wider, so that the logarithms cancel out.

4.6.4   *Computing dyadic intervals*

The Python code shown gives a decomposition of I into dyadic intervals, where we are given the large universe U and a range $1 \subseteq U$. First, we build a full binary search tree based on the universe interval, similar to figure 4.8, where each level corresponds to a level of dyadic ranges, and each node corresponds to a unique dyadic range. For instance, the root node represents the range $[1,n]$, its left child represents the range $[1,n/2]$, its right child represents the range $[n/2 + 1,n]$, and so on. The leaves represent the ranges of size 1, and there are n of them. We construct such a tree from the universe interval:

```
from collections import deque

class Node:
    def __init__(self, lower, upper):
        self.data = (lower, upper)
        self.left = None
        self.right = None
        self.marked = False

def intervalToBST(left, right):
    if left == right:
        root = Node(left, right)
        return root
    if abs(right - left) >= 1:
        root = Node(left, right)
        mid = int((left + right) / 2)
        root.left = intervalToBST(left, mid)
        root.right = intervalToBST(mid + 1, right)
        return root
```

Each node represents a dyadic range. ← (annotation for `class Node:`)

Transforms the interval [left, right] into a binary search tree ← (annotation for `def intervalToBST(left, right):`)

Given a particular range, we now compute a set of its dyadic ranges using the binary search tree we constructed. We also use a `marked` attribute at each node. The nodes that end up having a marked attribute of `True` will be the nodes that represent the dyadic subranges of the query range. The algorithm works by first marking each leaf that is a subrange of the interval I. Then it works in a level-by-level fashion going up the tree, and if a node has both children marked, we mark that node and unmark the children. The algorithm stops after we have processed the root node.

Consider a simple interval, $I = [1,5]$, in a universe interval, $U = [1,16]$. On the bottom level of the tree, we mark the nodes representing the following intervals: $[1,1]$, $[2,2]$, $[3,3]$, $[4,4]$, and $[5,5]$. Then we go one level up and find that for node $[1,2]$, both of its children, $[1,1]$ and $[2,2]$, are marked, so we mark $[1,2]$ (and unmark $[1,1]$

and [2,2]). Similarly, we mark [3,4] because [3,3] and [4,4] are marked and unmark [3,3] and [4,4]. On the third level from the bottom, we mark [1,4] because [1,2] and [3,4] are marked and unmark [1,2] and [3,4]. We also process nodes from all other levels all the way to the root, but we do not encounter any more nodes with both children marked as True. Therefore, there are two marked nodes left, and those correspond to the subranges [1,4] and [5,5], and we report them as our dyadic ranges. This functionality is illustrated in the following code:

```
def markNodes(root, lower, upper):
    if root is None:                          ◁───┐  First traverse the nodes
        return                                     │  in a level-by-level order
    queue = [root]                                 │  (BFS traversal).
    stack = deque()
    while(len(queue) > 0):
        stack.append(queue[0])
        node = queue.pop(0)
        if node.left is not None:
            queue.append(node.left)
        if node.right is not None:            ┐  The stack stores
            queue.append(node.right)          │  nodes in a level-by-
                                              │  level order, starting
    while(len(stack) > 0):                ◁───┘  from the leaves.
        i = stack.pop()
        if i.data[0] >= lower and i.data[1] <= upper and
        i.left is None and i.right is None:   ◁───┐  Each leaf inside
            i.marked = True                        │  the interval is
                                                   │  marked.

        if i.left is not None and i.right is not None:
            if i.left.marked and i.right.marked:  ◁──┐  Mark internal nodes
                i.left.marked = False                 │  whose two children
                i.right.marked = False                │  were both marked, and
                i.marked = True                       │  unmark the children.

def inorderMarked(root):          ◁───┐  Print dyadic
    if root is None:                   │  ranges.
        return
    inorderMarked(root.left)
    if root.marked:
        print(root.data)
    inorderMarked(root.right)
```

Here is how this implementation works on an example of universe interval $U = [1,16]$ and interval $I = [3,13]$:

```
k = 4
root = intervalToBST(1, 2**k)
markNodes(root, 3, 13)
inorderMarked(root)
```

The output dyadic intervals are

```
(3, 4)
(5, 8)
(9, 12)
(13, 13)
```

The time to complete the algorithm in the worst case is the time asymptotically required by the breadth-first search algorithm on the universe tree, hence $O(n)$.

Summary

- Frequency estimation problems commonly arise in the analysis of big data, especially in sets that have many occurrences of very few items and a small number of occurrences of many items. Even though in the standard RAM setting frequency estimation can be simply solved in linear space, solving this problem becomes very challenging in the context of streaming data where we are allowed only one pass over the data and sublinear space.
- Count-min sketch is well suited to solve the approximate heavy-hitters problem, as well as many other problems in sensor and NLP domains.
- Count-min sketch is very space efficient and has two error parameters, ε (controlling band of overestimate) and δ (controlling the failure probability) that are tunable and determine the sketch's dimensions. If the allowed band of overestimate error is kept as a fixed percentage of the total quantity of data N, then the amount of space in count-min sketch is independent of the dataset size.
- It is possible to do fairly accurate frequency estimates for range queries using count-min sketch by decomposing a range into a set of dyadic ranges and using $O(\log n)$ count-min sketches.

Cardinality estimation and HyperLogLog

This chapter covers

- Practical use cases where space-efficient cardinality estimation algorithms are used

- Teaching the incremental development of ideas leading up to and including HyperLogLog, such as probabilistic counting and LogLog

- How HyperLogLog works, its space and error requirements, and where it is used

- How different cardinality estimates behave on large data using a simulation via an experiment

- Insights into practical implementations of HyperLogLog

Determining the cardinality of a multiset (a set with duplicates) is a common problem cropping up in all areas of software development, and especially in applications involving databases, network traffic, and so on. However, since the expansion of internet services, where billions of clicks, searches, and purchases are performed daily by a much smaller number of distinct users, there is renewed interest in this fundamental problem. Specifically, there is great interest in developing algorithms and data structures that can estimate the cardinality of a multiset in one scan of data and in an amount of space substantially smaller than the number of distinct elements.

Today, cardinality estimation is used to determine how many distinct visitors are interested in a particular product, how many different users are using particular features of a web app, and how to detect sudden changes in the number of distinct source-destination IP addresses passing through the router (potentially indicating a denial-of-service attack). Because of the way in which information on the web is replicated over and over, measuring cardinality also helps us ascertain how many distinct pieces of content we are dealing with; for example, the number of distinct news articles or copies of a particular website content.

With the large datasets of today, there is a burgeoning interest in designing algorithms that can accurately approximate set cardinality in an amount of space substantially smaller than the set itself. This chapter will examine one such algorithm called HyperLogLog, but first, let's dive into one classic application of measuring cardinality to see why classic solutions to measuring cardinality do not measure up.

5.1   Counting distinct items in databases

Perhaps one of the most familiar examples of measuring cardinality comes from databases and how SQL uses the keyword DISTINCT. Applied to a single column in a table, SELECT DISTINCT returns all the distinct items in that column, while SELECT COUNT DISTINCT returns the number of distinct items in the given column.

Queries with COUNT DISTINCT are very common, especially in e-commerce when we want to obtain the usage statistics on a website. User visit data is often logged in the DAILY_VISITS table, which tends to grow very large, with attributes such as session_id, timestamp, product_id, user_ip_address, visit_duration, and others. By issuing the SELECT operation

```
SELECT COUNT (DISTINCT user_ip_address) WHERE product_id = 9873947
FROM DAILY_VISITS
```

we will receive the number of distinct IP addresses (i.e., users) accessing the product with the ID 9873947 on a given day. On a busy website, a daily visit table can grow to be a few billion rows long, and this particular query might take a while.

The delay is mostly due to the sorting operation that the classic COUNT DISTINCT does in most databases (e.g., Azure SQL/SQL Server), unless the column was previously ordered. After we sort the column, all duplicates land next to each other, and one sequential scan is sufficient to identify and count the distinct items. The sorting operation costs $O(n \log_2 n)$ on a table with n rows and doesn't scale well even on a few million, let alone a few billion, rows. To make matters worse, even simple queries do many COUNT DISTINCTs and GROUP BYs on different columns, and sorting one column does not help reduce the complexity of sorting another one. We could use a hash table to make things faster, but a hash table still requires linear space in the number of distinct elements k. Because k can go up to n, we cannot afford to use hashing either.

Even when we only need to know how many distinct items the multiset has, and don't have to list the distinct items themselves, the complexity remains. To convince yourself of that, consider the element-distinctness problem, in which, given an array of n elements, we are asked to determine whether all elements in it are distinct; this problem has a lower bound of $\Omega(n \log_2 n)$ [1].

To address scalability issues, the newer editions of database management systems and warehouses turn to cardinality estimates: SQL Server 2019 has the APPROX_ COUNT_DISTINCT operation (http://mng.bz/QWjm) that uses a very small amount of space and works fast. Google BigQuery goes a step further and makes this approximate and probabilistic approach the default in COUNT_DISTINCT, reserving EXACT_ COUNT_DISTINCT for situations where we absolutely need the exact answer (http:// mng.bz/y4PJ). Running underneath these estimators is the algorithm called Hyper- LogLog, originally invented by Flajolet et al. [2], that offers amazing space savings (think KBs) while processing trillion-sized datasets and keeps the error rate fairly low—on the order of $O(1/\sqrt{m})$ where m denotes the number of 5- or 6-bit-wide memory locations. One common choice for m is 2^{14}.

In this book, we have seen a number of examples of saving space in exchange for giving up some accuracy; however, HyperLogLog gives a whole new meaning to space efficiency, almost always staying in the range of a few kilobytes while hitting true cardinality, with a small error rate (e.g., ±2%), on average.

What follows in the next section is the incremental development of ideas that led to HyperLogLog. We will present the original algorithm and some examples, simulations, and mathematical intuition around it, as well as mention some of the ways in which HyperLogLog has been implemented and optimized by companies such as Redis, Google, Facebook, and others.

Is HyperLogLog a data structure or an algorithm (and does it matter)? Originally, HyperLogLog was referred to as an algorithm, and we will refer to it as an algorithm when we focus on the procedure that is performed on the input data. However, HyperLogLog also needs to store an array with values that are computed on the input data, and this structure is often stored for future use, as we will see in our aggregation example in section 5.5. In that context, we will also talk about HyperLogLog as a data structure.

5.2   *HyperLogLog incremental design*

The essential idea of HyperLogLog (HLL) is to use probabilistic and statistical properties of uniform random bit strings to guess the cardinality of a multiset. To that end, elements are initially hashed into bit strings: the original implementation of Hyper- LogLog uses 32-bit hashes, and the more recent Google reincarnation called HyperLog- Log++ [3] and the implementation by Redis (http://antirez.com/news/75) use 64-bit hashes to accommodate arbitrarily large cardinalities. Hashes are not random, and it is impossible to obtain random data from nonrandom data; however, they mimic randomness well enough for our purposes (i.e., they *look* random).

Given a multiset $M = \{a_1, a_2, ..., a_n\}$ with n elements and k distinct elements (we do not know k) and using a hash function $h{:}U \rightarrow \{0,1\}^L$, we produce a hashed set $h(M) = \{h_1, h_2, ..., h_n\}$ where $h_i = h(a_i)$ with hash length $L = |h_i|$. For a large enough L (e.g., $L = 64$), each distinct item will map to a distinct hash with high probability so that the number of distinct hashes will also be k or very close. Hashing by itself does not help us estimate cardinality just yet, but now we've switched from estimating the number of distinct input elements to estimating the number of distinct hashes.

We decided it would be best to demonstrate how HyperLogLog works by gradually building from the simplest algorithms, identifying their flaws, and getting to more and more sophisticated algorithms. To aid in understanding, we obviate some of the technical details by showing Python-like pseudocode as opposed to the code itself.

In other words, we will try to put ourselves in the mindset of HyperLogLog's inventors and start from something simple and gradually improve it. Our hope is that you will not only learn about the final product but about the iterative process of algorithm design and making little improvements at every stage. At some point, subsections 5.2.1–5.2.4 might start to feel a bit dense from a mathematical point of view. But don't worry; section 5.4 contains an experiment that tests the three versions of the algorithm that leads to HyperLogLog, and that should help you understand the ideas behind the algorithms and the need for respective improvements.

5.2.1   *The first cut: Probabilistic counting*

The roughest estimate, called *probabilistic counting* [4], observes the bit patterns in the hash by computing ρ_i for each hash h_i such that

$$\rho_i = (\text{the number of trailing zeros in } h_i) + 1$$

That is, ρ_i will denote the position of the first 1 encountered from the right (if the hash does not contain any 1s, then $\rho_i = L + 1$.) Without loss of generality, we will use right instead of left in this and other places in this chapter. For example, for $h_1 = 1100$, $h_2 = 0111$ and $h_3 = 0000$, the respective values of ρ_i are $\rho_1 = 3$, $\rho_2 = 1$, and $\rho_3 = 5$. The cardinality estimate E will depend on $\rho_{max} = \max(\rho_1, \rho_2, ..., \rho_n)$, and it's equal to

$$E = 2^{\rho_{max}}$$

Here is the idea of probabilistic counting expressed in Python-like pseudocode:

```
p_max = 0
for a in M              ◁——┤ M is a multiset whose cardinality
    h = hash(a)              we wish to measure.
    p = num_trailing_zeros(h) + 1
    if(p > p_max)
        p_max = p
return 2**p_max
```

Example 1

Figure 5.1 shows probabilistic counting in action where $n = 12$, $k = 7$, and the final estimate of $2^5 = 32$, with the lemon item significantly affecting the estimate.

Figure 5.1   A dataset of 12 items is hashed into 16-bit hashes. As we scan the dataset, we keep the running maximum of the ρ_i. In this example, the lemon item, whose hash is `1001 1111 0001 0000`, holds the maximum $\rho_{max} = 5$, and our cardinality estimate is $E = 2^{\rho_{max}} = 32$, but the true distinct count is $k = 7$.

This is not as close to the truth as we would like, but we are just getting started. The rough intuition behind probabilistic counting is that if we managed to get an unusual hash (i.e., a hash with many trailing zeros), then that would be an indicator of the presence of many other hashes in the set. Let's see why that is, but before we do, keep in mind that we are still far from the truth with this estimate, so do not get married to this method, and similarly, do not expect the mathematical explanation that follows to be the written-in-stone kind of truth; we are talking approximately.

Let's put on our probability hats: in a uniformly randomly generated set of k bit strings, on average about $k/2$ bit strings have 0 as their last digit, and the other $k/2$ have 1. Out of the former $k/2$, half, on average (i.e., $k/4$), have 00 as their two last digits and the other $k/4$ have 10, and so on. Ultimately, $k/2^i$ items, on average, have their last i digits as all 0s and another $k/2^i$ have their last i digits of the form 10^{i-1}.

Accordingly, the probability of generating a hash where $\rho_i = 1$ (hash ends with 1) is $1/2$, the probability of a hash where $\rho_i = 2$ (hash ends with 10) is $1/4$, and the probability of a hash where $\rho_i = i$ (ends with 10^{i-1}) is $1/2^i$. For the event that occurs with probability $1/2^i$, on average we need 2^i repetitions for it to occur, so working backward, having an element with $\rho_i = \rho_{max}$ on average implies the cardinality of $2^{\rho_{max}}$, which corresponds to the probabilistic counting estimate.

However, this is only the *average* behavior of random variables (i.e., expectation), and often the ground truth is far from average. Consider a dataset with two data points, 0 and 100; our average is 50, which says little about the actual values in the set. Similar things happen with random variables, where deviations from this average will occur, and even a small deviation can significantly affect the estimate, considering that ρ_{max} is in the exponent. In general, we observe the estimate error of HyperLogLog as the `relative error`—the fraction of the true cardinality by which the estimate is off in any direction ($\pm\frac{E-k}{k}$); this fraction can be very large for small cardinalities.

5.2.2 Stochastic averaging, or "when life gives you lemons"

There are a couple of problems with our first-cut solution: even without outliers affecting the estimate, all estimates are powers of 2, which for many cardinalities makes it impossible to get close to the right answer. To address the outlier issue, we will resort to a method called stochastic averaging, which divides the hash set uniformly randomly into $m = 2^b$ subsets of roughly the same size by throwing hashes into the buckets determined by the first b bits of each hash. Once each hash is assigned to a bucket, we perform probabilistic counting on each bucket individually: instead of 1 estimator ρ_{max}, we will have m estimators $\rho_{i,max}$, $1 \leq i \leq m$, where $\rho_{i,max}$ represents the ρ_{max} of hashes from the ith bucket.

You can think of partitioning into subsets as a poor man's hashing of the whole set m times and obtaining m estimators that we can further combine. In reality, we cannot afford m hash functions and the computational cost of hashing each item m times.

Now that we have m estimators, we will first compute their arithmetic average

$$A = \frac{\sum_{i=1}^{m} \rho_{i,max}}{m}$$

and use it to obtain the average bucket estimate

$$E_{bucket} = 2^A$$

the equivalent of a geometric mean of probabilistic counting estimates for individual buckets. To obtain the overall estimate E, we need to account for all m buckets:

$$E = m \times E_{bucket} = m \times 2^{\frac{\sum_{i=1}^{m} \rho_{i,max}}{m}}$$

Example 1 (continued)

Let's see how this works when $b = 2$, and hence there are $m = 4$ buckets. Figure 5.2 illustrates the contents and $\rho_{i,max}$ for each bucket. To compute the estimate, we first compute $A = (2 + 2 + 5 + 1)/4 = 2.5$. From there, we have that $E_{bucket} = 2^A = 2^{2.5} \approx 5.66$, and $E = m \times E_{bucket} = 4 \times 5.66 = 22.64$, which is more accurate than our earlier estimate of 32. The ultimate value we are aiming at is 7.

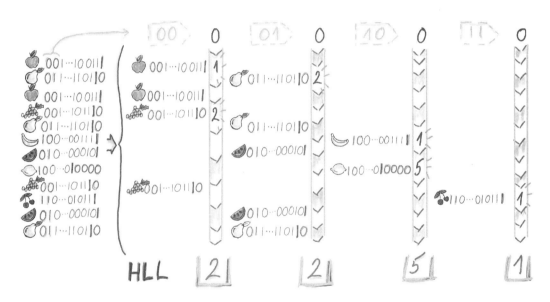

Figure 5.2 In this example, each hash is being mapped to a bucket based on its first two bits (e.g., the hash corresponding to the grape item is mapped to the bucket 00, while the hash corresponding to the pear item is mapped to the bucket 01. When this process runs on large datasets, we expect each bucket to receive the same number of distinct hashes. Each bucket computes its $\rho_{i,max}$, which in this case results in bucket values of 2, 2, 5, and 1. Now the hash of the lemon item is only affecting the value stored in bucket 10.

The following Python-like pseudocode shows how stochastic averaging works:

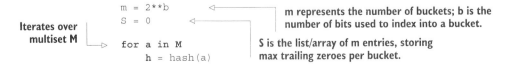

```
m = 2**b
S = 0

for a in M
    h = hash(a)
```

Iterates over multiset M

m represents the number of buckets; b is the number of bits used to index into a bucket.

S is the list/array of m entries, storing max trailing zeroes per bucket.

```
    p = num_trailing_zeros(h) + 1
    bucket = first_bits(h, b)  . . . .       ◁         Integer
    if(p > S[bucket])                                  decribed by
        S[bucket] = p                                  first b bits of h
sum = 0
for item in S
    sum += item

arit_avg = sum / m
return m * 2**avg
```

5.2.3 LogLog

The LogLog algorithm uses stochastic averaging in combination with a normalization constant $\tilde{a}_m$ that is introduced to undo the systematic overestimate bias that occurs when we estimate cardinality with a $\rho_{i,max}$ random variable (the maximum of geometric variables of parameter $1/2$). Hence, we modify the original estimate to the following formula

$$E = \tilde{a}_m \times m \times 2^{\frac{\sum_{i=1}^{m} \rho_{i,max}}{m}}$$

where the constant $\tilde{a}_m$ is parameterized by m and equals

$$\tilde{a}_m \sim 0.39701 - \frac{2\pi^2 + (\ln 2)^2}{48m}$$

For most practical purposes (specifically, when m $\geq$ 64), one can use $\tilde{a}_m = 0.39701$. More details on how the expression for $\tilde{a}_m$ is derived can be found in the original LogLog paper [5].

Example 1 (continued)

To obtain the LogLog estimate for our running example (from figure 5.2), we compute $\tilde{a}_4$ to be approximately 0.292, so the LogLog estimate is 0.292 × 22.6 ≈ 6.6, extremely close to the true cardinality of 7!

ERROR AND SPACE CONSIDERATIONS IN LOGLOG

Using statistical analysis, it has been found that the relative error in LogLog can be closely approximated by $^{1.3}\!/\!\sqrt{m}$. To put this in perspective, for many modern implementations, the value of m is often set to 2^{14}, and we can expect the relative error to be $^{1.3}\!/\!\sqrt{2^{14}} = 1.01\%$, regardless of the dataset size. If we take into account that 2^{14} 8-byte integer locations only take up about 130 KBs, LogLog might seem like magic!

Still, it is important to recognize that we do not need 8 bytes for bucket counters. In fact, we need five or six bits, depending on how large the cardinalities we're estimating are. If the upper cardinality limit of our dataset is k_{max}, then we need $O(\log_2 k_{max})$ to be the length of a hash to differentiate up to that cardinality, and then we need $O(m \log_2 \log_2 k_{max})$ bits to store the maximum value in the bucket (hence the LogLog). A safe upper cardinality limit is $k_{max} = 2^{64}$, so one bucket needs six bits. The total storage requirement of LogLog is

$$O(m \log_2 \log_2 k_{max})$$

When we plug in $m = 2^{14}$ for the common value, it turns out we need approximately 12 KBs to store LogLog.

To be more exact, we expect the maximum cardinality within one bucket to be closer to k_{max}/m (k_{max} is the worst case), which reduces the space requirement to

$$O\left(m \log_2 \log_2 \left(\frac{k_{max}}{m}\right)\right)$$

However, in our example, where $k_{max}/m = 2^{50}$, this does not help, as the logarithms are rounded up to their integer values (in this case, the logarithm of 50 will be rounded up to 6.)

SuperLogLog

One way to improve on the error rate of LogLog is to retain only a percentage θ of the lowest bucket values and base the estimate on those $m_\theta = \theta m$ buckets. This is called the *truncation rule*. A similar approach called the *restriction rule* uses only bucket values that are no larger than $\lceil \log_2 (k_{max}/m) + 3 \rceil$, which removes outliers but also allows us to use buckets that are $\lceil \log_2 \lceil \log_2 (k_{max}/m) + 3 \rceil \rceil$ bits wide. There is experimental evidence that the error rate drops to $1.05/\sqrt{m}$ when employing the truncation and restriction rules.

Even though it is an improvement over the basic probabilistic counting approach, the arithmetic mean in the exponent can still draw the final estimate arbitrarily far from the mean because the arithmetic mean is very sensitive to outliers. It is similar in the 3D context, where the centroid (the 3D version of arithmetic mean) can end up arbitrarily far from the center of the mass due to one point being far from all the others. Our final improvement, HyperLogLog, will use the harmonic mean of the bucket values to compute the estimate.

5.2.4   *HyperLogLog: Stochastic averaging with harmonic mean*

The formula for the harmonic mean applied to our buckets, which represents our new bucket average, is as follows:

$$E_{bucket} = \frac{m}{\sum_{i=1}^{m} 2^{-\rho_{i,max}}}$$

For the final estimate, we will apply the appropriate bias-correcting factor α_m and account for all m buckets:

$$E = a_m \times m \times E_{bucket} = \frac{a_m m^2}{\sum_{i=1}^{m} 2^{-\rho_{i,max}}}$$

The bias-correcting factor is different than that of LogLog, and it can be approximated as follows:

$$a_m = \frac{1}{2 \ln 2 \left(1 + \frac{1}{m}(3 \ln 2 - 1) + O(m^{-2})\right)}$$

For very large values of m, $a_m = \frac{1}{(2 \ln 2)} = 0.72134$ is a good approximation, but it is also useful to build some typical values of α_m into our code:

$$\alpha_{16} = 0.673$$

$$\alpha_{32} = 0.697$$

$$\alpha_{64} = 0.709$$

$$\alpha_m = 0.723/(1 + 1.079/m) \text{ for } m \geq 128$$

Example 1 (continued)

When we apply the harmonic mean to our running example from figure 5.2, we get

$$E_{bucket} = \frac{4}{\left(\frac{1}{2}\right)^2 + \left(\frac{1}{2}\right)^2 + \left(\frac{1}{2}\right)^5 + \left(\frac{1}{2}\right)^1} = \frac{4}{\frac{33}{32}} \approx 3.88$$

We also get $\alpha_4 = 0.541$ from the formula for α_m, which further gives the following estimate:

$$E = 0.541 \times 4 \times 3.88 = 8.39$$

This estimate is even further from the truth than our earlier LogLog estimate (6.6), but as datasets get bigger, as we will see in the simulations in section 5.4, HyperLogLog is a less biased estimator and has a smaller relative error. The statistical analysis shows that the relative error in the HyperLogLog algorithm is down to $1.04/\sqrt{m}$. For more details on how the error rate in HyperLogLog is derived, you can consult the original HyperLogLog paper [6].

   This is the end of our story about how we obtain the raw estimate in HyperLogLog, whose Python-like pseudocode is shown (the first part of the pseudocode snippet, excluding setting alpha parameters, is identical to the earlier pseudocode snippet).

There are a few minor tweaks after we obtain the raw estimate, specifically when the cardinality we are computing became too small or too large:

```
alpha16 = 0.673          ◁─────┐  Sets alpha for
alpha32 = 0.697                │  different values of m
alpha64 = 0.709
alpha_m = 0.7213/(1 + 1.079/m) for m>= 128

m = 2**b
S = 0

for a in M
    h = hash(a)
    p = num_trailing_zeros(h) + 1
    bucket = first_bits(h, b)  . . . .
    if(p > S[bucket])
        S[bucket] = p
sum = 0
for item in S
    sum += 2**(-1*item)

harmonic_avg = m / sum
E = alpha_m * m * harmonic_avg      ◁────── Raw estimate
```

Computes corrected estimate └→

```
if E <= 5*m/2           ◁──┐  Small range
                           │  correction
    V = num_registers_zero()    ◁──┐  Let V be the number
    if V != 0                       │  of registers equal to 0.
        E_final = mlog(m/V)
    else
        E_final = E              ┌── Intermediate range,
if E <= 2**32 / 30       ◁──────┘   no correction
    E_final = E
if E > 2**32 / 30
    E_final = -2**32 * log(1 - E/2**32)
    return E_final       ◁────┐  Corrected estimate with
                              │  relative error of ±1.04/sqrt(m)
```

Large range correction └→

In the case of very small cardinalities (in relation to the number of buckets), many buckets will remain empty, and in that case, we will resort to the probabilistic method called *linear counting* to establish true cardinality. This approach follows the logic of the balls-and-bins setup where, if we throw n balls into m bins uniformly randomly, based on how many buckets remain empty, we can estimate the total number of balls. More details can be found in the paper on linear counting [7].

An interesting artifact of using linear counting is that right at the cross-over point, when the cardinality becomes large enough to switch to the HyperLogLog estimate, there is a large spike in bias. The authors of HyperLogLog++ tried to alleviate this issue by experimentally ascertaining average amounts of bias for each cardinality around that point and then returning the estimate by that bias amount. Redis implementation uses polynomial regression that approximates the curve of the bias and then returns the estimates by that predicted amount.

Considering that our pseudocode reflects the original paper's implementation of HyperLogLog, one issue that might arise when using 32-bit hashes, as they are used in the original paper, is that for very large cardinalities, hashes start colliding, so we start losing accuracy even on the hashing level, and thus a correction to the estimate is needed. However, this is not a problem if we use a 64-bit hash, as it is used in all modern implementations by Google, Redis, Facebook (http://mng.bz/M2z2), and others.

ERROR AND SPACE CONSIDERATIONS IN HYPERLOGLOG

Statistical proofs show that HyperLogLog has a relative error of around $1.04/\sqrt{m}$. Space consumption is the same as in LogLog:

$$O(m \log_2 \log_2 k_{max})$$

And just like in LogLog, we can use six-bit fields for buckets. Are we being stingy by insisting on custom six-bit fields as opposed to standard eight-bit fields for an algorithm that already has a very small memory footprint, and are we sacrificing valuable CPU time by unpacking those bits? Answers to these questions are largely dependent on a particular application. For example, when embedding algorithms in hardware, or when aggregating a large number of HyperLogLogs into one, such differences add up, and every space optimization trick is very much worth it.

Before experimentally testing the features of data structures/algorithms introduced in this section, we will break up the technical discussion with an example of a context where HLL can be used.

5.3 Use case: Catching worms with HLL

Applications and intrusion detection systems that monitor network traffic keep track of changes in various network parameters that might reveal impending security breaches, for example, in an organization's network. One indicator of network health is related to the source-destination IP address pairs available on packet headers passing through a router.

Stable network traffic is marked by a (potentially large) number of packets exchanged between a much smaller number of pairs of computers. Having one source open a large number of connections to (sometimes random) destinations in a short time interval, or simply a significant rise in the number of distinct source-destination IP address pairs, might indicate a virus [8] (see figures 5.3 and 5.4).

Thus, embedding a HyperLogLog in software that is wired into a router can be very beneficial, especially due to the need for fast computation times and a small memory footprint. Another good place to strategically place a HyperLogLog and other data structures/algorithms that help analyze busy network traffic with small

Figure 5.3   A healthy network flow. A fairly large number of packets but a small number of different flows.

Figure 5.4   A suspicious flow—having many source-destination pairs, and one source opening a large number of different connections in a short amount of time

space and time requirements is an entry point in an organization's network, as shown in figure 5.5.

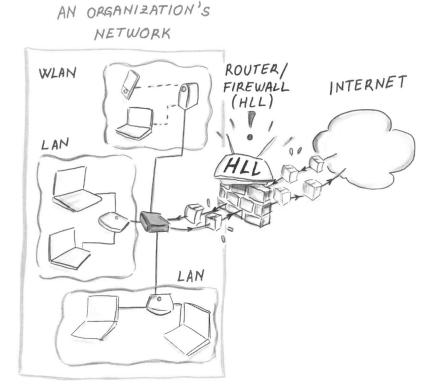

Figure 5.5 Placing a HyperLogLog at the entry point of the network within an organization can help us gather valuable statistics about the network traffic of that organization.

5.4 But how does it work? A mini experiment

In this section, we run simulations to gather some intuition on how various estimates—probabilistic counting, LogLog, and HyperLogLog—compare with respect to bias and accuracy when run on a reasonably sized dataset. We design an experiment to see how well the error bounds derived from probabilistic analysis correspond with numbers from the practical context. We are also interested in how much the normalization factors, $\tilde{a}_m$ (for LogLog) and a_m (for HyperLogLog), improve accuracy, as well as the effect of the number of buckets in HyperLogLog on the accuracy and width of the distribution.

Data for all plots in this section is derived from running the following experiment 1,000 times: we generate $N = 2^{16} = 65,536$ 32-bit strings where each bit is chosen uniformly randomly. We are starting from uniform random strings that act like hashes (and we will refer to them in future text as hashes) because we are interested in producing 1,000 hash sets of the same (or almost the same) cardinality. Considering that there can be 2^{32} hashes and our hash set size is 2^{16}, in most experiments we will not encounter hash collisions, and the total number of distinct hashes/items will be equal to the dataset size, $N = k = 65{,}536$; there is an occasional hash collision, but the distinct count k never goes below 65,531, marking a negligible difference in cardinality between different experiments. We designed the experiment without duplicates because they do not influence the estimates of our methods, so this experiment could also serve to demonstrate how even much larger hash sets than 2^{16} but with 2^{16} distinct items behave.

In our first plot, shown in figure 5.6, we compare the following methods:

- Probabilistic counting
- Stochastic averaging with arithmetic mean unnormalized ($m = 64$)
- Stochastic averaging with harmonic mean unnormalized ($m = 64$)

The *x*-axis shows the logarithm base 2 of cardinality; we indicate on the plot the position of true cardinality (at 16). The *y*-axis shows the count of the number of experiments.

The plot shows probabilistic counting to have the largest deviation of the three methods, having some instances of the experiment be as much as 12 units of log2 cardinality apart and 384 instances of the experiment (over a third) with log2 cardinality of 18 and over. Probabilistic counting is followed by stochastic averaging with arithmetic mean unnormalized, spreading about 1.5 units of log2 cardinality, and the stochastic averaging with harmonic mean unnormalized is the narrowest of the three.

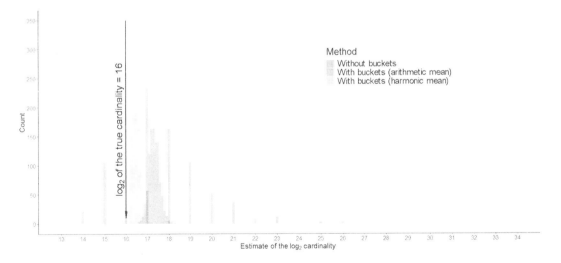

Figure 5.6   Plot shows the comparison of the probabilistic counting (without buckets), stochastic averaging with arithmetic mean (unnormalized; with buckets; arithmetic mean) and stochastic averaging with harmonic mean (unnormalized; with buckets; harmonic mean). All raw estimates show consistent overestimate bias; however, the least bias, on average, is shown by the harmonic mean method, followed by the arithmetic mean method and probabilistic counting. The largest deviation in the estimates (having different experiments vary in estimates by a factor of 2^{12}) is exhibited by probabilistic counting, which only has estimates that are powers of 2, followed by the arithmetic mean method, and then followed by the harmonic mean method.

The harmonic mean method is closest to the true estimate on average. The average log2 cardinalities in this experiment are 17.31 (probabilistic counting), 17.32 (stochastic averaging with arithmetic mean unnormalized), and 16.47 (stochastic averaging with harmonic mean unnormalized).

After we normalize the arithmetic and harmonic mean estimates with respective constants $\tilde{a}_{64} = 0.3907$ and $a_{64} = 0.709$, average log2 cardinalities drop to 15.97 (LogLog) and 15.93 (HyperLogLog), respectively, with an average bias from true cardinality in both cases around 13%. It is good that we obtain this result, considering that the estimated error rate in both cases is $O\left(1/\sqrt{m}\right) = O\left(1/8\right)$, approximately 12.5%.

5.4.1   The effect of the number of buckets (m)

Here we show the experiment with the same hash sets as before, but this time, we measure the effect of using three different choices for the number of buckets in HyperLogLog: $m = 16$, $m = 64$, and $m = 256$. As expected, figure 5.7 shows that the more buckets we have, the less variance we encounter in the obtained estimates.

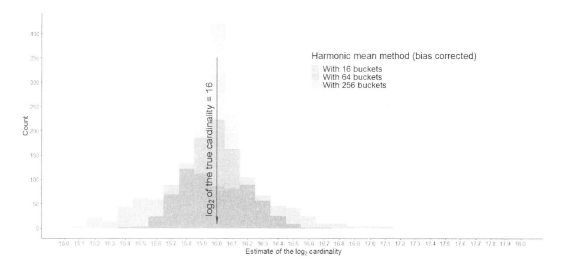

Figure 5.7   Effect of different values of *m* on the accuracy of the log2 cardinality estimate in HyperLogLog. The larger the number of buckets, the smaller deviation from true cardinality. In general, the harmonic mean method, once bias-corrected, rarely over-/underestimates by more than one unit of log2 in all three cases.

Because the bias-corrected harmonic mean from HyperLogLog gets very close to the truth, in figure 5.8 we show the same graph, but plotted as the bias from actual cardinality in each experiment (now the *x*-axis is the true cardinality not the logarithm).

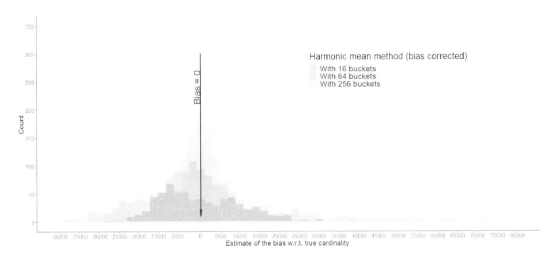

Figure 5.8   The effect of buckets on the cardinality estimate in HyperLogLog. A larger *m* implies smaller bias and a more properly Gaussian-looking distribution.

As observed in the original paper, the distribution of cardinalities appears Gaussian, with shorter tails when m is larger. A rough Gaussian distribution can help us draw the following practical conclusion:

> *Given the standard error (or relative error) of HyperLogLog as* $\sigma = {}^{1.04}\!/\sqrt{m}$, *then about 65%, 95%, and 99% of values, respectively (a value being the cardinality estimate for one dataset), will fall within* σ, 2σ *and* 3σ, *fractions away from the true cardinality.*

To verify that, we took the case of $m = 256$ buckets, hence $\sigma = {}^{1.04}\!/\sqrt{256} = 0.065$. Therefore, 6.5%, 13%, and 19.5% are, respectively, one, two, and three standard errors away from the truth. It turns out that in our experiment, 71%, 94.8%, and 99.2%, respectively, fall within the boundaries of the mentioned errors, roughly indicating Gaussian behavior (even a bit more tight). Thus, when we implement HyperLogLog, we can expect the estimates to behave in a predictable manner and most often be very close to the mean (true cardinality).

5.5   *Use case: Aggregation using HyperLogLog*

Let's revisit a previous example with tables of daily customer visits on a popular website. As we have seen, computing the distinct count on a column (e.g., finding a total number of users) in a large table is a challenge, but the real issue crops up when we need to aggregate those insights over days, weeks, months, and so on. Individual data is very costly to maintain for a long period of time, yet it is crucial for many businesses to be able to go back and pull relevant statistics from an arbitrary moment in the past. Unsplash, a photography website that hosts a large number of images and receives millions of visits per day, uses HyperLogLog to solve this problem (http://mng.bz/aDXJ).

One issue with calculating the distinct count on one or more columns in a table is that even if we are magically given the distinct counts, it in no way helps compute the aggregated count, as shown in figure 5.9.

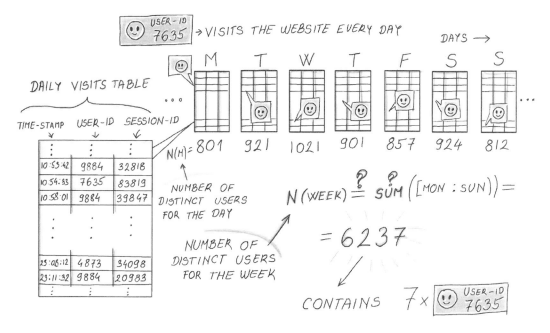

Figure 5.9   In a daily visit table, each row indicates one visit by a user, and each table maintains a separate distinct-count variable that tracks the number of different users. Considering that some users return to the website repeatedly, we cannot simply sum the individual counts to obtain the week's distinct user count.

However, if we can maintain one HyperLogLog per daily table instead of the distinct count, then we can aggregate the results over multiple days by performing a union operation between two (or more) HyperLogLogs of the same size and the same hash function, as shown in figure 5.10.

The union operation of two HyperLogLogs HLL1[1..m] and HLL2[1..m] works by creating a new HyperLogLog HLL_UNION[1..m], and assigning max(HLL1[i], HLL2[i]) to HLL_UNION[i] for each i, $1 \leq i \leq m$. For example, the union of two HyperLogLogs whose bucket values are (1, 4, 2, 5) and (2, 2, 5, 3) will produce another HyperLogLog with bucket values (2, 4, 5, 5).

What happens to the error rate when we aggregate a large number of HyperLogLogs? The relative error, being dependent on the number of buckets m, stays the same after aggregation, as the number of buckets remains unchanged. But as much as we might be tempted to think that in HyperLogLog the error rate does not depend on the size of the dataset, as it is often advertised, it is important to keep in mind (just like with count-min sketch) that the relative error *is* the percentage of true cardinality,

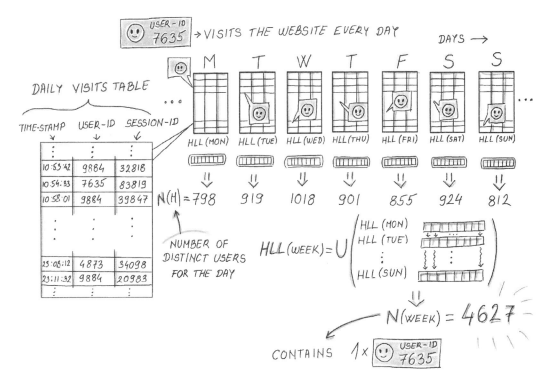

Figure 5.10   Maintaining one HyperLogLog per daily table helps us later aggregate the HyperLogLogs over multiple days to obtain an estimate for more tables. In fact, HyperLogLog can easily be encoded so that we can maintain a table of HyperLogLog schemas to be decoded later.

which generally tends to increase with dataset size. So even though the error rate stays the same after union, the constant by which the error increases actually grows proportionally with the number of distinct elements.

HyperLogLog has a simple encoding, which makes it conducive to being stored as a record in a table of HyperLogLogs, whose space requirements are dramatically smaller than maintaining the equivalent daily tables. This enables us to aggregate HLLs over arbitrary time intervals or at certain specific dates, as shown in figure 5.11.

Moreover, the estimates can be performed on many levels, where we can aggregate hourly HLLs into daily HLLs, then use daily HLLs to compute weekly HLLs, and so on (shown in figure 5.12). In the world of traditional databases, doing a number of groupings on different levels usually means having to scan whole data once for each grouping we want to do. With HyperLogLog, we only have to scan all data once to produce HyperLogLogs, and then we only read and combine HyperLogLogs.

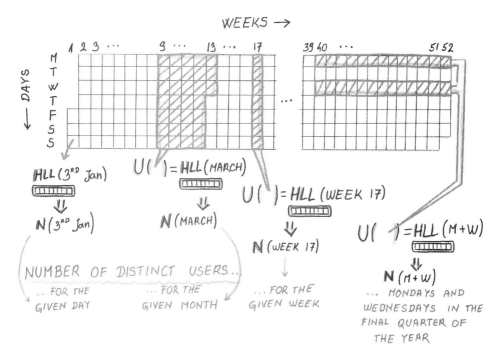

Figure 5.11   Once we have the daily HLLs that are stored, we can perform a union over the arbitrary choice of interest to obtain the aggregate cardinality estimate for a given period.

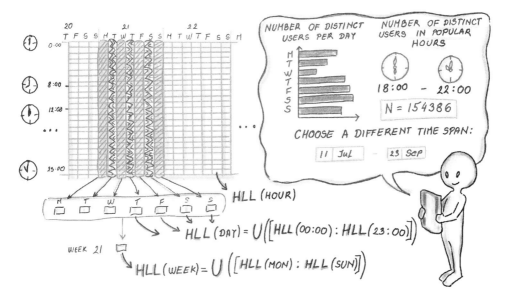

Figure 5.12   Aggregation happens over multiple levels, in this case hour, day, week, and so on. In databases it is common that when we group by different time spans, we do one scan of all data for each level of aggregation.

Summary

- Cardinality estimation arises in many areas of software development, primarily databases, network traffic, and e-commerce. Due to the volume of data, classic database functions for exact cardinality computation are being replaced with probabilistic methods that offer great space savings in exchange for a small error in accuracy.

- HyperLogLog is the algorithm/data structure that uses hashing and probabilistic properties of random bit strings to gauge the set cardinality. Its space consumption is $O(m \log_2 \log_2 k,)$ and its relative error rate $1.04/\sqrt{m}$.

- Many companies that run large systems have implemented HyperLogLog for their use and have improved and modernized various aspects of it (e.g., implementations by Google, Redis, Facebook, and others.)

- The estimates provided by HyperLogLog have a roughly Gaussian shape. In our simulations on a hash set of 2^{16}, we ascertained that HyperLogLog obeys the rules of Gaussian distribution by letting approximately 70% of data fall within one, 95% within two, and 99% within three standard errors.

- The true power of HyperLogLog is visible when doing aggregations of a large number of large individual tables that represent data over time. Instead of keeping the large tables, we can store a table of HyperLogLogs and choose to aggregate and merge HyperLogLogs for the periods of interest (e.g., week, month, quarter, etc.).

Part 2

Real-time analytics

Thus far, we haven't been concerned with the state in which massive data arrives at our disposal. All the algorithms we have gotten to know so far can be applied to continuously arriving data as well as to historical data residing in a big database system. The three chapters in part 2 present algorithms and data structures (sketches) whose design considerations and application context were driven by the continuous arrival of data tuples referred to as data streams. Here, due to the transient nature of the data at hand, algorithms have to operate efficiently and incorporate knowledge about the stream after each tuple seen. We achieve this by keeping sketches of a data stream. Some of them, like random samples, are general and can answer many queries about the data. Others, like the t-digest, are more specialized, and the algorithm/data structure is tailored to return a specific feature of the data, like different (tail) percentiles. All in all, imagining a lot of data arriving at nonuniform speeds and, once operated on, leaving into oblivion, is a good starting point for things to come.

Streaming data: Bringing everything together

This chapter covers

- Learning about the streaming data pipeline model and its distributed framework

- Determining where streaming data applications and the data stream model meet

- Identifying where algorithms and data structures fit in data streams

- Setting up basic computing constraints and concepts inherent to data streams

- Giving some probabilistic background for the next two chapters to follow

Previous chapters introduced a number of algorithms/data structures for sketching (an important characteristic) huge amounts of data residing in a database or, as you saw in the application of the HyperLogLog in network traffic surveillance, arriving and expiring at a lightning rate. In this chapter, we will round up these algorithms.

The first part of this chapter will zoom out of the very detailed view on massive data algorithms. Instead, we will do some bookkeeping and inspection of the wider context where the algorithms covered so far find their use. At this point, we need to start dealing with data streams, and, conveniently, one of data streams' natural habitats is streaming-data pipeline applications and their wider system architecture. If this sounds too vague, see *Streaming Data* by Andrew G. Psaltis (Manning, 2017). You shouldn't think that you bought a book that tells you to buy another book; we will introduce enough of what you'll need here. Skimming sections 1.1, 1.2, and 1.3 in Psaltis's book, though, should clear up anything that piques your interest further. We will use and show the streaming data system/pipeline model from Psaltis to stage and depict how and where Bloom filters, count-min sketches, and HyperLogLogs can be employed to save time/space in that particular architectural landscape.

In the past, streaming data was an exception reserved for systems controlling highly critical processes in nuclear facilities or airplanes where quick automatic reaction to anything unusual meant saving human lives. With the arrival of the internet, the myriad requests issued by users to the server or a cloud of their choice are easy to conceptualize as streaming data. With the arrival of the Internet of Things, any device that is sophisticated enough to measure and then report its current state over some distance becomes one of many producers feeding a centralized server or a cloud with a constant stream of data. This happens at rapid rates and in an unpredictable and volatile fashion.

We may visualize streams as never-ending sequences of data and huge datasets made up of many tiny pieces, but most of the time we are not particularly interested in the tiny pieces. "What was the exact temperature recorded by the sensor ID 1092 at 11:34 p.m. on May 15, 2003?" sounds like a question someone might only ask in court. And for such purposes, data is stored in archival storage. But what we care about on a daily basis is the imperfect big picture reported in real time. This setup stands in contrast to how we are used to thinking of traditional databases taking great pride in providing perfect accuracy, but on their own clock. Figure 6.1 [1] is a rough depiction of the streaming model algorithm researchers use.

We are ready to elucidate how components of this high-level view on streaming data (figure 6.1) correspond to specific components of a fully implemented and functional streaming data application.

Anyone trying to explain a streaming data algorithm would plant it in the *analysis tier* of the streaming data pipeline model (figure 6.2). There, in the heart of this system, is where its designers imagined its use. For purposes of understanding an algorithm, such "zooming in" is helpful, but it blurs our vision when we want to develop intuition about when to use a Bloom filter as our solution.

Say we need to sample some data tuples from a stream of requests issued to a cloud that hosts a popular webpage or service (say, Google or Amazon). We would probably design the algorithm to operate on some unique ID of each request. These requests would pass the *data-collection* and *message-queuing* tier and actual random sampling of the stream of requests would happen in the analysis tier (figure 6.2).

Sometimes users send the request but fail to receive acknowledgement of receipt. Perhaps they walk out of the reach of their Wi-Fi signal. The logic in the device might

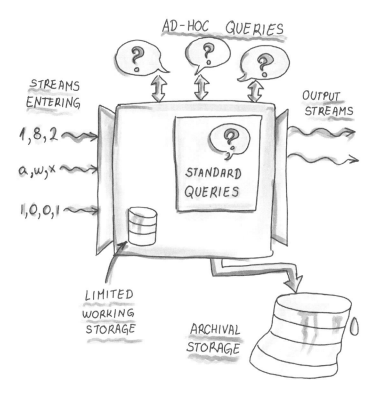

Figure 6.1 Streaming data model. The streaming data model differs from the traditional database management system in that data passes through the processor and a small amount of working storage, and it is either never stored or stored into the archival storage that is usually too large and slow to be indexed and searched. Items can be found there, but we should not count on doing this often and quickly. All the real-time analysis is done on the fly. There are standard (or standing) queries, ones that need to be computed all the time, and ad hoc queries that show up at unexpected times and have their content externally controlled.

resend the identical request. We end up with two basically identical requests received. We have a problem now, because we don't want our sampling to be affected by such an extraneous process. If we leave the duplicates in, our sampling algorithm will pick those duplicates many times more often, as there are identical copies, compared to requests that were received only once. Remember, we started in the analysis tier, but it seems that to use our out-of-the-box version of the sampling algorithm, some preprocessing of the streaming data, upstream of the analysis tier, is necessary. It helps to take a step back and observe our sampling plan in a system. It just went from being a vanilla, out-of-the-box, plug-in-here algorithm confined to the analysis tier to a composite preprocessing plus sampling algorithm that spreads wider over the streaming data architecture (figure 6.2). The necessary deduplication will happen in the message

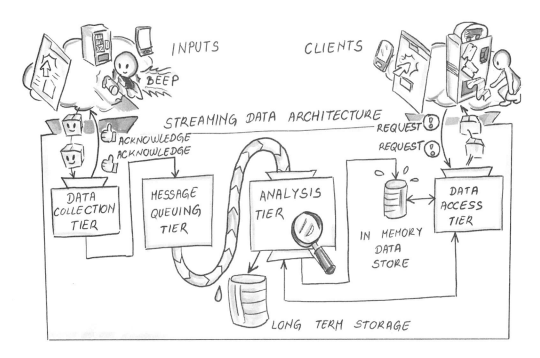

Figure 6.2   The general model of a streaming data pipeline is shown. Data producers are initiating connections by interacting with retailer's application.

queuing tier, hence our sampling algorithm has become possible, but only if we can do deduplication fast enough. Suddenly, we might think of Bloom filter–enhanced deduplication, which we describe later in the chapter.

Even though BloomFilter, HyperLogLog, and stream sampling algorithms are designed to be used in the confines of the safe, controlled analysis tier when applied, they organically create an environment of interdependent problems that can be solved by applying these in a sequence or ensemble.

We started with the theoretical view used to build these algorithms (figure 6.1), but they became too simplistic on their own to solve the problem of sampling from the stream. We then zoomed out and saw that the streaming data application is a natural habitat of such algorithms, with all its tiers. This is the only way a novice in the area can recognize commonalities in different areas of application, with these commonalities the key to successfully developing practice-relevant skills on the topic. We already saw illustrative use cases in previous chapters for each algorithm/data structure, but with a streaming data pipeline (figure 6.2), we have a chance to see them in close juxtaposition, used for different purposes but contributing to the same global task.

We will use figure 6.2 to describe the common evolution of data through a streaming data pipeline. Data is consolidated in a centralized data center that integrates data possibly coming from different geographical areas. Here, some transformation, data augmentation, and pre-processing might happen. Data is then sent to message-queuing servers (in-house or commodity hardware gathered around a cloud service) that check and, if possible, reestablish structural, temporal, and perhaps causal consistency of the data. Through the message-queuing paradigm, this layer establishes and maintains the balance between the ingestion rate of data from the collectors and the consumption rate from the side of the *analysis tier*. This may happen because the analysis tier is more computation-intensive compared to what producers have to do when passing data to the collection tier. This can easily lead to data congestion, or *load shedding* (deliberate dropping unprocessed tuples), and hence loss of data. Finally, data reaches the analysis tier, where different synopses of the data (sub)streams are calculated and kept, streams are sampled, and continuous and ad hoc queries are answered. The stream of query results from the analysis tier are then forwarded to supply different data consumers on the "edge" of the streaming data system, such as data dashboards, a real-time ad-bidding application, or some automated industrial production control application. Phew! That was a lot, but we fit the whole streaming data application in there. Take your time with it, and know that what follows is a lot less loaded.

Section 6.1 exemplifies the organic habitat that a streaming data application makes for the algorithms we've covered thus far. They crop up in the streaming data application very naturally. Use cases in this section should contribute to your ability to recognize which problems, in an inherently massive data context, such as a streaming data pipeline, are well suited to solve by applying our previous acquaintances (Bloom filter, count-min sketch) and our future ones, which we will get to know in the chapters that follow. We hope that this will help you develop the skill of homing in on parts of the system that represent solutions for a narrow, localized problem and the skill of zooming out to a bird's-eye view on the data-intensive distributed applications from their "source" to their "sink." For those of you who are still inexperienced in streaming data applications, this will be a chance to safely see the "belly of the beast."

In section 6.2, we introduce concepts native to data streams that drive algorithm design and define inherent constraints under which such algorithms are developed. Figuratively, we will zoom in on parts of figure 6.1. We should be able to recognize those constraints as an immutable feature of our data-generating procedure to devise a solution operating within them. To achieve this goal, our recommendation is to read Psaltis's book, which, in combination with this one, creates a well-rounded and powerful streaming data toolbox.

Section 6.3 revisits some probability theory behind sampling and estimation as we prepare to introduce stream sampling algorithms in chapter 7. If you need to know how to modify the original algorithms and set parameters so that they are customized to your particular situation, you should probably fight through this part, as if you find yourself in front of a large amount data, even a small tweak can mean large savings in space/time. Otherwise, you can skim this material so that your eyes get used to the notations, because we will make use of them in chapter 7.

6.1 *Streaming data system: A meta example*

Figure 6.2 shows the model of the streaming data pipeline. Keep in mind that the depicted tiers are not so clearly discernable from one another in practice. As we will see, these tiers often overlap: some parts of the system integrate tasks that cannot be clearly attributed to a single tier.

This should not come as a surprise after our request sampling example. Streaming data pipelines have vast numbers of data tuples fly by along their whole length. The only difference, as you will see, is which components of the data tuples that are being sent, emitted, queued, transported, received, and analyzed are operated on by our algorithms.

We know that the most general model of sending data along some network entails at least two components, metadata and payload. We will see that, depending on where we are in the streaming data pipeline, the metadata and payload can change their connotation. This means that, along the data pipeline, payload (requests) sometimes become overhead of the data tuple, while metadata (unique request IDs) become relevant for the analysis depending on where in our streaming pipeline we currently are.

6.1.1 *Bloom-join*

Imagine a large retailer that sells its products online and in stores. Walmart or Whole Foods fit the profile. The company may want a (close to) real-time analysis of the functional association between click patterns on its URLs and its sales transaction data. Maybe they would like to optimize their strategy for bidding in real-time ad campaigns (http://mng.bz/g4pR). These days it is not uncommon to have these types of data in two different database systems to make a so-called hybrid warehouse. The sales data is more valuable for the company; hence it often resides in a parallel database on high-end servers or enterprise data warehouses (EDWs), while for the click-stream data, a commodity server network like a Hadoop Distributed File System (HDFS) might suffice.

For now, we will assume that the click stream data tuples arrive and are stored in HDFS, and we want to join the click stream data and the data on sales made online. We will do this by using the IP address column as the join key. Here, for the sake of brevity, we are abstracting away the necessary time proximity that the join has to take into account. Only clicks close in time to an online purchase from the same IP are matched with that online purchase. In this case, we would have to join purchases made from IP addresses with clicks made from the same IPs around the time the purchase was logged (see figure 6.3).

We can assume that both databases are very large, but that the HDFS side is larger, which is a plausible assumption. We concentrate on minimizing the size of the tables that we need to broadcast between these two systems in order to implement the desired join operation. This saves bandwidth and time, particularly when the local predicates and/or projections applied to the tables are not highly selective (we end up with tables that are not much smaller than all the data that the storage systems hold).

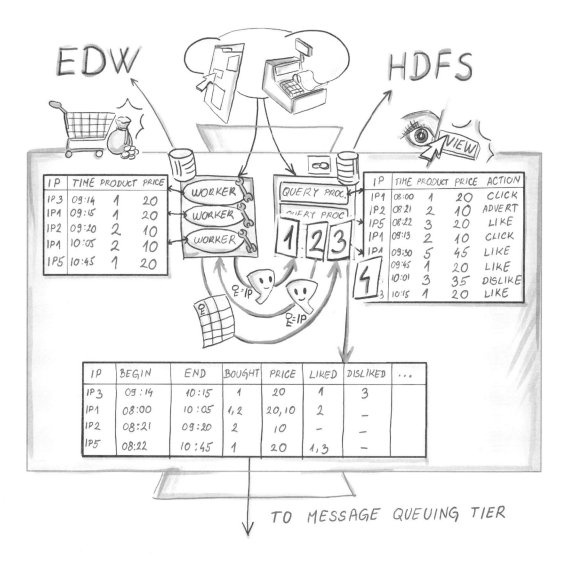

Figure 6.3   The pre-join communication between the EDW implemented with a fast parallel database (on the left) and an HDFS (on the right). Before the data for financial transactions is sent from the EDW side, an exchange of Bloom filters, which both storage systems make for the mutual join key (IP address), is made. Bloom filters are used by each side as a criterion to identify tuples that will participate in the final join. HDFS can then shuffle only necessary data among its nodes and move a minimum amount of data to the node that will execute the join to come. EDW will identify which IP addresses didn't appear in the HDFS and send only those that will participate in the final join. This way, purchase data is augmented with the click-stream component from that IP address and can be further used as a data source in a hybrid data streaming pipeline.

The common strategy in such a case is for each side to first make a Bloom filter (BF) of the join key. Let us assume that the final join happens on the HDFS side; then a global BF_{EDW} on the EDW side calculated for the IP address column is sent to each

HDFS query processor (HQP) (not a bad time to glance at figure 6.3). Here, it is used as a type of a predicate (filter) to identify the resulting smaller table that will participate in the final join. In case data needs to be shuffled among HQP processors, only data with a join key in BF_{EDW} needs to be moved (up to the false positive rate of the BF_{EDW}). Then the HDFS side makes its global BF_{HDFS} and sends it to the EDW side, which uses it to further reduce the number of rows that need to be sent. After all this is done, the EDW side sends the resulting table after applying the predicates, projections, and BF_{HDFS} on its original table. Through this two-way use of Bloom filters, only those records that participate in the join will be sent over the network, and only the necessary shuffles of data between HQPs on the Hadoop side need to be executed.

EXERCISE 1

We concretize our Bloom-join now. Assume, for clarity, that a purchase is tuple saving: time in milliseconds (occupying 4 bytes), IP address (4 bytes), list of items purchased (their codes, etc.) (64 KB), and grand total bill (8 bytes). Clicks on the HDFS side are as follows: Spartan tuples save time in milliseconds (4 bytes), IP address (4 bytes), and URI (64 KB). We can assume that purchases and clicks are "intertwined" at constant rates that keep the ratio of clicks to purchases constant; in our case, 45 clicks/purchase. All people click, but they don't all purchase something.

Assume that the next join happens after 1 million distinct purchases were made. What would be the size of the communicated data that we would save by employing a Bloom filter here with a false positive rate of 0.1%?

Let's look at where, in the streaming data pipeline, all of this just happened. Such Bloom-joins can be anchored somewhere in the collection tier of our schema from figure 6.2. This is a type of a data augmentation/preprocessing step to generate data that is apt for answering the question of interest from the business domain of the company. The resulting table created on the HDFS side saves pairs of temporally proximate clicks and purchases from the same IP address (figure 6.3) or, more accurately, all their fields. This process can then serve as a type of a continuous producer for a data stream–processing framework (e.g., Apache Kafka). The pairs (rows in the resulting table; figure 6.3) are then passed on to be queued, analyzed, and used for perhaps (close to) real-time individualized ad campaigns.

6.1.2 Deduplication

Due to the high ingestion frequency from data producers and the consequentially large flow of (perhaps) preprocessed data through the pipeline, each of the tiers shown in figure 6.2 is made up of a large number of nodes (machines) connected through a network. These computation nodes are implementing the task of their tier in parallel, as fast as possible. The message-queuing tier is there to prevent congestion, loss of data (due to different rates at which data is produced and consumed), implement deduplication, if necessary, and so on. These safety mechanisms inherently entail some resolution steps between the nodes that keep track of what data has passed through to the analysis tier and what should be next.

Nodes in the message-queuing tier are commonly called *brokers*, and in addition to keeping message queues consistent, they complete other preprocessing steps. As in our requests example, a customer might, while interacting with a retailer's website, lose wireless reception or enter an elevator. They would miss the acknowledgment from the server side of the submitted payment, and the mobile app would try to send the same payment request again. This would cause a duplicate payment. Neither customers nor corporate systems like seeing duplicate payments. Some systems, especially e-commerce ones, have deduplication mechanisms to keep such redundancies out. The percentage of duplicates in realistic scenarios is not too large (maybe 1%), but in a system that logs billions of events, these can lead to inefficiencies reflected as a significant loss of profit.

We already solved one deduplication problem in the previous chapter. Can you remember the example with large file storage and backup services? This reality, where a small portion of messages is duplicated, is well suited for another Bloom filter application that allocates "intercept" nodes into the streaming application, built, perhaps, on Apache Kafka Streams. These worker nodes are connected to high-speed databases. Aside from permanently saving all (or just a window of) messages to facilitate a possible rollback in case data is lost, they keep a Bloom filter of all the IDs of the messages they save. Each message that arrives is checked against the filter, and if it's reported present (subject to a BF false positive rate), worker nodes discard them. Deduplicated message streams proceed to queue in, possibly, Kafka output topics (https://segment.com/blog/exactly-once-delivery/), where they can then be forwarded by a load-balancing node to several brokers leading to the analysis tier (figure 6.4).

Figure 6.4   Intermediate nodes connected to fast databases implementing deduplication to remove the repeated messaging instances in a streaming data pipeline. Each node keeps a Bloom filter of messages it saved, and at the arrival of the next message, checks the message ID hash against its Bloom filter. If the Bloom filter reports that the message already exists, this message's data is discarded; otherwise, the message is saved and propagated onto the message-queuing tier.

6.1.3 *Load balancing and tracking the network traffic*

As in any distributed computing system, in streaming data applications, load balancing among the brokers is of paramount importance. Giving brokers unbalanced loads can cause one of them to receive disproportionately more connections, requests, and so on. Considering that the service is as fast as the slowest broker, this can cause high end-to-end latencies and interrupt real-time applications. Near-real-time detecting of overused resources in a network is a classic network traffic/distributed queuing problem, and it boils down to detecting outliers/anomalies instantly. Such outliers come in the shape of overloaded packet flow patterns and are typical of denial-of-service attacks on servers. Modern defense strategies rely on statistical methods to detect them in real time.

One such class of algorithmic solutions for this issue in network traffic relies on the monitoring of package headers in the network. The least the algorithm would need for this is the basic information about each flow (FL =[source IP, source port, destination IP, destination port, protocol]). Monitoring this form of stream of requests allows us to identify a small number of flows that constitute most of the network traffic, the so called heavy hitters. In practice, we want to detect a number of them whose rate (nr of packets/requests (bytes) in a unit of time) is above some threshold.

In chapter 5 we saw a HyperLogLog-based solution for a worm detection problem in a generic network. Another solution might be to employ a count-min sketch that counts the aggregate size of the flow by adding the size of each packet sent through that flow (flow here is a pair of source/destination determinants). Keys hashed into a count-min-sketch are packet headers, and the counter is incremented by the size of the current packet.

In the more specific case of a broker in the data-streaming application, the counter would be incremented by the number of requests queued for the same broker. This could happen due to some momentarily increasing number of producers (called *sudden bursts* in this context). The traffic-measuring or load-balancing application would then estimate min counts: how "heavy" is each flow, or how "busy" is each broker? These would be periodically divided by the length of the measurement period. This gives us flow/queuing rates. A network administrator or a data pipeline engineer would then discriminate good flows from bad by applying some threshold informed by their use case. After identifying the culprits they can apply some curtailing strategy.

Due to the count-min sketch algorithm, the flows under the threshold are, by definition, not malicious, while, out of those identified, some may be false positives due to the overestimate inherent to count-min-sketch. We could then quickly check the exact size/rate of the small number of flows breaching the threshold and remove false positives, leaving only the true culprits in the set.

EXERCISE 2

Let's revisit the deduplication use case for a Bloom filter in the e-commerce system. Assume you were given an assignment by your superior to inspect and finish a solution started by an engineer who recently left the company. You understand the logic of the solution, as it seems to save time and prevent charging the customer twice. Nevertheless, there is a "price" to pay. What happens once the Bloom filter delivers a false positive related to a particular request carrying information about a like, submitted comment, or a clicked ad? What if the client app submitted a payment? Is there anything there we should watch for? What happens when the Bloom filter returns a false positive for an actual intended payment?

A generic network-traffic-monitoring application can be found in a cloud service on which your streaming data application is running, while the load-balancing use case pertains to the inner workings of the streaming application itself (see figure 6.5).

Figure 6.5   A cloud computing architecture servicing different client data pipelines. A network-traffic–monitoring application installed to monitor the communication of data producers (or any communication attempts originating outside the cloud) is implemented with the help of a count-min sketch. CMS identifies network flows that exhibit flow rates above a certain predetermined threshold and acts accordingly. Similar problems of load balancing between the brokers of the message-queuing tier are solved analogously by applying another CMS at the load-balancer node in the message-queuing tier. Notice that both these CMSs are operating on the package/message headers and that the payload of the packets/messages, namely data on clicks issued by the user, is not analyzed until it reaches the analysis tier. There, other Bloom filters, HyperLogLogs, sampling procedures, or other synopses are calculated.

The purpose of this short and surface-scratching excursion into realistic streaming data architecture was to give you some insight into the omnipresence of the algorithms and data structures that we've covered so far in state-of-the-art streaming data applications. Aside from that, we hope we helped you see all accompanying problems that need to be resolved in such an inherently distributed computing landscape. We hope to have weaved a "*rug to tie the room together*" for you so far.

Our second goal was to relate the level of abstraction needed to develop streaming data algorithms (figure 6.1) and the level necessary for building a realistic streaming data application/pipeline (figure 6.2). We know that the former crops up in several places in the latter and that streaming data glues them naturally together, each becoming visible at different "image resolutions."

6.2   *Practical constraints and concepts in data streams*

Next, we introduce some computing and streaming data concepts that the streaming data algorithm designers have to observe, and by which their algorithms are evaluated.

6.2.1   *In real time*

Designing a streaming data application is a task that takes our conception of time from a philosophical pastime to a very practical time-keeping exercise. The first question that comes to my mind and, judging by some posts on data analytics forums, the minds of others, is whether real-time analytics ever exist. Any semirespectable streaming data reference will tell you that data in a data stream is continuously received (from possibly numerous producers) at such a pace that both saving it and making more than one pass over each data tuple is infeasible. In some applied domains, such as the analysis of financial data streams to make trading decisions, having this unrealistic option to save and query the whole history is deemed useless, since decisions will depend on only the data from the most recent week, perhaps even from the last minute. Hence, it is reasonable that typical requirements for streaming data algorithms are for them to operate in *one pass* in *small time* and in *small space*.

Let's revisit our question of the existence of real-time analytics. Even if our algorithms are built under these requirements, computation (not to mention security, communication, scheduling, and load balancing—all part of a typical cloud-based streaming data application) costs time. Strictly speaking, the only data that really is real time comes as the sensory stimulation from the events we are immediate witnesses to. If this sounds like hair splitting, you're probably right; it would be hard for me to come up with a convincing argument to the contrary, but please bear with me. I have good news: we will resolve this. Let us agree that real time and the notion of (near) real-time analytics is decided by the state-of-the art solution for a particular streaming data business problem. If it produces results and drives decision-making that keeps the company competitive, we wouldn't be off by much if we called it real time. In other words, users/clients have a final saying in what is (near) real time for them, even when they over- or underestimate their needs.

If we think about it, when witnessing live events in our lives, we are all experiencing identical latency when it comes to our sensory and cognitive appreciation of the events happening in front of us. This is why we agree so easily about the concept of real time; we are all equally "late." Now that we've settled this dilemma, of perhaps disputably pressing importance, we can continue with what we mean by small time and small space.

6.2.2 *Small time and small space*

For our considerations, small space will be defined with respect to the available working memory depicted in figure 6.1 as *limited working storage*. In it we have to keep any data the stream-query processing engine needs to answer the ad hoc or continuous queries, in time. Here is where all the different data synopses, Bloom filters, Hyper-LogLogs, results from sampling algorithms (buffer) on data streams, histograms of the stream, and so on need to fit.

Small time refers to the processing time of the algorithm per each new arrival, as well as the time needed to issue an answer to a particular query (*query processing time*). Small time usually means sublinear, typically poly-logarithmic in N, where N is the length of the substream that we can fit in the limited working memory.

6.2.3 *Concept shifts and concept drifts*

As much as a data stream is continuous in its time component, the data-generating mechanism can and will exhibit discontinuities.

Let's take a real-time streaming data application at Facebook that has the task of warning users of an immediate local threat due to an armed conflict, natural disaster, or similar imminent danger that affects a large geographical area. Assume further that the application keeps counts of word occurrences in substreams of user announcements on the platform. Substreams may be defined using some geographical criteria that makes warnings about such events relevant for people in the area. Any solution would need to implement the logic for calculating rates (count divided by the length of the logging period) of occurrence of particular reserved words. An imminent local threat to human lives in the area would translate to the sudden increase in rates of word occurrences related to such a disaster. Streaming algorithms should be able to detect such abrupt changes in the data stream, know in literature as *concept shifts*.

Data stream behavior similar to concept shifts but that is exhibited over a longer period of time and characterized less by abrupt and more by gradual changes is called *concept drift*. Detecting this is a less trivial problem compared to *concept shifts*, and it has been a long-standing research topic. (For a good review of available methods see an article by Sebastiao and Gamma [2].)

Both concepts are intimately related to the notion of a windowed data stream, one of the mechanisms for accounting for recency in a data stream.

6.2.4 *Sliding window model*

Theoretically, a data stream is infinite. It is assumed that the stream processing begins at some well-defined time t_0, and that at any time t the queries are answered while taking into consideration all observed tuples seen between t_0 and t. This model of a data stream is referred to as a *landmark stream*.

Hopefully by now you feel that this is impossible, since we know that we cannot keep the stream in working memory and cannot make multiple passes on its data—at least not in time to deem the answer relevant for practice. Luckily, the phrase "taking into consideration" means that the synopses that we make of the "galloping" data persist to be a function of *all* tuples seen thus far. Hence, even the older data tuples that appeared long ago and, due to a limited working memory, were discarded or retired in archival storage (figure 6.1) contribute with the same weight as the new ones.

For some applications, like financial data streams, having old data govern current answers to queries is useless at best and a liability at worst. When faced with concept shifts and drifts, queries in landmark streams are prone to inertia and can be too slow to "react" to changes in concept. For this purpose, different time-decay mechanisms have been introduced that relate the age of the data tuple and the weight with which it influences the answers to queries.

One of the most prominent is the *sliding window model* that considers only a certain number (a window) of the most recently arrived data tuples. Data tuples outside of the window are automatically removed from the analysis or given a weight of zero. Be aware that they can theoretically still be in the limited working memory if the sliding window is designed to be smaller than what we can fit in the space available to us for one-pass computing.

Sliding movement of the window can be either time- or count-based. In time-based windows, any data tuples that arrived in the last W time units are in the window, while for count-based windows, sliding movement is governed by maintaining a constant number of W items in the window (it will be clear what we mean by W for each future mention). Figures 6.6 and 6.7 show both the models on a generic data stream example for three of the most recent sliding window movements.

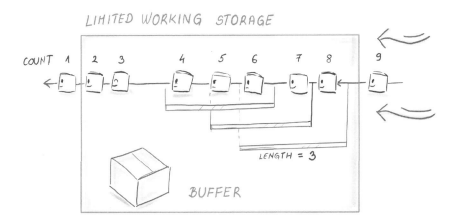

Figure 6.6   Last three sliding movements by the count-based window. Notice that window length is not necessarily all that we can fit into our working storage, but that is the maximum we can cover. Hence, in applications where we want "as much history as possible" to influence our data stream analysis, we would extend the length of the window to "everything we can fit." Keep in mind that aside from a substream that we need to operate in one-pass mode, we need to preserve space for our synopses and the computation needed to build and update them. This is indicated by the buffer space show.

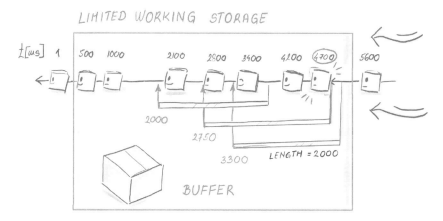

Figure 6.7   Here, we can see the time-based sliding window of length W = 2000 ms and its three last sliding (meaningful with respect to the arrival times of the data tuples) movements. We started the data stream at time 0 ms and at time 1 ms when the first data tuple arrived. Then two more arrived at 500 ms and 1000 ms. Here, we observe the stream after 5,500 ms. The three last movements of the window are indicated, which changed the content of the window: from 1,400 to 1,401 ms (data tuple arrived at 3,400 ms and entered the window), from 2,700 ms to 2,701 ms (notice that this movement resulted in 4 data tuples in the window), and from 2,800 ms to 2,801 ms (data tuple at 2.800 ms is discarded).

Our list of constraints related to data streams is not exhaustive, but we can fare well through the next couple of chapters without having to leave loose ends for any of the algorithms we learn.

The next section is intended as a review of sampling theory. This should make it easier for the more technically curious to appreciate the nuances of chapter 7.

6.3   *Math bit: Sampling and estimation*

The idea of sampling came out of being unable to answer questions about logistically intractable large sets. For example, if you and someone you share an IP address with surf the internet, your requests are received from the same IP, but using different browsers will leave a different HTTP fingerprint. We might be interested in the average number of HTTP fingerprints over all possible IP addresses. There is no chance we would be able to get a correct answer, but even an estimate would be more than what we knew when the idea popped into our head. To get an estimate we would sample from the IP space.

The first recorded use of this idea came in 1786 as an attempt by Pierre Simon Laplace to estimate the population of France. Naturally, the estimate was not correct, but what Laplace did, and what made sampling a powerful tool, was provide an upper bound on the chance that his sampling-based estimate was too far from the correct answer. Providing an estimate was not that novel, but adding to it a structured way to measure, and perhaps curb, the uncertainty of the estimate compared to the truth was new and, luckily, a generally applicable idea.

To define a sampling process in practice, we need two components: a (finite) *population* that we are interested in (or some aspect of it) and some way to pick random members of that population, a final, "materialized" artifact called a *sample*. You will find that the word *sample* is often used for individual elements/observations that make up the sample. We find this confusing. Therefore, we will call the individual elements of the sample elements/observations/members, while the collection of them will make up a sample. Depending on the way we acquire these random members, sampling can be *representative* (unbiased) or *biased* with respect to the population.

If every subset of k elements from the population has the same chance to become our final sample of size k, then the sampling process is representative of the population. In our IP space, this translates to making sure that each subset of k IP addresses has an equal probability of being picked for our sample. This also means that every individual member of the population has the same chance of being selected, independent of anything else about that member. If we can guarantee this, we have a *simple random sample* (SRS).

Let's think about how this translates to our IP space example. In reality, rates of requests over IP addresses are different. *Crawlers* (scripts visiting and cataloging websites automatically) send requests perhaps more often than a human who is browsing during a single session. If we were to pick IPs in the following manner, "sample a random request and add its IP address to the sample," crawlers would have a higher chance of getting into our sample. Once we decide that the sample is big enough, we might have an overrepresented set of IPs related to crawlers compared to the number of those used by humans. This would translate to having the wrong idea about the true average number of fingerprints per IP. If we make sure that each IP address has the same chance of making it into the sample, independent of anything else about that IP address, this can't happen. This is what we're usually after, because this allows us, like Laplace, to believe we have a good estimate and to calculate those bounds on uncertainty of the estimate. Our original sampling strategy to sample IP addresses directly via all requests received is a *biased sampling strategy*.

6.3.1 Biased sampling strategy

To describe what makes a sampling process biased, we will use a hypothetical population of bills logged by a large retailer. For now, it is of no relevance how this data is available to us. It can reside in a database, or it might be data received from a data stream. We denote the number of these individual purchases N. We want to know the proportion of purchases made via a loyalty card. If our marketing department makes plans and informs us beforehand that they need this information, saving and updating this information with every newly seen purchase is easy, but if they suddenly decide they want this (an ad hoc query), we can get a good estimate by keeping a sample and returning the sample proportion of the loyalty card purchases.

The purchases are partitioned into purchases with and without the use of a loyalty card. The true value (l) of the proportion of purchases with a loyalty card (L) is clear;

it is the number of members with L divided by N. In our sample of size k, this translates to having i of elements with L, and j of elements without L, with $i + j = k$.

We will describe two sampling processes in this context. The first is unbiased, while the second is a biased sampling process on the population of purchases that were logged. We will use the example with $N = 10$, $k = 5$, and $p_L = 4/5$. Let the set represent the population:

$$\{x_{1L}, x_{2\bar{L}}, x_{3L}, x_{4L}, x_{5\bar{L}}, x_{6L}, x_{7L}, x_{8L}, x_{9L}, x_{10L},\}$$

In the index for each element, we can read off some form of ID and an indicator about the presence/absence of the characteristic L (in this case, elements with IDs 2 and 5 are bought without presenting a loyalty card). For any 5-element subset of these 10 elements, a simple combination argument can be made about the probability of picking that specific subset. Introductory notes for either probability theory or a discrete math course teach you in the first few weeks that there are (10 choose 5) = 252 different 5-element subsets, and if each is supposed to be equally probable, then the probability of picking any specific one is $1/_{252}$. Now imagine we have a 252-sided die showing numbers 1, 2, . . . , 252, and we (in any arbitrary way) enumerate all 252 5-element subsets. Throwing this die and picking the subset indicated on the side of the die after it lands is a representative sampling strategy.

It is helpful to know the probability for each x_i, $i = 1, 2, ..., 10$ to be selected into the sample. For this sampling process, it is simply 0.5 for any of them, independent of whether a loyalty card was used.

Any five-element subset (our sample) that you can imagine belongs to one of the three types. We will call the sample type 5 when all five purchases turn out to be made via loyalty card. Type 4 is made up of one purchase made without the loyalty card and four purchases made with it. And last is type 3, which has two purchases made without the loyalty card and three purchases with it. Estimates of true $p_L = 4/5$ from these three types of the sample are 1, 4/5, and 3/5, in that order.

Let's assume a different sampling strategy: we first roll a three-sided biased die (each side showing the number of purchases with the loyalty card; hence 3, 4, 5) to decide which type, 5, 4, or 3, of a sample we will draw. We then reach into partition L and partition $\bar{L}$ separately and draw as many purchases as decided by the first biased die. If we roll 4, for example, we know that we need to take 1 from partition $\bar{L}$ and 4 from partition L. For picking actual purchases, we will use the representative strategy described. This time we will need three pairs of dice for the second stage. We need a pair because we have to representatively sample from partition $\bar{L}$ and partition L. We need three of them because, depending on the type of sample we rolled using our first biased die, we will draw a different number of purchases from partition $\bar{L}$ and partition L. This leads to (8 choose 5)-sided and (2 choose 0)-sided dice for sample type 5, (8 choose 4)-sided and (2 choose 1)-sided dice for sample type 4, and (8 choose 3)-sided and (2 choose 2)-sided dice for type 3. If you remember counting techniques, you will notice that the first and third pair are actually the same two dice; hence you need only four additional dice.

Let's see the probability of picking a five-element subset of a specific type 5, 4, or 3. Let's assume that the sides corresponding to sample types 5, 4, and 3 are seen with probabilities $\frac{2}{5}$, $\frac{2}{5}$, and $\frac{1}{5}$, respectively (this is where the bias of the first die comes into play). For the sample of type 5, we have

$$\frac{2}{5} \times \frac{1}{\binom{8}{5}} \times \frac{1}{\binom{2}{0}} = \frac{1}{140}$$

For the sample of type 4, we have

$$\frac{2}{5} \times \frac{1}{\binom{8}{4}} \times \frac{1}{\binom{2}{1}} = \frac{1}{350}$$

For the sample type 3, we have

$$\frac{2}{5} \times \frac{1}{\binom{8}{3}} \times \frac{1}{\binom{2}{2}} = \frac{1}{280}$$

Hence, it is easy to see that this sample strategy is not representative, or it is biased, since not all five-element subsets are equally likely to be "materialized" into a sample. The same goes for the number of requests issued introducing bias into our request sampling strategy; the biased die allowed samples with more purchases made with a loyalty card more probable than those with fewer loyalty card purchases. Let us now see what it does to the probability of selecting a single observation. Remember that for the representative sampling strategy, probability of selection into a sample for *any* single x_i was 0.5, independent of the feature L. For the biased sampling strategy, we don't expect this to be the same since a biased die "prefers" samples with a higher number of purchases made with a loyalty card. This bias will "trickle down" to the level of a single observation and will "tilt" its chances to be part of the final sample depending on its L feature. In this case, we need to calculate probabilities of selection separately for elements with L and elements without it. We leave the derivation of the exact probability for selection of a single x_{iL} and $x_{i\bar{L}}$ as an exercise and just state here that for each x_{iL}, this probability is 0.525, while for $x_{i\bar{L}}$, it amounts to 0.4.

EXERCISE 3

Calculating selection probabilities for x_{iA}, $A \in \{L, \bar{L}\}$ in the case of our biased strategy can be done via an iterative expectation method. We separately calculate for each

$A \in \{L, \bar{L}\}$ a probability that x_{iA} is selected into the sample given what the biased die shows. Go through the steps to get to the same answer we did for x_{iA}, $A \in \{L, \bar{L}\}$.

EXERCISE 4

What probabilities for the three sides of a biased die correspond to the representative sampling strategy with the line at 0.5 in figure 6.8? We could use the second biased strategy with specifically chosen probability weights for each side and emulate a representative sampling strategy.

This is where we can truly visualize the bias, because we see the "tilt" away from 0.5 for each observation in the population depending on the feature L. Figure 6.8 shows the bias in selection probabilities p_i^{BS} for differently biased dice compared to $p_i^{SRS} = 0.5$ selection probabilities under a representative sampling strategy.

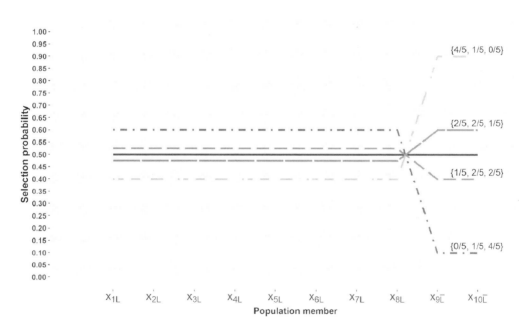

Figure 6.8 Selection probabilities for differently biased die from our example. The probability of drawing a sample of type 3, 4, and 5 is shown on each line that shows the probability of selection for all x_{iA}, $i = 1, ..., 10$ and $A \in \{L, \bar{L}\}$. Notice that for any biased sampling strategy, via the three-sided biased die, the selection probabilities move away from 0.5. The direction of the movement depends on loyalty card existence A with respect to the particular purchase x_{iA}. Our original biased die corresponds to the shift denoted by 1/5, 2/5, 2/5.

6.3.2 *Estimation from a representative sample*

Of course, sampling without the estimation step that follows it doesn't serve much purpose by itself, so we will see what the subsequent estimation step from a representative sample looks like. Assume we want to know the exact number of purchases performed by presenting the loyalty card; the correct value of this characteristic for our population is $\theta = 8$, and we get it if we add 1 for every element in the population with the characteristic L and 0 for all those without it:

$$\theta = \sum_{i=1}^{10} c_{iL} = 8$$

We will estimate this population sum by utilizing its random sample counterpart, "sample sum":

$$\hat{\theta} = \sum_{j=1}^{5} I_{jL}$$

Sample S is a random subset of size 5, so we have to take into account that instead of fixed values c_{iL}, we are now dealing with random indicator variables I_{jL} for $j = 1, 2, 3, 4, 5$. After some specific sample is materialized, we can speak of fixed values. I_{jL} is 1 if the jth element of the sample has characteristic L, and 0 otherwise. For any possible sample, the value of this sum depends on our sample type from before (sample of type 3, 4, or 5). All samples of type 3, 4, and 5 will have values 3, 4, and 5 for this sum, respectively.

Since the sum is random, let us check the expectation of the sample sum (its long-term behavior in an experiment where we draw a random sample of size 5 repetitively). The expectation of a single I_{jL} for any $j = 1, 2, 3, 4, 5$ under our representative sampling strategy is $8/10$ (we leave this as an exercise), and five of those make four. With four, we seem to be off from our aim by a factor of 2. But we can see that this is exactly the factor by which our population and sample size are off, too. The population has $10 = N$ members, while the sample S has $5 = k$. Hence, if we scale $\hat{\theta}$ up by N/k, we will be on target with the expectation. Our final form of the estimator is

$$\widehat{\theta_{su}} = \frac{10}{5} \sum_{j=1}^{5} I_{jL}$$

which makes it an unbiased and consistent estimator of our population sum θ (as the sample size increases, $\widehat{\theta_{su}}$ converges to our true value $\theta = 8$). This general form of the scale-up estimator in the last equation is known as the *Horvitz–Thompson type estimator*.

EXERCISE 5
How would you go about calculating the expected value of I_{jL}? Could you show that it is what we claim?

The scaling–up step is a general strategy, and we can use it to estimate other population sums too, such as the total amount spent on online purchases in the last month (what is the population of interest here?). Or, if you want to know how many purchases were higher than $100 in the last month, you can use our scale up estimator with the characteristic L substituted by "purchase higher than $100." Population sums like θ look specific, but they can be used to define any linear transformation of it (any average). Notice that if you divide θ by 10, you get $p_L = 4/5$, which is a type of average too, so you can use $\widehat{\theta_{su}}$ to estimate p_L as well. Hence, representative sampling strategy and the "scale–up" estimator are powerful general tools to get a good estimate of the corresponding population parameter.

The population of interest can be classical, as Laplace had it; it can be all the purchase tuples from last month residing in a database or all purchases that arrived in the last 24 hours from our producers to our streaming data pipeline. The probabilistic argument is the same for all three, but the technical implementation of a sampling process within these three domains is of course different.

Summary

- A streaming data pipeline is a natural environment for showcasing algorithms and data structures.
- Distributed computing and the imperative of real-time delivery of results in streaming data applications create numerous opportunities for shortening the end-to-end latencies by the smart use of hashing, Bloom filters, count-min sketches, and HyperLogLogs. Tasks like joining large tables saved across heterogeneous storage systems, deduplication in the stream, monitoring network traffic, and load balancing are all real examples of such opportunities.
- Real-time analytics is possible if stakeholders can agree on a level of tolerance for latency in such systems. Data-generating mechanisms are prone to periodic or incidental changes, and our streaming data algorithms should be able to accommodate and detect those in time. There are data stream models like count-based or time-based sliding windows to allow for recent adjustments to detect such phenomena, known as concept shifts and concept drifts.
- Sampling is a powerful and long-established technique for answering questions about an intractable set by systematically forming its subset and answering the same question from it. Long- and well-established theory for statistical inference from the unbiased or biased sample can help to decide on the sample size and choose an estimator for the query answer to guarantee accuracy and precision.

Sampling from data streams

This chapter covers

- Sampling from an infinite landmark stream
- Incorporating recency by using a sliding window and how to sample from it
- Showcasing the difference between a representative and biased sampling strategy on a landmark stream with a sudden shift
- Exploring R and Python packages and libraries for writing and executing tasks on data streams

We are ready to fully appreciate sampling as a single task staged in the analysis tier. Although we have already shown that this division of the streaming data architecture is not so clear-cut, we will imagine the stream processor sampling the incoming stream in this tier. This will help to introduce the sampling algorithm without any additional complexity coming from deduplication, merging, or general preprocessing of the data. In our fingerprint-rate example, the incoming requests will first go through IP deduplication and then appear in front of the stream processor that will materialize a representative sample. The current state of the sample is then used to answer a continuous or an ad hoc query approximately but quickly. We will use our IP sampling use case to illustrate each algorithm.

Theory for sampling from a stream developed naturally from database sampling. Database sampling comes with a long and rich research and publication record, starting as early as 1986 with work by Olken and Roten [1]. One of the research directions in database sampling, *online aggregation*, served as an inception platform for our main topic in this chapter, *sampling from data streams*. We will introduce specific algorithms operating on different stream models discussed in section 6.2.

7.1   Sampling from a landmark stream

We will dip our fingers and try to "tap" into our first stream of data via sampling from a landmark stream model. This is a continuous stream of data that is not *windowed*. Data items arrive continuously and are operated on and disappear forever. Well, perhaps forever is too strong, since it usually moves to slow, massive, secondary memory storage. Sampling from such a stream "only" needs to somehow ensure that at every moment in the stream evolution, we are keeping a representative sample of the data seen thus far. This is an easier task compared to sampling from a windowed (sequence- or timestamp-based) data stream. Here, we don't have to implement the logic for updating the sample once an element of the sample has exited the window (ages out). This inevitably costs time and brings us to the criterion for evaluating the "goodness" of the sampling algorithms we will present. An algorithm that answers the query well should be able to create and/or update the sample in a single pass over the elements of the stream. It should also give an approximate answer to the (continuous or ad hoc) query using the sample of size polylogarithmic in N (N being the number of stream elements seen thus far, for landmark streams). This notion of *approximate* must be concretized when algorithm designers want to be able to compare their solutions. The approximate answer then means that the answer should be within ε absolute/relative error of the correct answer, except for some small failure probability, δ, when it is not. We want to be ε– accurate $100 \times (1 - \delta)$ percent of the time. For windowed streams, the size of the window ω takes the role of the parameter N when we talk about polylogarithmic size. We assume that ω is too big for us to fit all tuples between t and in $t - \omega$ in memory.

7.1.1   Bernoulli sampling

Bernoulli sampling is a classical sampling strategy. (Daniel Bernoulli lived in the 18th century, when a sheet of paper with data on crop yield over time in different parts of a county was the closest concept to a database). It is also a representative sampling strategy that lived through its second spring once easily and quickly accessible data elements (the rise of database sampling) were available. The easiest way to exemplify the strategy is to imagine playing the modified game of picking petals one at a time off a flower (with the underlying audio track wondering about the existence of affection toward you). Once you ruin a perfectly fine flower, you stop with the game. What you've also done is sample the petals according to a degenerated version of *Bernoulli sampling*: you picked each petal with probability $p = 1$. Naturally, *Bernoulli sampling* of practical use will have $p \in (0,1)$ with p representing the true sampling fraction for any number of elements so far encountered in the stream.

If we take our stream of deduplicated IP addresses, we can pick every 1/pth that will pass. Here lies the beauty of the simplicity of this method: at any moment we can be sure that our sample is a completely random sample of size pN, where N is the number of elements seen thus far. We can then use those to calculate an estimated number of fingerprints per IP in all the IP space.

For each arriving IP-address, we will toss a coin showing heads, with probability p, and tails with $1 - p$. If we introduce the currently seen IP address each time we see heads, each IP will have p chance to be in the sample. To exemplify, with a fair coin we will, on average, take every second IP seen. Notice an inevitable feature here: although p remains constant, the size k of the sample is a binomially distributed random variable, and its expected size Np grows with N. We can now define *Bernoulli sampling* more formally: given a sequence of elements, $e_1, e_2, e_3, ..., e_i, ...$, from a landmark stream, include each element e_i of the stream with probability $p \in (0,1)$ independently from any other element already passed or yet to come. Figure 7.1 illustrates this idea.

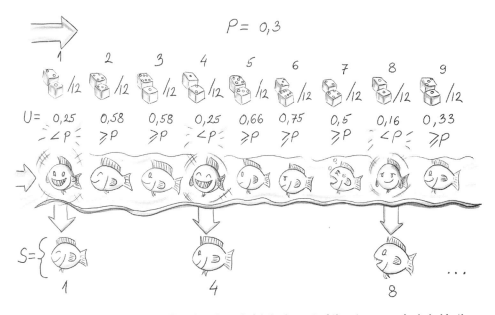

Figure 7.1   **You can see how the first, fourth, and eighth element of the stream are included in the sample, since the corresponding pseudo-random value uniform on [0,1] turned out less than p = 0.3.**

If you are not into nitty-gritty parts of the implementation, you now have all the necessary information about Bernoulli sampling to skip to the bottom of the next page. Naive implementation invokes a pseudo-random number generator algorithm (PRNG) for each element seen, produces a uniformly distributed random number between 0 and 1, and includes the element into a sample if the number is less than p.

Getting into the theory behind PRNGs would be a sudden and time-consuming change of context at this point. Luckily, all we need to know about PRNGs to appreciate what's to come is that these are efficient deterministic algorithms producing a sequence of pseudo-random numbers. These numbers, if the algorithm preserves some assumptions from number theory, become indistinguishable, for practical purposes, from a sequence of real random numbers. It's also important that they, although efficient, do cost some time, and because we are in the streaming data context, we don't want to call them more often than necessary.

It is nice to notice that PRNGs are actually anathema to randomness (as J. von Neumann said, "Anyone who considers arithmetical methods of producing random digits is, of course, in a state of sin"), but the number theory behind them is nothing short of fascinating, so if you haven't already, it's in no way a waste of time to read up on them. Not the easiest, but probably the best place to do this, is chapter 3 of D. Knuth's *The Art of Computer Programming*, Volume 2: Seminumerical Algorithms (1998, Addison-Wesley Professional).

To save on calls to PRNGs, our implementation will use the fact that the number of elements to skip after the last inclusion is a geometrically distributed random variable. Instead of having to do something each time a new element in the stream is seen, we'll only operate when a new element is included in the sample. This is because we generate a "skip" of indices that we will let by each time, leading us to the next element to include.

We make use of a very general theorem from probability theory called *inverse probability integral transform*. (Sorry for the lofty words there!) For our case, this says that if a U is a uniformly distributed random variable on the interval $(0, 1)$, then $\Delta = \left\lfloor \log U / \log(1 - p) \right\rfloor$ gives the number of elements to skip before the next element that it is to include ($\lfloor x \rfloor$ denotes the smallest integer less than or equal to x) if we are to include every pth one. Phew! Following is the pseudocode:

```
S = []          | Initialize an empty buffer S to keep the sample
p = 0.01         | in, and set the sampling probability p.
j = 0           | Set j, the index of the next element to include, to
i = 1           | 0, and the i index of the current element to 1.
```

```
U = PRNG_unif(0,1)        <---| Uniformly draw
                               | the first U.
```

$$\Delta = \left\lfloor \frac{\log U}{\log(1-p)} \right\rfloor \quad \text{<--- Produce the first skip.}$$

```
j = Δ + 1        <---| Calculate the index of the
                     | first element to include.
```

```
while (True):
    while (i! = j ):     | Pass all indices between the
        i += 1      <----| last and the next inclusion.
```

```
S.append(e_i)              ◁────┐   Include the current
U = PRNG_unif(0,1)              │   element in the sample.
```

$$\Delta = \left\lfloor \frac{\log U}{\log(1-p)} \right\rfloor$$

```
j = j + Δ + 1
```

At any time t, the sample S is a Bernoulli random sample from all tuples seen so far, with inclusion probability p. As you can see from the pseudocode, we call the PRNG and log function only at times of inclusion of a new element into the sample S.

A generalized version of Bernoulli sampling uses, for each item, separate and unique inclusion probability p_i. This sampling scheme is called *Poisson sampling*, and inclusion of X_i is a Bernoulli trial with success probability p_i. If we have a fairly good idea about the multiplicities of X_i (i.e., in the problem of estimating the total sum of dollars from purchases, some amounts X_i show up more often than the others, say X_j), we can let them be reflected in the probabilities for inclusion. X_i with higher multiplicities will have higher p_i, while those amounts that appear only rarely will have correspondingly smaller p_i. This type of *biased sampling* allows for building a Horvitz–Thompson type of an estimator straightforwardly and reduces the variance of the estimate. Unfortunately, generating skips for Poisson sampling is not a trivial task.

In a distributed computing environment, in which any industrial streaming data application operates, a sampling algorithm should offer itself simply to parallelization over a number of stream (sampling) operators. The advantage of Bernoulli sampling should be obvious: sampling r substreams via Bernoulli sampling with inclusion probability p will result in a representative sample from the whole stream after the r samples are pooled at a designated master node.

The main drawback of Bernoulli sampling, as well as Poisson, is the random sample size; a landmark stream can, in theory, grow infinitely. Some attempts were made to combine Bernoulli sampling and a sample size-curtailing strategy for deleting some elements from the Bernoulli sample or using reservoir sampling once the sample size exceeds a certain threshold. Such strategies introduce some bias into the original sampling algorithm. In the case of Bernoulli sampling, the sampling strategy becomes biased, with a different bias $p_i^{BS} - p$ for each element i. There is often no closed functional form of this bias, which we can use to recover p_i^{BS} by adding that bias to p, and hence it becomes difficult to correctly use a Horvitz–Thompson-type estimator.

7.1.2   Reservoir sampling

Reservoir sampling solves the problem of variable sample size. The algorithm was popularized among computer scientists in a 1985 paper by Vitter [2]. For any number of elements read from the stream, a sample, selected using reservoir sampling, will be uniformly distributed among all samples of size k. Proof for this claim is widely available, so we won't show it here. Consequently, we get an SRS strategy of a fixed size k from an infinite landmark stream. Magic!

Reservoir sampling algorithm operates on a data stream as follows. First, k elements of a stream are included in the reservoir deterministically (simply append the first k elements). For every additional incoming element with index i, the probability of inclusion is i/k for any $i > k$. If we are to include an element with index i, another element currently residing in the reservoir is removed uniformly at random to make place. If we add a similar shortcut that we used before to traverse elements by generating skips between those to include, instead of inspecting each, you have all that is necessary to test your understanding of the algorithm (see figure 7.1). If you are not going to implement the algorithm, but merely use it, you can still appreciate the figure. It depicts reservoir sampling for the first seven elements of the stream, using a reservoir of size $k = 3$.

Before we discuss the runtime of the reservoir sampling algorithm, we will describe, in detail, one possible efficient implementation of this sampling strategy. If you are not interested in this level of detail, you can safely skip the next couple of pages.

Vitter gives an efficient implementation of the algorithm using the same idea of generating the number Δ_i of skipped elements after the element with index i is included in the sample. Notice that here the number of skipped elements is equipped with an index; hence skips have a different distribution depending on how much of a data stream has been seen thus far. They change as the stream evolves. Generating such skips is more involved than for Bernoulli sampling because of the unequal (decreasing) probability of inclusion as the stream evolves. The theory behind it is not too hard and can be surveyed either in the original paper or in section 2.3 by Haas in Garofalakis, Gehrke, and Rastogi's manuscript [3] (we will refer to this work as GGR from now on).

The method makes use of our familiar inverse probability integral transform to generate skips Δ_i for "early" i's. For "later" i's, the *acceptance-rejection* method [4] is used in combination with the *squeezing* argument.

For the latter, we have to know the exact functional form of f_{Δ_i}, which we hardly ever do. Luckily, for reservoir sampling, Viter derived the exact form for us to use. Nevertheless, we still have to evaluate it to sample with it, and that costs time. So we don't want to call it too often. Instead, we sample using a different, easy-to-evaluate function, and use a probabilistic argument to proclaim that some of the elements sampled come from f_{Δ_i} indirectly. That's the high-level idea.

More specifically, we find an integrable "hat" function, h_i, over the range of f_{Δ_i}, which is the probability mass function of Δ_i. To serve as a hat for f_{Δ_i}, we have to have $f_{\Delta_i}(x) \le h_i(x)$, meaning that the probability of Δ_i being X is always smaller than $h_i(x)$. We then normalize h_i with the finite value α_i, which is its integral over the range of f_{Δ_i}, to get a valid probability density function $g_i(x) = h_i(x)/a_i$. It makes sense to sample from the range of f_{Δ_i} using $g_i(x)$. We draw a random value X from $g_i(x)$ and a uniformly distributed U from $(0,1)$. If $U \le f_{\Delta_i}(x)/a_i g_i(x)$, we take X, the current realization of X, to be a random deviate from f_{Δ_i}; otherwise, we generate the next pair (X, U) until the condition is fulfilled. If we abuse the notation and theory heavily, we could say that $g_i(x)$ conditioned on $U \le f_{\Delta_i}(x)/a_i g_i(x)$ is the same as f_{Δ_i}.

We now have one more detail to cover. Remember that we want to eschew evaluating f_{Δ_i} due to its cost. *Squeezing* introduces a "reversed" hat or perhaps a bowl (bathtub?) function that "props" f_{Δ_i} "from beneath."

Squeezing, then, is finding a function r_1 that is inexpensive to evaluate, such that $r_i(x) \le f_{\Delta_i}(x)$ for all x in the range. Then, asking $U \le \frac{r_i(x)}{a_i g_i(x)}$ can be confirmed by the affirmative answer to $U \le \frac{r_i(x)}{a}$, and only in the case of a negative answer does the more expensive $U \le \frac{f_{\Delta_i}(x)}{a_i g_i(x)}$ have to be evaluated. We will use f_{Δ_i}, g_i, a_i, r_i, and the cumulative distribution function G_i as Vitter derived them for us. In particular

$$f_{\Delta_i}(m) = P(\Delta_i = m) = \frac{k}{i-k} \frac{\prod_{j=0}^{m}(i-k+j)}{\prod_{j=0}^{m}(i+1+j)}$$

$$F_{\Delta_i}(m) = P(\Delta_i \le m) = 1 - \frac{\prod_{j=0}^{m}(i+1-k+j)}{\prod_{j=0}^{m}(i+1+j)}$$

$$a_i = \frac{i+1}{i-k+1}$$

$$g_i(x) = \frac{k}{i+x}\left(\frac{i}{i+x}\right)^k$$

$$G_i(x) = 1 - \left(\frac{i}{i+x}\right)^k$$

$$r_i(m) = \frac{k}{i+1}\left(\frac{i-k+1}{i+m-k+1}\right)^{k+1}$$

```
S = [None] * k
j = 0
i = 0
Δ = 0
```
Initialize an empty buffer (reservoir) S of size k. Set j, the index of the next element, to include the i index of the current element and the first skip Δ to 0.

```
while (i<k)
    i+=1
    S[i]=e_i
```
Include first k elements of the stream; e_i is the load.

```
i = i + 1
```
Move the index after the repeat block.

Draw U for the first skip.
```
U = PRNG_Unif(0,1)
```

Draw the first Δ from $F_{\Delta_i}^{-1}(U)$.

```
while  | 1 - (∏_{j=0}^{Δ}(i+1-k+j)) / (∏_{j=0}^{Δ}(i+1+j)) | > U :  Δ = Δ + 1
```

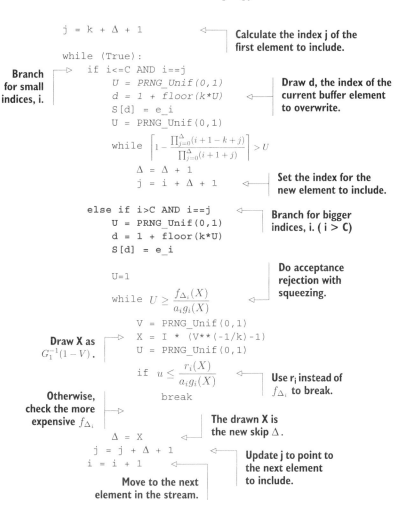

```
j = k + Δ + 1                    ◁──┐  Calculate the index j of the
                                    │  first element to include.
      while (True):
        if i<=C AND i==j
            U = PRNG_Unif(0,1)          ┌─  Draw d, the index of the
            d = 1 + floor(k*U)     ◁────┤   current buffer element
            S[d] = e_i                  │   to overwrite.
            U = PRNG_Unif(0,1)
```

$$\text{while } \left[1 - \frac{\prod_{j=0}^{\Delta}(i+1-k+j)}{\prod_{j=0}^{\Delta}(i+1+j)} \right] > U$$

```
            Δ = Δ + 1
            j = i + Δ + 1       ◁──┐  Set the index for the
                                   │  new element to include.

        else if i>C AND i==j    ◁──┐  Branch for bigger
            U = PRNG_Unif(0,1)      │  indices, i. ( i > C)
            d = 1 + floor(k*U)
            S[d] = e_i
                                       ┌─  Do acceptance
            U=1                        │   rejection with
```

$$\text{while } U \geq \frac{f_{\Delta_i}(X)}{a_i g_i(X)} \quad ◁── \text{squeezing.}$$

```
            V = PRNG_Unif(0,1)
            X = I * (V**(-1/k)-1)
            U = PRNG_Unif(0,1)
```

$$\text{if } u \leq \frac{r_i(X)}{a_i g_i(X)} \quad ◁──┐ \;\; \text{Use } r_i \text{ instead of}$$

```
                break                     f_{Δ_i} to break.
```

$$\Delta = X \quad ◁── \begin{array}{l}\text{The drawn X is}\\ \text{the new skip } \Delta.\end{array}$$

```
        j = j + Δ + 1    ◁──┐  Update j to point to
        i = i + 1       ◁──┘  the next element
                              to include.
```

Branch for small indices, i.

Draw X as $G_1^{-1}(1-V)$.

Otherwise, check the more expensive f_{Δ_i}

Move to the next element in the stream.

The pseudocode shows efficient implementation of reservoir sampling. Sample size k should be set to some value. Using the example from figure 7.2, you can connect the code to your understanding of the algorithm.

Techniques like inverse probability integral transform, the acceptance–rejection method, and squeezing are general methods for efficient sampling from any probability distribution, so although you might need a bit of perseverance to understand how they are used, once you understand, you can tackle a wide domain of sampling tasks efficiently. Notice that the algorithm works for any number of elements coming from the stream and can be stopped at any time, resulting in a simple random sample of size k of all elements seen up to that point.

The runtime of the reservoir sampling algorithm is $O\left(k + \log \frac{n}{k}\right)$, so time and space requirements fit our "small space, small time constraint"—at least, in principle, since n in a landmark stream is infinite. It might be better to think about a continuous query, which uses the sample, after some specific number of elements has been seen.

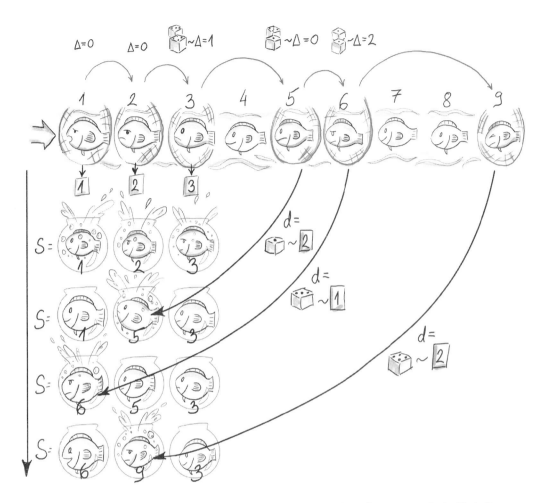

Figure 7.2   The figure shows the content of the reservoir after each of the first seven arrivals. First, three elements are included in the sample deterministically. Subsequently, e_4 is skipped (this corresponds to Δ_3, the number of elements to skip after e_3 is included, being 1). e_5 then randomly replaces e_2 in the reservoir (d = 2). The next element, e_6, is included at the random position 1 in the reservoir and replaces e_1 (notice that this means that Δ_5 was 0). Δ_6 is bigger than 0, since at least one element, e_7, is skipped.

For the difference analysis between the runtime of the naive implementation and the one we presented with geometric jumps, see "Non-Uniform Random Variate Generation" ([chapter 12], http://www.nrbook.com/devroye/).

To understand how the reservoir sampling algorithm delivers an SRS, we will visualize a very fine balance between two sequences of probabilities. The first one is $k/i := p_i$ the probability that ith element is included (we have referred to it as *inclusion probability*). The second is the probability that the ith element is not removed from the reservoir, once it is included, if we see $N - i$ elements after it. The second probability pertains to the event when all e_j (j in index) that show up at the "door" after e_i (i in the index), fail to remove element e_i (i in the index) that sits in the reservoir.

For one specific e_j, this second probability is the sum of the probability that e_j was not selected for inclusion in the first place (e_j is skipped in this case) and the probability that, if it was selected for inclusion, it failed to remove the e_i. This sum is written as

$$q_{ij} = 1 - \frac{k}{j} + \frac{k}{j}\left(\frac{k-1}{k}\right) = 1 - \frac{1}{j}$$

Hence, the probability that e_i is part of the reservoir after N elements are seen is

$$P_N(e_i \in S) = \min\left(1, \frac{k}{i}\right) \times \prod_{j=\max(i,k)+1}^{N} \frac{j-1}{j}$$

We will call this the *probability of residing at N*. The first part of the product (left from $\times$), which we denote as p_i, is *inclusion probability* for e_i. The second part (right from $\times$) is the cumulative product (we will denote it as π_{iN}) that captures the probability that none of the later elements remove e_i (assuming we see N elements in total). We used min to generalize the expression to accommodate the first k elements (that are included deterministically) as well. Figure 7.3 shows these two opposing forces and the resulting $P_N(e_i \in S)$ for every e_i, $N = 100$, and $k = 10$.

You might remember that there aren't many realistic data streams where we want the distant past to influence our current query to the same degree as the more recent past. This different weighting of elements based on their arrival time cannot be accomplished with reservoir sampling, so researchers try to "tilt" the balance, as shown in figure 7.3, to where more recent elements are more likely to be a part of the final sample compared to those that arrived earlier. This way the black line goes up as it approaches the current moment. This leads us to our next sampling algorithm, *biased reservoir sampling*.

7.1.3 Biased reservoir sampling

To bias the sample, we will focus on the probability of residing at N, $P_N(e_i \in S)$, which determines if the element e_i at time N resides in the reservoir once it has seen $N - i$ elements after it. We would like to be able to tilt the $P_N(e_i \in S)$ from the representative equilibrium where all e_i's have equal $P_N(e_i \in S)$ (see figure 7.3). One way to do this is to assume that $P_N(e_i \in S)$ decreases every time a new element arrives from the stream. We are aging out the elements nondeterministically. This way, when e_i becomes the ever more distant past and we would rather not have it in our current reservoir, the probability of that happening becomes very small. In our IP example, you might be interested in the average number of fingerprints per IP over only the last day of traffic. In this case, you want a mechanism to govern the residing probabilities that will allow day-old elements, but no older, in the reservoir.

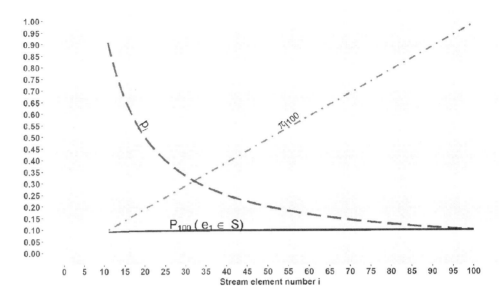

Figure 7.3 **We can see the balance between probabilities of inclusion (curved, dashed line) and probabilities of removal up to the point N = 100 (straight, dashed line) reflected in $P_{100}(e_i \in S)$ (solid line), which is approximately constant for all elements seen so far (when the reservoir is of size 10). This means that each element, no matter when it has been seen, has the same chance of being in the sample.**

To achieve this, we model the probabilities of residing using some memoryless bias function $f(i, N)$. Even though this function has two parameters, i (-th element from the stream), and N (number of elements seen thus far), it evaluates equally for all pairs (i, N) that have the same distance $(N - i)$ between them. Therefore, $P_N(e_i \in S)$ $= P_{N+k}(e_{i+k} \in S)$, meaning that e_i after we have seen N elements has the same probability of residing in the reservoir as e_{i+k} after we have seen $N + k$ elements. We are inquiring about elements that are at the same distance in the past from their two respective querying moments, N and $N + k$. The fact that we saw k new elements in the meantime leaves the two *residing probabilities*, $P_N(e_i \in S)$ and $P_{N+k}(e_{i+k} \in S)$, untouched. This is what is meant when we say *memoryless*. The function does not "remember" what absolute moment in time it is; it just needs to know how far in the past we are inquiring about.

You can imagine tilting $P_N(e_i \in S)$ (see where the fixed $N = 100$ is set in figure 7.3). Notice that $P_N(e_i \in S)$ stays constant for increasing i. This is what we expect from a classical reservoir sampling algorithm. Biased reservoir sampling would have $P_N(e_i \in S)$ be larger as we approach the current moment and smaller toward the start of the stream ("beginning of time").

In the original paper for biased reservoir sampling, Aggarwal [5] makes use of the memoryless exponential bias function $(i, N) = e^{-\lambda(N-1)}$. Do you notice $(N - i)$ in the negative exponent? When we observe the expression, we notice that the wider the gap, the bigger the exponent (and hence the smaller the negative exponent). This makes the whole expression, which is our residing probabilities, smaller $P_N(e_i \in S)$. For financial data streams, or any stream for which aging elements out is beneficial, this is what we want.

The parameter λ serves as the *speed of aging* factor. Figure 7.4 shows $P_N(e_i \in S) = f(i, N)$ for several different values of λ. We will equip you with some intuition about λ. As a part of an exercise, know that $P_N(e_i \in S)/P_N(e_{i+1} \in S) = e^{-\lambda}$. In other words, after a single new element arrives, the residing probability of the current element decreases by the factor of $e^{-\lambda}$. The edge case $\lambda = 0$ means "never forget," and this, for our purpose, is a useless value of λ, but it helps to observe what happens near it. If we part from $\lambda = 0$ to the right in small, increasing steps (i.e., $\lambda = 0, 0.001, 0.01, 0.1 \ldots$), $e^{-\lambda}$ takes up values 1, 0.999, 0.99, and 0.9, in that order. Here, we see how λ governs the speed of aging; a single new element's arrival makes the residing proba- bility 99.9%, 99%, or 90% of what it was before the arrival. From this progression governed by λ, we can now deduce how many elements have to arrive for p_i to age out completely. If we extrapolate the reasoning, we see that $e^{-\lambda(N-i)}$ is the inverse of the number of elements that need to arrive to decrease $P_N(e_i \in S)$ by the factor of e^{-1} (which is multiplication by approximately 0.36; see figure 7.4). Phew! What a mouthful!

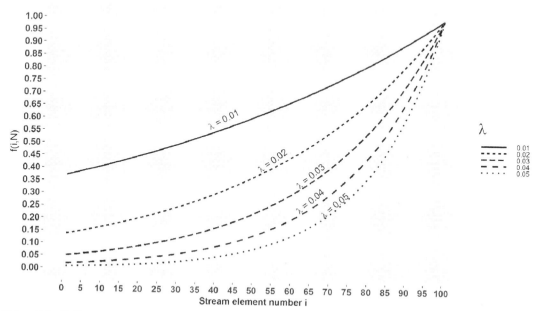

Figure 7.4 Notice that for $\lambda = 0.01$, we need 100 elements to reduce f(i,N) by the factor of 0.36, while for $\lambda = 0.02$, this number is 50. So, the higher the λ, the easier it is to forget old elements.

Example 1

For our average number of fingerprints per IP use case, we might have a constant arrival rate of 12 elements per second. We would like to know the average number of fingertips per IPs that appeared in the last 24 hours. That is 86,400 seconds, in which we see 12 x 86,400 = 1,036,800 IP addresses with their FP. Our λ needs to decrease $P_1(e_1 \in S)$ from 1 so that $P_{1036801}(e_1 \in S)$ is effectively 0. This means that after we see 1,036,801 elements, the residing probability of the first one has to effectively fall to 0. For our application, what would be the value of λ that would make this happen? This is equivalent to the question "For which λ is $e^{-\lambda \times 1036800} = 0$?" Through trial and error, you can check that for $\lambda = 10^{-6}$, $e^{-\lambda \times 1036800}$ is 0.35, while for $\lambda = 10^{-5}$, this becomes 3×10^{-5}. So, between these two values is where our λ is if we want to "cling out" elements gradually over a day.

We will now see how one such particular λ governs the sample size too. This biased sampling scheme does not come for free, and to maintain a sample over a landmark stream, we have to meet some minimal space requirements; we have to know how the sample size grows with elements seen. Authors of the original paper denote the sample $S(n)$ to indicate its dependency on the number of seen elements. Conveniently, they also prove that for large N (conforming with realistic streams), the size of the sample is bounded above by $1/1-e^{-\lambda}$. From that, we bound the maximal sample size needed to achieve rates λ at which $P_N(e_i \in S)$ reduces appropriately slow (or fast). That first bound can be replaced by $1/\lambda$ (using a basic calculus theorem), so all we have to facilitate is enough space for our specific, application-driven λ to govern our bias. If the λ we calculated in the example fits this constraint, we can use the exponential bias function with that λ. In our case, the maximum sample size is somewhere between 10^4 and 10^5. For the case where we can hold the entire maximal size of the sample within the (efficient) space constraints of the stream application, we can use the following simple algorithm to maintain a biased sample over any number of elements from the stream.

Assume that the jth element in the stream just arrived, and denote the occupied proportion of the reservoir by $F(j) \in (0,1)$. The new element e_j is added to the reservoir deterministically. This can happen in two ways: with probability $F(j)$, e_j substitutes a randomly chosen element from the reservoir, and with complementary probability, e_j is appended to the reservoir without resulting in any removals. The pseudocode for this version of biased reservoir sampling is shown in the code snippet on the next page. Figure 7.5 shows biased reservoir sampling for a reservoir of size $k = 3 \left(\lambda = \frac{1}{3}\right)$ for the first seven elements of the stream.

e_1 is included deterministically, and e_2 is inserted without removing any existent elements from the reservoir due to the values $F(2)$ and U_2. Since the portion of the reservoir that is occupied grows, the probability of including the next element at the expense of one existent element is higher ($U_3 < F(3)$); hence e_3 is saved at the first spot ($d = 1$). Notice that there are two possible positions for this: 1 and 2. e_4 is

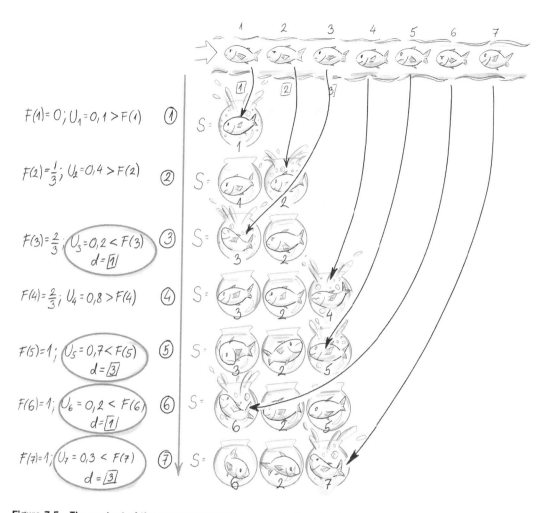

Figure 7.5 The content of the reservoir for first seven arrivals under the biased reservoir sampling strategy

included at the third position without removing any elements ($U_4 < F(4)$). Since at this point the whole reservoir is occupied, elements e_5, e_6, and e_7 are included, all at the expense of elements saved in positions 3, 1, and 3, in that order:

```
S = [None] * 1/λ          Initialize an empty buffer (reservoir) S of size k = 1/λ. Set i,
COP = 0                   the index of the current element, to 1 and the currently
i = 1                     occupied proportion (COP) of the reservoir to 0.

while (True)
    U = PRNG_Unif(0,1)
    if U < COP
        U = PRNG_Unif(0,1)
```

```
        D = 1 + floor(k * COP * U)
     ⊳    S[d] = e_i
   else
        d = 1 + floor(k * COP)
        S[d] = e_i
        COP += 1/k
```

Draw index d between **1** and the maximal occupied index **k * COP** of the reservoir.

Append the current element to the reservoir. In this case, we have to update the COP too.

Save the element e_i at that random index in the occupied part of the reservoir.

You can go through the pseudocode and use the example from figure 7.5 to check your reasoning. Notice that once the reservoir is full, the COP is 1, and the `IF`-branch is always executed after that.

EXERCISE 2

Implement biased reservoir sampling using the provided pseudocode and the R package `stream` introduced in section 7.3 or using Python 3.0.

When $1/\lambda$ cannot fit into our available working buffer memory, the algorithm is modified to "slow down" the insertions by introducing a $p_{ins} = k\lambda$ probability of insertion instead of $p_{ins} = 1$. This allows us to implement the same bias in the sampling, but with a lower sample size, p_{ins}/λ.

This modification introduces the issue of the initial filling of the reservoir too slowly. This can lead to long waiting times to answer the sample size queries that guarantee the acceptable accuracy and precision standards. Aggarwal gives a strategy to solve this problem, so, if necessary, see his paper [5], if necessary, to implement this.

7.2   *Sampling from a sliding window*

We will first discuss how to sample from a sequence-based window. Here, the recency is measured in an ordinal sense as a number of arrived elements. In our IP addresses stream, the IP addresses could come at different times, but the window would be 1,000 of them long, no matter how that number spans on the time scale. We will be dealing with a sequence of windows (hence, sliding), W_j, $j \geq 1$, where each indexed window entails n elements, e_j, e_{j+1}, e_{j+2}, ..., e_{j+n-1}. This n does not change with stream evolution as N does. The gaps between two arrivals can generally be different in absolute time units, but sequence-based windows deem these irrelevant and log the elements in consecutive integer positions. We will maintain a sample of size k from the current window. Notice that we now have to devise a strategy for updating the sample not only when we decide to insert a new element in the sample, but also every time the oldest current member of the sample exits the current window (is "aged out"). We don't assume that the size of the window n can fit our working memory; therefore, it makes sense to sample from it.

7.2.1   *Chain sampling*

First, we explain how to select a random sample of size 1 from the current window and update it as the window moves. The algorithm for a random sample of size k is then just a simultaneous (parallel) execution of k instances (chains) of the strategy for keeping just one random element.

The initial phase of the algorithm that lasts n discrete time steps (length of the window) is the regular unbiased reservoir sampling, with some additional operations. Each arriving element e_i will be selected as the sample $S = \{e_i\}$ with the probability i/j. This is the reservoir sampling part. The addition that handles the sliding window will pick the element that will substitute e_i when this one is aged out. We did not do this in the reservoir sampling algorithm. Hence, each time we pick a random future index, $K \in \{i + 1, i + 2, ..., i + n\}$, and add $(K, .)$ to the chain. We know that the Kth element will be saved there once it enters the window. This becomes the second element of the chain. The first element (i, e_i) saves the current sample of size 1. After the whole window W_1 has been seen (n elements pass), we are in possession of a simple random sample from W_1 of size 1, because reservoir sampling guarantees that. In addition, we have the latest K, the index of the tuple that will replace it, once the sample of size 1 expires. Now, for each arriving element, i $= n + 1, n + 2, ...,$ we have options:

- With probability $1/n$, we discard the current sample, $S = \{e_j\}$, and its associated chain, saving the index K and element e_K that was supposed to inherit it once e_j expires.

- We replace it with $S = \{e_i\}$. Now e_j has to have a successor to take over after e_j expires, so we sample a random future index, $K \in \{i + 1, i + 2, ..., i + n\}$, and add it as the second element in the newly created chain.

- With probability $(1 - 1/n)$, we check if i is the next replacement element to be saved in the chain ($K = i$?). If so, we save the ith tuple into the (last) chain element. We sample a random future index, $K \in \{i + 1, i + 2, ..., i + n\}$, of the element that will replace e_j once it expires and add it at the end of the chain. This is how the chain grows. In the case of $= j + n$, meaning e_j is leaving the window, the second element in the chain moves up, while the expired sample, $S = \{e_j\}$, is removed from the top of the chain.

These options deliver, at every discrete window-update moment i, a simple random sample of size 1 from the window W_{i-n+1}. Figure 7.6 shows chain sampling for first seven elements and the size of the window $n = 3$.

You should try to follow figure 7.6 as you read. First, the element e_1 is included deterministically. We then pick a future index, K, that will replace e_1 when e_K arrives. K seems to be 2. After we finish with the first element, the chain entails $(1, e_1)$ and $(2, .)$. At that moment, e_1 is the random sample of size 1. But to continue our example, element 2 arrives, and we notice that it is supposed to be saved as the successor of e_1. This is immediately done, and the chain now saves $(1, e_1)$ and $(2, e_2)$. These successor bookkeeping operations are done even before we decide to do them if we will sample e_2 with probability ½ (reservoir sampling) and discard e_1 and its chain altogether. We throw a die and $U > 1/2$ (in our case, $U = 0.7$); hence e_2 does not cause us to discard the existent chain. To finish dealing with e_2, its successor is drawn, and it turns

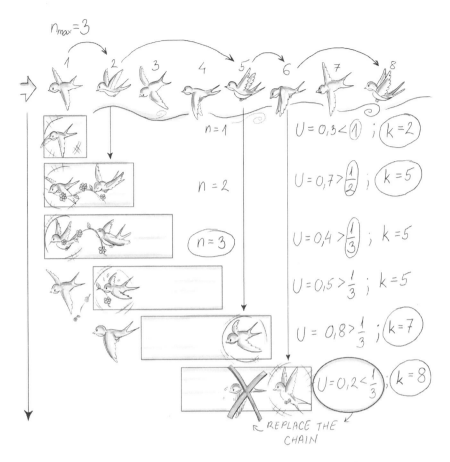

Figure 7.6   The content of the chain (list L) for the first seven elements from a sequence-based windowed stream of size n = 3

out to be $K = 5$. Hence, the current chain is $(1, e_1)$, $(2, e_2)$, and $(5, .)$. e_3 will not cause the deletion of the existent chain, either, since $U_3 > 1/3$. Since e_3 is nobody's successor, it won't be included in the chain, and we move on. At the fourth arrival, since the length of the window is $n = 3$, e_1 expires. We first need to update the current sample element with its successor in the chain. The role is taken over by e_2. e_4 does not cause us to discard the existent chain $(U = 0.4 > 1/3)$, and it was not chosen as anyone's successor, so we move on. Notice that e_4 is the first element in the second non-reservoir sampling phase. At the fifth arrival, two things happen. First, e_5 is added to its designated position in the chain, and its successor index is also included, $= 7$, so the chain is $(2, e_2)$, $(5, e_5)$, and $(7, .)$, and it is at the peak of its length. Second, since e_2 expires, the next element in the chain, the newly added e_5, replaces it. Once we finish with e_5, we have $(5, e_5)$ and $(7, .)$ as the current chain and e_5 as the current sample of size 1. When e_6 arrives, we randomly choose to discard the current sample and start a new one ($U = 0.2 < 1/3$). The current chain, together with the sample, is discarded, and e_6 is added to the new chain and becomes the new sample. The index of its successor K is drawn, which is 8 in our example. e_7 does not cause the chain to be discarded, and since it is not anyone's successor (it was e_5's, but that chain was disbanded), we move past it. At each moment of the stream evolution, you can read off two important points from figure 7.5: the sample of size 1 (the shiny sparrow) and which sliding window it represents (the window it is in). The sample is always the top element of the list.

Extensively commented pseudocode for selecting a sample of size 1 using chain sampling is shown next. You can follow the code in figure 7.6 and see where the chain gets longer and when its elements are discarded to start a new chain:

```
L = []          L is empty at the start. Set the i index of the
i = 1           current element to 1. Set K, the index of
K = 0           the future replacement element, to 0.

while i<=n                          Reservoir sampling
    U = PRNG_UNIF(0,1)             decides to keep eᵢ.
    if U < 1/i
        L.clear()                   Remove the current
        L.append([e_i, i])          sample and its chain.
        U = PRNG_Unif(0,1)
        K = i + floor(n*U) + 1      Add the current element e_i
    else                            to the chain and determine
        if i == K                   its successor K.
            L.append([e_i, i])
            U = PRNG_Unif(0,1)
            K = i + floor(n*U) + 1
    i+=1

while True                          The second phase for
    if (i==j+n)                     I = n + 1, n + 2, , , ,
        L = L.pop(1)
    U = PRNG_Unif(0,1)              Remove the top element of
    if U < 1/n                      the list because it expires
        L.clear()                   from the window.
        L.append
        U = PRNG_Unif(0,1)
        K = i + floor(n*U) + 1
    else if i==K
        L.append([e_i, 1])
        U = PRNG_Unif(0,1)
        K = I + floor(n*U) + 1
    i+=1
```

The first phase with n elements

Reservoir sampling decides to skip e_i, so we see if it is anyone's successor.

EXERCISE 2

Implement chain sampling for a window of length 100, sample size 1, and any $N > 100$.

Analysis of the space complexity for keeping k independent chains can be found in the original technical report by Babcock, Datar, and Motwani [6] or in GGR [7]. Expected memory consumption for k chains is $O(k)$, meaning that all of them have at most a length bounded by a constant. The space complexity of the algorithm does not exceed $O(k \log n)$ with probability $1 - O(n^{-c})$, hence by our criteria it is efficient.

Notice that each chain in the chain sampling algorithm delivers a simple random sample, at each time point, without a replacement of size 1 from the current window. Nevertheless, when we maintain k parallel chains at a time, the algorithm will deliver a simple random sample with replacement of length k, but this is not a limiting factor.

We will now present a similar algorithm for keeping a sample of size k from a timestamp-based sliding window.

7.2.2   *Priority sampling*

When we are dealing with timestamp-based windows, we don't know the exact number of elements n in the window, so it is not possible to anchor our algorithm on that parameter. To keep a simple random sample (SRS) of size 1 over a timestamp-based window, we generate a priority p_t for each arriving element e_t as a uniform draw from the interval $(0,1)$. The element with the highest priority in the window (now $- \omega < t <$ now) is our SRS of size 1. As we did with chain sampling, we will keep successors to inherit the sample once the current one exits the time-based window.

The first element e_{t_1} becomes our sample deterministically since there is no priority to beat ($p_0 = 0$). When the second element, e_{t_2}, arrives at time t_2, we check if $p_{t_2} > p_{t_1}$; if true, e_{t_2} replaces e_{t_1} (e_{t_1} is removed from memory). Otherwise, (e_{t_2}, p_t) is saved in a linked list and as the first element of the list (the sample is saved separately and is not an element of the list). After e_{t_3} arrives, there are three different scenarios for ordering the priorities in memory p_{t_1}, p_{t_2}, and p_{t_3} of the newly arrived element e_{t_3}:

1 $p_{t_1} > p_{t_2} > p_{t_3}$: e_{t_3} is added to the tail of the list that keeps replacements in case the element e_{t_1}, the current samples, expires. The list is ordered by descending priority and, per creation, ascending time.

2 $p_{t_1} > p_{t_3} > p_{t_2}$: e_{t_3} is added behind e_{t_1}, while all the elements (currently this only includes e_{t_2}) with lower priority and (inevitably) a lower timestamp are removed from the list/memory. The list remains ordered by descending priority and, per creation, ascending time.

3 $p_{t_3} > p_{t_1} > p_{t_2}$: e_{t_3} is added at the beginning while all other elements are removed from the list/memory. The list remains ordered by descending priority and, per creation, ascending time.

The first case adds the new element at the end of the sorted list (by priority) and keeps the whole list. The second case keeps the part of the list that has a higher priority than the new element. The third case discards the previous list and adds the new element at the top of the new one. The rest of the elements are discarded, and the new element is saved last.

The algorithm continues to update the list with each arriving element in one of the manners described. At each moment, l, on the top of the list is the element e_t, with the second highest priority among elements from the window $W_{l-\omega}$ where ω is the duration of the window ($l - \omega < t < l$). The current sample is the element with the highest priority within the time t ($l - \omega < t < l$). The element from the top of the list substitutes the current sample and becomes the new SRS of size 1 once the current sample exits the timestamp-based window. Figure 7.7 shows the priority sampling for six elements arriving at indicated times t_is for a window size of 600 ms.

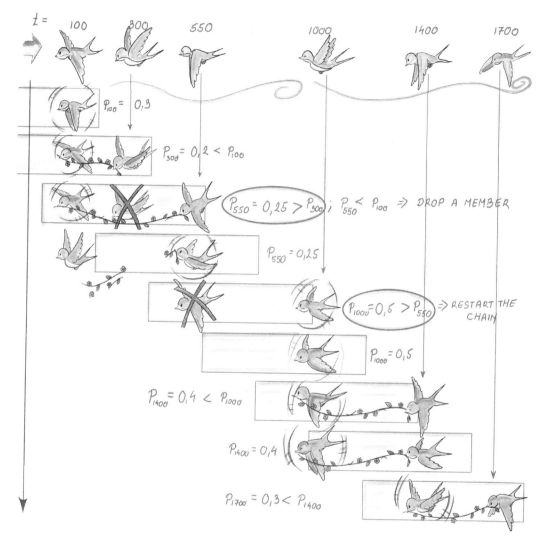

Figure 7.7 Content of the list of successors and the current sample for first six arrival times in ms for a timestamp-based window of length 600 ms

We will gradually explain what happens in figure 7.7, so it is a good idea to keep it in front of you while you read. The first element arrives at 100 ms, and p_{100} is drawn to be 0.3. e_{100} is set to be the current sample, while the list with the successors stays empty. At 300 ms, when e_{300} arrives, its priority, p_{300}, is set to 0.2. Since it is smaller than the priority of the current sample, it is added in the list as the first element with its priority and time of arrival. Upon arrival, e_{550} will break the priority list there, where elements that have lower priority ($p < p_{550} = 0.25$) start. This causes e_2 to be discarded from the list. The new content of the list is e_{550} only, with its priority and time of arrival. This probabilistic trimming of the list ensures the priority list doesn't grow too large.

Since $p_{550} < p_{100}$, the new element does not substitute the current sample; it simply becomes its new and only successor, for now. At time 700 ms, no element arrives, but since e_{100} expires, we have to replace the current sample with its successor. e_{550} becomes the current sample, and the list is empty. At 1,000 ms, the new element arrives. Its priority is 0.5, which is higher than the priority of the current sample. This causes e_{550} to be removed and replaced by e_{1000}, with its priority and time of arrival. The list with successors remains empty. e_{1400} does not have a higher priority than the current sample; hence it is added to the list as the only element so far. At 1,600 ms, the current sample e_{1000} expires and is inherited by e_{1400}. The list is now empty again. When e_{1700} arrives, its priority is set to 0.3, so it is lower than $p_{1400} = 0.4$. Therefore, e_{1700} is added to the list as the first successor of e_{1400} once it expires.

The pseudocode and detailed comments for priority sampling of sample of size 1 are shown next. This solution will work if the inter-arrival time between any two elements of the stream is always less than ω, the window length:

```
L = []
i = 1
p = 0
```
L is empty at the start. Set the i index of the current time point to 1. Set p, the priority, before any elements are seen, to 0.

```
while True:
    if len(L) == 0
        p = PRNG_unif(0,1)
        t = t_i
        L.append([e_{t_i}, p, t_i])
    else if ( t_i - t ≥ ω )
        L = L.pop(1)
        p = PRNG_unif(0,1)
        if p ≥ L[1][2]
            L.clear()
            t = t_i
            L.append([e_{t_i}, p, t_i])
        else
            j = 0
            while p ≤ L[j][2]
                j+=1
            L = L[0:j]
            L.append([e_{t_i}, p , t_i])
    i = i + 1
```

Handle the first element.

If the current sample element expired at time t_i, remove the top-first element of the list

Does the element that just arrived have a higher priority than the top-first element of the list?

Empty the list and append the new element as the only member of the list. Update the time t of the current sample.

Find where to break the list and discard the "tail."

We have to break the priority list somewhere beneath the top-first element.

Discard the tail and append the current element in its place.

Move to the next timestamp (arrival time).

The expected number of elements stored in memory for this strategy at any given time is $O(\ln n)$. To maintain a sample of size k, we can keep k lists; assign k priorities, p_{t_1}, p_{t_2}, p_{t_3}, ..., $p_{t_{ik}}$, to each arriving element e_{t_i}; and repeat the algorithm as many times with e_{t_i} as there are lists. For this algorithm, the expected memory cost is $O(k \log n)$, while, with high probability, the cost does not exceed $O(k \log n)$ (the space complexity analysis can be found in the same references as chain sampling).

Notice that the algorithm with k lists delivering a sample of size k generates a simple random sample with replacement from a timestamp-based window.

To try out sampling from the stream in practice before we get to the actual implementation of the sampling algorithm, we first have to have a framework to handle data streams as objects. Setting up such an environment using low-level OS functions, or even using special R or Python libraries, to communicate with a streaming framework like Apache Kafka can be quite time-consuming, especially if you are just trying to quickly check if your streaming algorithm works as it is supposed to.

In the next section, we show you how to use these algorithms in the R programming language within a simple data stream framework. We will spare ourselves some groundwork with the help of the R-package `stream`. We give some references for a similar framework in Python.

7.3 Sampling algorithms comparison

Now that we have gotten to know a few algorithms for sampling from a stream, we will demonstrate how to use some of them in the R programming language, and in particular the R-package `stream` [8]. This puts a data streams framework with data stream data (DSD) objects at your disposal. These can be wrappers for a real data stream, for data stored in memory or on disk, or for a generator that simulates a data stream with known properties for controlled experiments. Once we define what kind of data we will receive from the DSD object, we implement the task. In our case, this will be to maintain a random sample over the stream and use it to estimate the average value. For this we will use the class *data stream task* (DST).

7.3.1 Simulation setup: Algorithms and data

We will compare how well biased and unbiased sampling strategies adapt to sudden and gradual changes in the data stream. We will generate a stream with a sudden change in concept to check the robustness of the sampling algorithms with respect to this characteristic of a stream. The two algorithms operate on landmark streams, so we can talk about a random sample of size k from what we've seen so far. Biased reservoir sampling puts more weight on more recently seen elements, and the bias function and parameter lambda in particular determine how fast the older elements are aged out.

To simulate a sudden change in concept, we create a stream with the help of the function `DSD_Gaussians()`. This generator of normally distributed data creates 10^6 Gaussian deviates. The observations from the data stream change their distribution from $N(1, 1)$ to $N(3, 1)$ in a single step. This means that the stream source simulates a sudden shift at one point. We split the stream in half for this purpose. We receive 500 K random values from $N(1, 1)$, followed by 500 K random values from $N(3, 1)$. We will try out two sample (reservoir) sizes, $\in \{10^4, 10^5\}$.

We first create the stream and then save it permanently as a csv file. This is done so that we can sample the same data with our two algorithms:

> **Remove possible leftover objects in the workspace.
> If the package stream is not installed already, install
> it. Then bind the package to the workspace.**

```
rm(list=ls())
if (!'stream' %in% installed.packages()) install.packages('stream')
library(stream)
```

```
setwd(" ")                                ⊲─── Choose the path where you would like
set.seed(1000)                                 DStream.csv with the data to be saved.
stream_FirstHalf <- DSD_Gaussians(k = 1,            ⊲─── Make a DSD object
                                  d = 1,                  for the first half of
                                  mu=1,                   the stream.
                                  sigma=c(1),
                                  space_limit = c(0, 1)
                                  )
```

**Set the starting position of
a PRNG so that the same
random data is created
every time.**

```
write_stream(stream_FirstHalf, "DStream.csv", n = 500000, sep = ",")
```

```
stream_SecondHalf <- DSD_Gaussians(k = 1,          ⊲─── Make a DSD object
                                   d = 1,                for the second half
                                   mu=3,                 of the stream.
                                   sigma=c(1),
                                   space_limit = c(0, 1)
                                   )
```

**Write 500 K elements
from the DSD object to
the file DStream.csv.**

```
write_stream(stream_SecondHalf, "DStream.csv", n = 500000, sep = ",", append=TRUE)
```

**Append 500 K elements from the DSD
object to the file DStream.csv.**

Implementations of the biased and unbiased reservoir sampling algorithms presented in this chapter are available in the package `stream` in the form of the function `DSC_Sample()`. In our simulations, we use two different sample sizes, 10 K and 100 K elements. We load the stream from the file using the `DSD_ReadCSV` class. The stream is processed in batches of 100 K elements; hence the whole stream is processed in 10 steps. In each step, we call the function `update(CurrentSample, stream_file, n=100000)`. It expects a data stream mining task object, a DSD object, and the number of new elements to read from the stream. The paradigm behind `update()` is that there is a task we are executing on the stream. In our case, it is sampling from the stream. Once we read 100 K new elements from the stream, we have to adjust the current sample accordingly. Hence, calling `update()` makes sure our sample object has integrated the new 100 K elements into its current state. Since we call `update()` 10 times, we have 10 snapshots of the sample, each after additional 100 K elements have been seen. At these 10 stops, we calculate the average of the current sample and save it. We will use this later to evaluate how well the samples from biased and unbiased reservoir sampling adjust their averages to the sudden shift in the average of the stream data. We repeat this scenario for biased and unbiased reservoir sampling with sample sizes 10 K and 100 K for both. Remember that for biased reservoir sampling, λ, the speed of the aging factor is reciprocal of the sample size:

Create a DSD object stream_file from our DStream.csv.

```
rm(list=ls())
if (!'stream' %in% installed.packages()) install.packages('stream')

stream_file <- DSD_ReadCSV("DStream.csv")
CurrentSample <- DSC_Sample(k=10000, biased=FALSE)


MeanResults_Size10K <- NULL

for(i in seq(1,10)){
    update(CurrentSample, stream_file, 100000)

    names(CurrentSample$RObj$data) <- "sample_so_far"

    current_sample_avg <-
      mean(as.numeric(CurrentSample$RObj$data$sample_so_far))

      MeanResults_Size10K <- c(MeanResults_Size10K, current_sample_avg)
}

reset_stream(stream_file, pos=1)

CurrentSample<-DSC_Sample(k=100000, biased=FALSE)
MeanResults_Size100K<-NULL
for(i in seq(1,10)){
  update(CurrentSample, stream_file, 100000)
  names(CurrentSample$RObj$data) <- "sample_so_far"
  current_sample_avg <-
     mean(as.numeric(CurrentSample$RObj$data$sample_so_far))
  MeanResults_Size100K<-c(MeanResults_Size100K, current_sample_avg)
}
close_stream(stream_file)
```

Annotations:
- **Make a data mining task object that implements reservoir sampling with the option "biased" set to FALSE and the sample size to 10 K.**
- **An empty vector to save 10 averages from the 10 consecutive snapshots of the sample**
- **Update the sample with 100 K new elements.**
- **Rename the variable where the sampling object saves the sample to something more informative.**
- **Calculate the sample average.**
- **Save the sample average in the vector.**
- **Reset the stream for unbiased reservoir sampling with the sample size 100 K.**
- **Close the DSD object.**

`CurrentSample` is an object of a `DSC_Sample` class, which is a subclass of the *data stream task* (DST) class. One can therefore use a `DSC_Sample` class to implement any sampling strategy as a task on a data stream. The code for the biased version of the reservoir sampling is identical, with the parameter `biased` set to `TRUE`. The λ parameter governing the bias toward new arrivals is $1/k$ in that case.

Figure 7.8 shows sample averages during the evolution of the stream for these two sampling strategies. We can see how the sample average changes for reservoir sampling and biased reservoir sampling and the reservoir sizes $k = 10^4, 10^5$ on a landmark stream with the sudden shift at $i = 500K$.

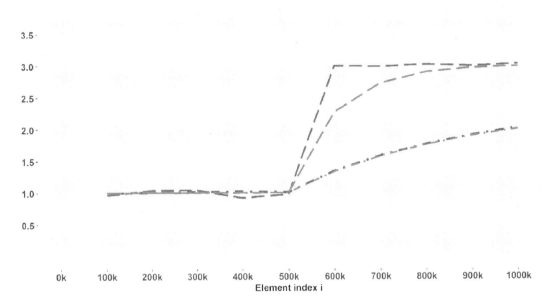

Figure 7.8 Dashed lines connect averages of samples selected using biased reservoir sampling. Upper, with λ = 10^{-4}, and lower, with = 10^{-5}, dotted and dashed lines track sample averages at every 100 K new elements for two unbiased reservoir sample sizes.

We see how biased reservoir sampling, due to uneven weighting of the recent and distant past, adapts to the sudden shift and estimates the mean very quickly and in an unbiased manner after the shift, while the unbiased reservoir sampling fails to do this. How quickly the biased strategy can detect the shift depends on the parameter λ. For $\lambda = 10^{-4}$ the probability of remaining in the sample decreases by e^{-1} every 10,000 elements, so this $\lambda = 10^{-4}$ forgets faster, or has a shorter reach into the past. Therefore, the biased sample with $\lambda = 10^{-5}$ is slower in moving toward the current true mean. This simulation hopefully gave you some sense of the realistic conditions under which you will be sampling from a stream and the decisions you need to make given the data at hand.

For those of you who would like to try out sampling from the stream using Python, there are two options. The first is more lightweight and allows you to deploy a simple Python-based Kafka producer that reads from a .csv file of time-stamped data. The repo can be found on GitHub under MIT license (github.com/mtpatter/time-series-kafka-demo). The second is Faust, a library for building streaming applications in Python (faust.readthedocs.io/en/latest). This is a very well-documented and rich library better suited for production-level processing of data streams. If you just want to convert a .csv file of time-stamped data into a real-time stream that is useful for testing your sampling algorithm, this might be too much.

Summary

- We have gotten to know five algorithms for sampling from a data stream (three for landmark streams and two for windowed streams). Bernoulli sampling is a very simple and representative sampling algorithm, but if you want to use it, you have to think about some sample size-curbing strategy, without introducing much bias.

- Reservoir sampling solved our problem of variable sample size and delivered an SRS from elements seen at any moment. If we want to accentuate more recent elements in our sample, biased reservoir sampling is one way to go, but we need to think about our desired speed of aging and how it relates to our available space. This depends on the realistic parameters you face in your own application.

- The other option to accentuate recently arrived elements in the stream is via the sliding window. We learned how to implement chain sampling for sequence-based windows and priority sampling for time-based windows if we need to sample from that window due to its size.

- We saw how biased reservoir sampling in our simulation managed to adjust to sudden shifts in concept, while reservoir sampling was unable to react to this change and led to a biased answer of the query about the recent true average of the stream data. Remember that you do need to adjust the speed of the aging parameter so that it suits the notion of sufficient recency for your particular use case.

Approximate quantiles
on data streams

This chapter covers

- Reviewing the concept of exact quantiles and understanding constraints imposed by streaming data context
- Understanding different types of errors for approximate quantiles
- Applying t-digest and q-digest algorithms to a data stream
- Comparing t-digest and q-digest on realistic data on length of visits to a website

Different algorithms presented in the previous chapter allow us to select an (un)biased sample from all data-tuples that have arrived up to the current moment. In a way, a sample is a very flexible datasketch: you form it once, and you can then use it to claim that its mean, or any other feature, is a good estimate of that same feature of all the data from the stream so far. Remember why we moved from Bernoulli sampling to sampling procedures that keep a sample of fixed size: because the Bernoulli sample grows with the number of elements seen and in combination with streaming data, it is just not practical.

However, what you get with Bernoulli sampling, and don't get with others, is a constant sampling rate for any value of N. You take on average every $1/p$th element, and this won't change no matter what N is. You "pay" for this nice property by having an average size of the sample pN. Why is it good to have the sample size grow? The central limit theorem says that any estimator from our sample has a standard error (precision) that decreases with the square root of the sample size. So, statistically, it is good to have a higher sample size. The problem is, as we see more and more elements from the stream, the density of the sample does not change for Bernoulli sampling, but it does for others. For algorithms that keep a fixed sample size of k, the density of the sample inevitably diminishes, since we always have k/N density while N grows.

This density, loosely defined, measures how well the points we took in our sample are spread among all points in the stream. (If you are interested in a more formal treatment of this concept of "density" of sample, read the introduction in this article: https://arxiv.org/pdf/2004.01668v1.pdf.)

Algorithms in this chapter aim to "marry" the finite size constraint and a specific notion of *constant density* (or precision) as N grows to answer queries about *approximate quantiles*. Although this might sound magical, under assumptions that don't affect algorithms' practical importance, this can be achieved.

8.1   Exact quantiles

Uninterrupted online presence and continuous contact and service for customers are of paramount importance for companies today. This is why a business or organization is highly invested in making the availability of content and access to their websites continuous and fast. One of the features of interest for an operating website is the time a user spends browsing it. From this data, we can determine the average time a user spends on the website. From some stable average profile, we could then identify pathologic examples of website time-spent data.

We simulated some data that tracks the distribution of the real data described and shown on the Apache DataSketches site (http://mng.bz/gwoG). The data there shows real data extracted from one of their backend servers. It represents one hour of website time-spent data measured in milliseconds. Data on the original scale has a very long right tail; hence showing it on a single milliseconds scale as a regular histogram is not something any ophthalmologist would support. Such data is better shown in a bar graph, like in figure 8.1. The actual bin widths increase as we move from left to right. Nevertheless, we draw them as equal-width bars. This way, we can enjoy the visual representation. Note that this is technically a bar chart, not a histogram.

Each time a user visits the website, the backend servers hosting it log the beginning and the end of each visit. The data shows the length of stay in milliseconds for around 26 million visits. There is a large proportion, around 14%, of visits whose time spent is logged as 0.

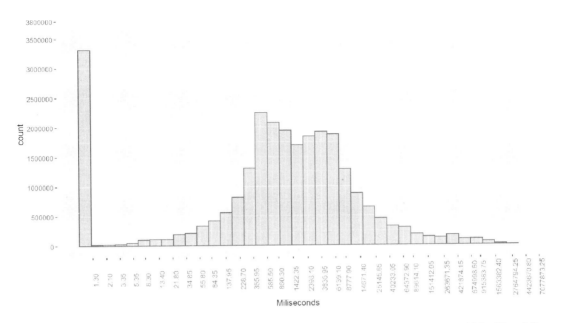

Figure 8.1   Bar chart (manipulated histogram) showing the length of stay in milliseconds for around 26 million visits

For now we don't care how this data arrived, from a stream or from a database, but we might be interested in the answers to the following questions:

- What is the median length of stay for visits hosted by a single backend server?
- What is the 95th percentile of the length of stay for visits hosted by a single backend server?
- What is the 95th percentile of the length of stay for visits over all backend servers that host this site?

The purpose of such queries is clear: I want to know when my website's *gripping power* starts attenuating or when it becomes a liability in the form of prolonged server latencies (which, of course, we can query in a similar fashion directly). This can be revealed by the movement of the median over time (or, for that matter, any other quantile you decide is of specific importance to track in order to optimize some business process).

What is this thing, a *quantile*, that can lead our decision ship through the angry sea of data? Unsurprisingly, the concept of a quantile was domesticated into human collective experience way before there was any big data around. Consequently, it carries around a scent of chalk-dusted sleeves. In other words, you will have to put up with some Greek letters and theory to understand the concept. The theoretical quantile, ϕ (*phi*), of some (continuous) probability distribution (density $f(x)$) is an inverse of the cumulative distribution function $F(x)$:

$$\phi_x = F(x) = P(X < x) \Leftrightarrow F^{-1}(\phi_x) = x$$

Let's now illustrate using our time-spent data. It helps if you insert the values we discuss into the expression. If we take $\phi_x = 0.5$, we then want to know below which time-spent x is 0.5 (half) of all the durations of the visits logged. This means that half of all visits are shorter than this length x. This is the median of our data. We can calculate any ϕ–quantile of our website length of stay data by sorting it and then picking out the ϕN th element in the sorted sequence. For example, with 25,961,440 visits, the median length of stay is the 12,980,721st record in the sorted sequence. This record has the value of 1150.592 milliseconds ($R(1150.592) = 12980721$). The last expression in the parentheses is read as the rank of 1150.592 ms is 12,980,721st.

We would go about calculating any other exact quantile (e.g., the 95th percentile has 95% of data "below" itself) similarly. The problem of calculating quantiles is known in computer science as the *sorting and selection* problem; by the name itself you can assume that it comes with a long history of intellectual efforts and research.

Finding the minimum or maximum (respectively, ranks 1 and N) requires only linear-time and constant extra space. The same goes for ranks that are near the edges of the data (i.e., finding any rank that is a constant away from a minimum or a maximum is similarly simple; e.g., rank c or $N - c$ for some constant c). To find other, less trivial ranks, we can easily employ sorting, where after having sorted the array $A[0, \ldots N - 1]$ in $O(N \log N)$, we find the rank r by accessing the element $A[r - 1]$ of the array (i.e., constant time). The high price for sorting will pay off if the data is largely static, and we expect to perform many rank queries. However, if we need to locate only a few specific ranks and/or the data is frequently modified, sorting becomes an expensive hobby.

Indeed, it is sufficient to spend $O(N)$ to find any a priori fixed rank on a given unsorted dataset. The deterministic worst case, $O(N)$, time *median of medians algorithm*, devised by Blum, Floyd, Pratt, Rivest, and Tarjan (BFPRT) [3], works recursively by splitting data into groups of size 5, selecting a median of each of the $\lfloor n/5 \rfloor$ groups (linear time operation!) and recursing on the medians until a single element remains. This element is then used as a high-quality pivot and is input to the quick-select algorithm (highly reminiscent of quick-sort) that rearranges data around the pivot and recurses on the side of rank r. Given that we are provided high-quality pivots from the BFPRT recursive scheme (that splits data conveniently into two equal fractions), quick-select runs in $O(N)$.

At this point you might say, "Well, there is our algorithm; why not just use that?" Advising against such an idea is a result as classic as 1980 itself, derived by Munro and Paterson [2]. They show that any algorithm that calculates the median exactly using at least p passes over the data requires at least $O(N^{\frac{1}{p}})$ working memory. It's easy to identify the p that we have to work with in a streaming data setting. Namely, we get just one pass over the data. This means we need linear memory in the size of the input. This sobering result should make it easier for us to accept some error ε when estimating ϕ_x for streaming data.

8.2   *Approximate quantiles*

Now that we know that it is not possible to get exact quantiles under streaming data constraints, we can, in a glass-half-full way, talk about the error. Algorithms developed for this setting always have to give some guaranteed error bounds. All algorithms calculating approximate answers should come with those, for that matter. There are three types of errors you will encounter if you sift through the (un)published research in this area:

- Additive error of the approximation of the rank
- Relative (multiplicative) error of the approximation of the rank
- Relative error in the actual domain of your data

8.2.1   *Additive error*

Most of the algorithms developed for this problem operate so as to guarantee a fixed additive error of εN in rank approximation *for any* $\phi \in [0,1]$. Here, N is the number of elements seen so far. This leads us to *ε-approximate ϕ* quantile. This implies that if we ask for a quantile $\phi_x \in [0,1]$, we will always get an element z with a rank of $R(z) \in [\phi N - \varepsilon N, \phi N + \varepsilon N]$. ϕ_x implies in notation that the ϕ quantile of the data is actually x and not z, hence the bound on error around ϕN. A closer inspection of the error bound reveals that z "promises," in the name of its rank $R(z)$, not to be further than εN away from the true rank, ϕN, of the element x we are actually interested in but didn't get to see. With this guarantee on $R(z)$, for any returned z, we can at least rely on

$$|\phi N - R(z)| \le \varepsilon N$$

If we allow some randomness in our algorithm, this error bound still needs to hold, except for some small failure probability δ (delta). Designers of nondeterministic algorithms deliver probabilistic proof that, under some loose assumptions, the algorithm won't fool you too often. That's where δ hails from.

Notice two important consequences of such a definition of an approximation error:

- The error is measured by the units of rank, not the units of your underlying data domain.
- The error is constant for fixed N, but since for streaming data our N will increase with each new arrival, the allowed actual error for the ε-approximate ϕ quantile will increase in the absolute sense as well.

This is something to keep in mind. To illustrate the concept of additive error, we will use a set of lengths, in milliseconds, for 10 visits to the website:

$$55.3, \quad 43.1, \quad 70.4, \quad 64.6, \quad 52.3, \quad 72.4, \quad 89.2, \quad 82.6, \quad 67.7, \quad 95.6$$

We first sort this set:

$$43.1, \quad 52.3, \quad 55.3, \quad 64.6, \quad 67.7, \quad 70.4, \quad 72.4, \quad 82.6, \quad 89.2, \quad 95.6$$

For ε = 0.1, x = 50 and $R(x)$ = 2. Legal ranks are then all from the interval $[R(x) - 0.1 \times$ 10, $R(x) + 0.1 \times 10] = [1,3]$. Returning 1, 2, or 3 as the rank of 50 miliseconds respects the additive error bound. The ε-approximate 0.1 quantile can then be 43.1or 52.3. Notice that the absolute errors on the scale of our actual data measured in miliseconds are $|43.1 - 50| = 6.9$ and $|52.3 - 50| = 2.3$ miliseconds.

EXERCISE 1

We continue the example involving additive error. If we receive 90 new elements (in addition to the 10 we have used to illustrate the concept) via data stream, this will increase our set size to 100 (for simplicity and reproducibility, assume that all are larger than 95.6). What would now be the approximate ranks and ε-approximate 0.1 quantiles that respect the additive error bound?

8.2.2 Relative error

Under the name *relative error*, you will find the following definition of the error z is carrying around:

$$|R(x) - R(z)| \leq \varepsilon R(x)$$

The word *relative* here comes from the fact that the error is proportional to the actual rank you want to estimate and not to the number of elements you have seen.

The only rank whose precision does not change between the relative and additive error is obviously the maximum: x_{max} ($R(x_{max})$ = N). The ε-approximate quantile for the minimum is allowed to be only ε away from the true rank 1. Let's look at our sorted example data again:

$$43.1, \quad 52.3, \quad 55.3, \quad 64.6, \quad 67.7, \quad 70.4, 72.4, \quad 82.6, \quad 89.2, 95.6$$

If we are to ask for the 0.1-approximate minimum of this data, ($R(x)$ = 1 and x = 43.1), the best approximation would be 52.3 with its rank 2. This does not preserve the definition of 0.1-approximate quantile in the relative error sense. Therefore, 2 is the best we can do and is not good enough if we want to keep the relative error bound. For ε = 0.1, the only order statistic we would be able to hold the relative error bound for is the maximum. You can check that.

Hence, guaranteeing relative error, in general, is harder than holding the additive one: the same ε algorithm that holds the relative (multiplicative) error bound, will trivially hold the additive error bound, but not the other way around.

Relative error is important for accurately estimating quantiles in the tails of the distribution. Most of data produced online are long tailed (our website visits data is too). When $R(x) \ll N$ or $N - R(x) \ll N$ (corresponding to the left and right tail quantiles, respectively), we want the accuracy of the estimates to be high, since percentiles like 99th, 99.5th, or 99.975th can exhibit large absolute differences. Remember how we had to extend bar widths as we went further into the right tail of website data? It is because of this increasing difference. In another use case, network latencies monitoring, the few very bad response times can cause a lot of problems for a portion of users, who might take their frustration to their favorite social network page. Even though latencies experienced by the majority of users are not long, this majority is silent. The long-tailed data might have a large difference between the 99.5th and 99.975th percentiles, in absolute terms, say, more than 30 seconds. This is why we would like to have an option of higher fidelity with respect to quantile estimation in the tails of the distribution. Multiplicative relative error bounds are better than additive error notions at gauging this unusual tail behavior.

8.2.3 *Relative error in the data domain*

The third type of an error you might encounter is the relative error with respect to values of your actual data items. For a quantile ϕ with $R(x) = \phi N$, we want to see an element z such that

$$|x - z| \le \varepsilon x$$

holds.

This sort of an error concept is fixed to the actual scale of your data and is applicable only to numerical data. Both of the previous error definitions, since defined with respect to the ranks, can be used to bound errors for any datum that can be ordered. Due to this lack of generality, not many researchers decide to develop algorithms whose quality is judged by this error type.

Now that we have established not only that that we're always wrong, but also how wrong we are, we can ask how we mechanistically implement sketches or digests that will serve this purpose.

8.3 *T-digest: How it works*

All algorithms for approximate quantiles that you will encounter are a form of self-organizing, data distribution–reactive data structures. They will go by the names *summary*, *digest*, or *sketch*. On a very high level, they save some small portion of observed data with some metadata for every saved data item. They then use this to answer a query about an approximate rank of an item or, conversely, returning an (approximate) data item for a particular quantile query.

It often occurs that an efficient method is proposed before one can provide a disclaimer of sorts in the form of error guarantees. For example, the random forest algorithm was used extensively (for around 13 years) before the asymptotic behavior (consistency and standard error) of this nonparametric estimator was proven. The first algorithm we will present comes from this heuristic-flavored part of a theoretical computer science town. Like with any other well-behaved and efficient heuristic, it has been widely adopted by the community since it was presented in 2013. According to their official documentation pages, the t-digest is used in many prominent databases and streaming data/distributed computing frameworks and libraries such as Apache Kylin, Apache Druid, Apache DataSketches, PostgreSQL, and Elastic Search. T-digest, by its construction, offers *empirical* relative errors in the quantile space that appear to be more than acceptable for a wide variety of applications. But for the formal proof for the error bound, the jury is still out. Let us first define a digest.

8.3.1 Digest

If you know how the famous magazine *Reader's Digest* started off, then you can draw a loftier analogy here compared to a simple one involving actual digestion. This thing has to consume some data and then decide what to save and what to integrate through metadata before discarding. This metadata is the data structure itself. You can imagine it as a series of equidistant blobs along the milliseconds axis, like clusters that span the range of the data. In the case of our website data, the query about the median involves data represented by clusters below the middle of the distribution. The number of these clusters is usually set before any data arrive, and it subsequently factors into the space requirements of the algorithm.

Figure 8.2 shows what a digest with five clusters looks like for $N = 10$ elements that arrived in that order. We have no reason to believe these will come in any particular order. We first partition the data items into sets π_i according to their consecutive, non-overlapping *arrival index* intervals. This corresponds to the ant level of figure 8.2. π_1 is {52.3, 72.4, 83.2}, and it spans arrival indices 1 to 3. These partitions are referred to as clusters, and we calculate for each the mean length of visit, called the *centroid*, and the number of data points contributing to this mean, called the *weight*. You can observe this in the first leaves level in figure 8.2. We then sort the clusters according to their mean. Notice that the second leaves level is sorted on size. In addition, for each cluster, we note the sum of the weights left and right of it. We now have a digest that has less information compared to our original received data.

We could use this resulting structure to answer a query about $R(72.4)$. We would find the first mean equal to or larger than 72.4. If we added all the weights left from this cluster, we would have some estimate of an approximate rank. In figure 8.2, we would return 8 and be off, from the true rank 7, by 1.

We call a digest strongly ordered if

$$i < j \Rightarrow x \leq y \text{ for } x \in \pi_i \text{ and } y \in \pi_j.$$

A digest is weakly ordered if

$$i + \Delta < j \Rightarrow x \leq y \text{ for } x \in \pi_i \text{ and } y \in \pi_j.$$

For some positive integer, $\Delta \geq 1$. Figure 8.2 shows the resulting weakly ordered digest. Notice that the 74.2 is bigger than 64.6, although the centroid of the cluster 64.6 is larger than the centroid of the cluster that 74.2 is part of. Hence, by definition, it is not strongly ordered. Intuition says, then, that the clusters are probably not very tight around their centroid, with some ambiguous data points "floating" between them. The parameter Δ is indirectly the measure of this tightness of the clusters. It determines how

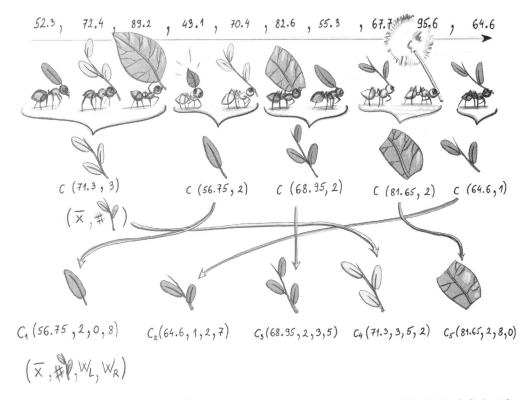

Figure 8.2 A digest for 10 elements. We order the clusters according to their mean. Clusters 1, 2, 3, 4, and 5 consist of 3, 2, 2, 2, and 1 data point, respectively. Each, aside from count, saves the mean value as well. W_{left} and W_{right} keep the number of data items left and right from each cluster. Notice that this digest is not strongly ordered.

many clusters i and j need to be away from each other so that all elements represented by the ith cluster are smaller than all elements represented by the jth.

EXERCISE 2

What is the smallest parameter Δ in figure 8.2 that make the digest weakly ordered (for that specific Δ)? Is there one? In other words, is there a number of clusters that, if we skip all elements from the ith cluster, are smaller than all elements in the jth?

Trivially, restricting the cluster size to 1 (by choosing singletons as a partition) will make the resulting digest strongly ordered. Smart, dynamic cluster size choices are the heart of the t-digest algorithm. We will now see how cluster sizes are governed indirectly by mapping them with forethought to the widths of intervals that partition the quantile range [0,1].

8.3.2   Scale functions

The ingenious part of the t-digest is how sizes (related to weights, but not being the weights themselves) of clusters are dynamically updated as new data comes in. To explain this we will *feed* the data into a t-digest in a sorted, ascending order. This can be done for a small, finite (with respect to available working memory) number of observations by having a buffer of working memory at our disposal and sorting the observations before inserting them into the t-digest. It will become clear that this is not a restricting assumption at all.

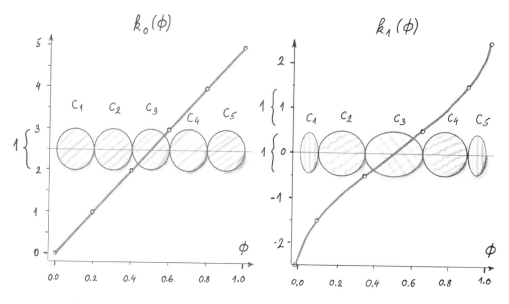

Figure 8.3 $\mathcal{K}^{k_1}$ and $\mathcal{K}^{k_0}$ differ between k_1 and k_0. The k-sizes for both functions allocate five clusters (both t-digests are shown as an ordered set of clusters that are fully merged; no two consecutive clusters can be combined without violating the weight bound). The k-size clusters in both cases are 1; nevertheless, the subintervals the clusters inform are different, and for k_1 they are variable with smaller clusters around the edges and larger in the middle. For k_1, they inform the same width subintervals of [0,1].

The key lever here is functions that determine which cluster needs to merge with their neighbor and when. At each moment, the cluster distribution along the axis is determined by the scale functions. Figure 8.3 shows how clusters partition the quantile range [0,1] for two different scale functions. In both cases, the quantile range [0,1] is covered, but the widths of the intervals pertaining to same clusters are different between them. We'll see why one is better than the other for our purposes of estimating an approximate quantile.

In figure 8.3, clusters grew to their widths by repetitive integration with neighboring clusters, until this new merge-result cluster reached a maximal width. This process of growth stops when the resulting cluster oversteps the size bound that is determined by the scale function. Good scale functions don't hold the size bound the same for every cluster. They make it depend on their position in the subinterval of the quantile range [0,1]. In other words, the size bound above which clusters can no longer merge depends on where in the quantile range [0,1] cluster merging of the two clusters is attempted. It is different if two merging clusters are close to the middle of the range than if merging happens at the edges of the interval. Therefore, the exact subinterval of the quantile range [0,1] that a cluster at each moment "informs" is determined by the scale function.

There are several functions suggested for these purposes. Those given in the original paper for t-digest (https://arxiv.org/abs/1902.04023) are as follows:

$$k_0(\phi) = \frac{\delta}{2}\phi$$

$$k_1(\phi) = \frac{\delta}{2\pi}\sin^{-1}(2\phi - 1)$$

$$k_2(\phi) = \frac{\delta}{4\frac{\log n}{\delta} + 24}\log\frac{\phi}{1 - \phi}$$

$$k_3(\phi) = \begin{cases} \frac{\delta}{4\frac{\log n}{\delta}+21}\log 2\phi, & \text{if } \phi \leq \frac{1}{2} \\ \frac{\delta}{4\frac{\log n}{\delta}+21}(-\log 2(1 - \phi)), & \text{otherwise.} \end{cases}$$

Here, n is the current number of data items received. These do look cryptic, but all you need to do is understand k_0 for a fixed δ (it is a simple line with a slope $\delta/2$). You can glance over the others if you are curious. They all share the same shape of the curve illustrated in figure 8.3. For our purposes, only think about the shape.

Remember those sizes we talked about? We will now explicate their dependence on the scale function k and refer to the size of the cluster C_i as its k-size $\mathcal{K}_i$. All these scale functions are monotonically increasing, as you can see, and they are defined for any quantile $\phi \in [0,1]$. We will use them to calculate differences $k(\phi_{\text{right}}) - k(\phi_{\text{left}})$ for (sub)ranges $[\phi_{\text{left}}, \phi_{\text{right}}]$ of $[0, 1]$. The first cluster for scale function, k_0, in figure 8.3 spans $[0, 0.2]$, for example. Its k-size is $k(0.2) - k(0) = 1 - 0 = 1$. Two different k functions don't share a domain, as you can see.

k-size $\mathcal{K}_i$ of a cluster C_i is related to the width $\phi^i_{\text{right}} - \phi^i_{\text{left}}$ of the subinterval that C_i currently informs. The boundaries of the subinterval ϕ^i_{left} and ϕ^i_{right} are

$$\phi^i_{\text{left}}\frac{\mathcal{W}_{\text{left}}(C_i)}{n}f$$

$$\phi^i_{\text{right}} = \phi^i_{\text{left}} + \frac{|C_i|}{n},$$

where $\mathcal{W}_{\text{left}}(C_i) = \sum_{j<i}|C_i|$ is the sum of the weights of all clusters to the left of the ith one in the ordered set. The bound on the k-size for each cluster C_i is then

$$\mathcal{K}_i = k\left(\phi^i_{\text{right}}\right) - k\left(\phi^i_{\text{left}}\right) \leq 1$$

You can see that the k–size is the difference between k-values of the boundaries. As soon as a single cluster reaches k-size 1, it cannot continue admitting any more neighboring singletons or neighboring clusters. This is how scale functions govern the cluster sizes. Beware—on the y-axis in figure 8.3, k-values are shown, not k-sizes. K-sizes are calculated as differences between the k-values (1s hiding behind left-hand curly braces).

The asymmetric concept of clusters admitting clusters into themselves is implemented in the t-digest by merging the clusters (integrating neighboring clusters into one). This is the way they grow in absolute weight($|C_j|$) and k-size. In a fully merged t-digest, no two (neighboring) clusters can be merged, since that blows their k-size bound of 1:

$$\mathcal{K}_{i,i+1} = \mathcal{K}_i + \mathcal{K}_{i+1} > 1$$

For scale function k_1, say you pick the parameter $\delta = 10$, $k_1(0) = -\frac{10}{4}$ and $k_1(1) = \frac{10}{4}$, as in figure 8.3. That means that k_1 spans 5 units on the k-size scale, while its argument moves a single step, from 0 to 1.

You might have figured out that this is a story of a derivative of k_1. On the periphery of the [0,1] interval, k_1 changes faster, and then the rate of change attenuates to a minimum somewhere around the middle. There it becomes linear with a constant slope (notice that k_0 has this constant slope behavior on the whole [0,1] interval). After that, it starts picking up again and ends with the same large rate of change as when it began. This way, the width of the subinterval [0,1] that the cluster is informing is inversely associated with the rate of change of the scale function on that subinterval. The steeper the function on the specific subinterval, the smaller the actual size of the clusters. The fast changing function on the "steep" parts reaches the maximal k-size of 1 faster, and the clusters are many but small.

Consequently, as you saw in figure 8.3, we have smaller cluster sizes on the edges of the interval and larger ones in the middle. Notice also that k_0 keeps all cluster sizes equal, no matter which subinterval of [0,1] you're in. This reveals bounds on the minimum number of clusters we keep at any point. Figure 8.3 shows the minimum number of clusters you can have for $\delta = 10$. It is five; hence the minimum is the range that the scale function spans, since within each unit at most one cluster is allowed due to the k-size bound of 1. These five clusters must be at their maximum size.

Hence, k_1 offers an opportunity to "zoom in" on those tails close to the minimum and maximum of the data, where unusual things happen (like in anomaly detection applications). For the quantiles ϕ that are close to 0 and 1, $k_1(\phi_{\text{right}}) - k_1(\phi_{\text{left}})$ is rounded up to 1 any time $k_1(\phi_{\text{right}}) - k_1(\phi_{\text{left}})$ turns out less. It can happen that the k-size reaches 1 without one whole data item allowed in the cluster, and you can't put half of the data item in a cluster. This is a numerical artifact of the scale function and the number of data items seen so far, so we don't want to have (and physically cannot have) less than 1 data item per cluster.

EXERCISE 3

What is the maximal number of clusters we can have for $\Delta = 10$? How do k-sizes look when we have a maximum number of clusters (knowing that each time two neighboring clusters ascertain that their integration will stay within the k-size bound, they will merge)?

8.3.3 *Merging t-digests*

Now that we understand what a scale function does, the algorithm is incredibly simple. Here, we describe the merge version of the algorithm. The algorithm is the same for updating a single t-digest with a newly arrived set of data items and for merging two t-digests. There are two phases that happen consecutively: sorting and merging.

We assume, aside from space allocated for t-digest S_n, that we have an extra buffer to receive a finite number l of incoming data items $X_L = [x_1, x_2, x_3, ..., x_l]$. As they arrive, we concatenate them with S_n (for the time being, we use noncapitalized n for the number of elements so far). We put them side by side. You can imagine this as an unordered union of a t-digest and X_L that represents l singletons with means identical to the data x_i with a weight of 1.

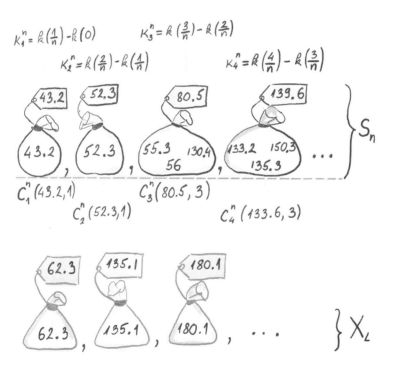

Figure 8.4 Strongly ordered t-digest S_n (superscripts on K and C denote the number of elements from the stream seen so far). Notice that the argument of the k-function appears in steps of $1/n$. X_L represents l new elements we are adding to the t-digest from the stream (we are showing only the left tail of X_n and S_n).

We then sort all $|S_n| + |X_L|$ clusters by their mean and do a following check from left to right. Is there a neighbor to the right of the cluster with which it could merge, while staying within its *k*-size bound of 1? If two neighboring clusters can merge like that, they proceed to do so, from left to right. If a cluster can merge with its neighbor, then the new resulting cluster will have the mean equal to the weighted mean of the centroids of the two merging clusters. The weight of the resulting cluster will be the sum of weights of individual ones.

After sorting according to the centroid value, we move from left to right and check if adding the cluster to the right will increase the *k*-size over the bound of 1. This time, the argument of the *k*-function is incremented by $1/(n+l)$. The $\mathcal{K}_i^n$ in figure 8.4 were calculated with advancing by $1/n$ for every element represented by the cluster. This is because we now have l new elements to account for.

Figure 8.5 shows the starting point after the sort phase. This becomes the input on which the merge starts working.

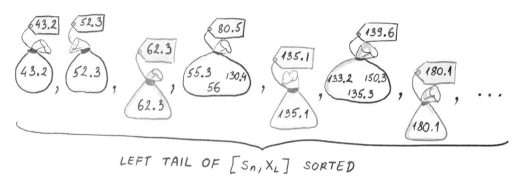

Figure 8.5   Sorted lower end of [S_n, X_n] before the merge phase begins

Figure 8.6 shows the merge process in incremental steps for the left tail of S_n and X_L. In other words, we show only the lower ends of the whole S_n and X_L, but since the merging phase starts from left and moves to the right, this should be enough for getting a grasp of how it's done. Between this and the pseudocode in the original paper, you should have a good basis of the concept if you ever want to implement it yourself.

Figure 8.6 shows that the attempt of the first cluster to assimilate its neighboring singleton fails because the resulting *k*-size is too big. This means that we stop and form the first cluster from the left as a singleton (with the same value and weight as before the merge). The next attempt at merging is performed by the second singleton toward its right neighbor (see figure 8.6, time point 3). This goes well, as judged by the *k*-size of the potential new future cluster. The same process continues, and now the tendency to merge is widened toward the next cluster to the right. The next cluster with centroid 80.5 has a weight of 3. When added to the weights of singletons 2 and 3, it will cause the *k*-size to be bigger than 1. This means we ought to stop and merge the two singletons that remain within the legal *k*-size bound (figure 8.6, time

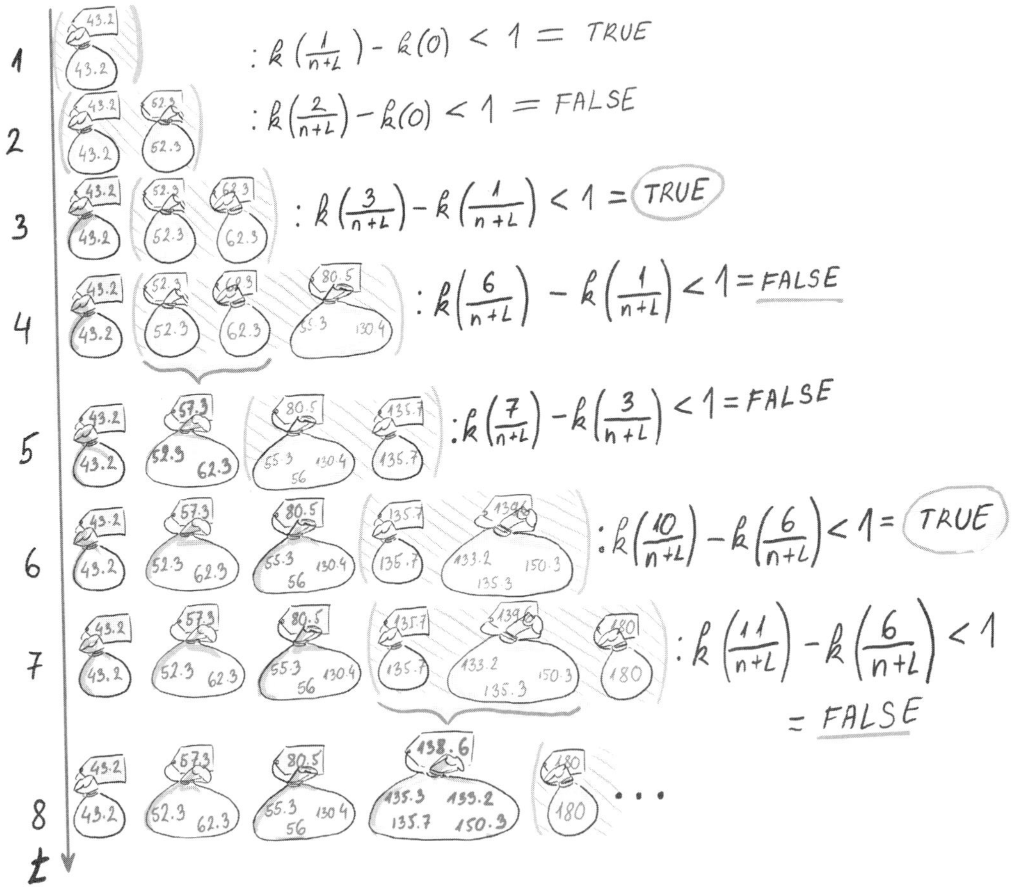

Figure 8.6 The merge phase of the t-digest algorithm. Each time the assimilation of the cluster to the right is not allowed (indicated by the negative answer to the *k*-size query), we form a new cluster (indicated by the closed [darker] bag). The current attempts to merge with the neighbor(s) to the right are indicated by the green parentheses at each time point. The clusters at the time point 8 are the first four clusters of the new S_{n+1}.

point 5). Simultaneously, the cluster with centroid 80.5 starts looking to the right and inquires if the sum of its weight and the weight of the singleton to the right of it causes a sustainable increase in *k*-size. It seems that it doesn't, and at time point 6 (see figure 8.6), we create a new *old* cluster with centroid 80.5 and weight 3. The process then continues analogously. Every time a new cluster is created, if it is a result of merging one or more clusters, its centroid is newly calculated and its weight updated.

Numerical values on the labels of the bags from figure 8.6 are what we actually save, while observations from the stream (shown in the bag) are discarded. The raw values in the bag are not kept by the algorithm, but we show them here for clarity. In addition, we save every new cluster's weight as well.

Notice that when we do the merge, a strongly ordered t-digest can become a weakly ordered one: 62.3 milliseconds is larger than 55.3 milliseconds; nevertheless, 62.3 milliseconds is part of C_2 (in S_{n+1}), while 55.3 is represented by C_3 (in S_{n+1}) after the merge phase is over. This can be even more drastic when we use this algorithm to merge two t-digests with singletons replaced by actual clusters of the second t-digest. Large Δ values (remember that Δ decides how well ordered the digest is) in this case can increase the error, but it seems that this doesn't happen often in practice.

The case of merging two t-digests proceeds just as it did in figure 8.6, but now we are not dealing with l singletons from the stream, but with some m_2 number of clusters of the second t-digest.

The fact that we can get a t-digest for "two worlds," $D_1 \cup D_2$, by merging t-digests built on D_1 and D_2 separately, is very powerful, since it allows the use of MapReduce computing architecture. Say our data about length of a visit to a website is partitioned into substreams based on the geographical location where the visit is coming from. If the data is huge, and it might be with popular sites like social networks or search engines, then you will probably have to parallelize the task of approximating tail quantiles. You can send the substreams according to a geographical split to different nodes in a streaming application. They would make their t-digests built on disjoint sets of data and send them to their master node. There the t-digests would be aggregated by merging them to approximate quantiles of all the data. Such a characteristic of a sketch or a summary is desirable, and good algorithms keep this feature, called *merge-ability*: the ability of a summary to merge with other summaries, but prevent the error of the resulting summary to grow, as formally defined in a paper by Agarwal et al. (http://mng.bz/p2NG). This paper is quite technical, but if you can follow the ideas in it, it makes for a very exciting read and is thus warmly recommended.

8.3.4   Space bounds for t-digest

If we look at the space bounds of this algorithm, for a single t-digest we only have to keep m clusters, and each cluster saves a constant amount of information, mean and weight and perhaps some housekeeping metadata, if necessary. So, the space needed for a t-digest is bounded by the maximum number of clusters we keep at any time. The maximum number of clusters can be derived for function k_1 as follows: since each time cluster is allowed to merge, they will merge, and the maximum number of clusters occurs when clusters are *almost* allowed to merge, but not quite.

This means that merging neighboring clusters takes the *k*-size just above 1 (e.g., 1.01). If this is true, the average *k*-size of a cluster is not less than 0.5; otherwise, at least one pair could merge. If $n > \delta$, the maximum number of centroids is δ the parameter of the scale function (remember the minimum was $\delta/2$). More detailed analysis of the number of clusters and the maximal weight of each cluster can be found in a short paper by Ted Dunning (https://arxiv.org/abs/1903.09921), one of the creators of t-digest.

We seem to have a constant space bound of $O(\delta)$ for any number n of data items that arrived. The δ parameter of a t-digest is called the *compression parameter*, for obvious reasons. This is pretty close to magical for the majority of the applications that use t-digests, if you ask me (leaving out the fact that the error needs to be empirically ascertained for each application anew and no universal guarantee exists).

8.4   Q-digest

In this section, we will present a different quantile digest (or q-digest) introduced by Shrivastava et al. [3], which is a precursor to the t-digest heuristic that offers worst-case guarantees on error and space. Apart from soothing our algorithmic souls, a q-digest serves as a good example of a data structure that most accurately answers queries for the elements with the highest frequencies. This is a desirable feature when working with frequency data, yet it is not shared by many other data structures. Recall from chapter 4 that the count-min sketch gave an identical overestimate range both for the bestsellers and the books that never got sold.

The q-digest can be used when elements have a prespecified range of legal values, $U = [1, \sigma]$. Essentially, you need to know the possible maximum your data has to use it. This is a realistic assumption for any data generated by some logging or smart device. The goal of the q-digest is to summarize the dataset S that comes in the form of key-value pairs, $S = \{a_1:c_1, a_2:c_2, ..., a_\sigma:c_\sigma\}$ where a_i is an element from U and c_i is the weight/frequency of the element a_i. Also, $\sum_{i=0}^{\sigma} c_i = n$ (total sum of observations).

Here is a rough idea of how the q-digest blurs accuracy to save space: if an element is deemed to have too low of a count to be separately stored as a key-value pair, its count information will be merged with that of a similarly low-count neighboring element to preserve information about the number of items in the relevant range but will lose information on counts of specific elements.

For instance, depending on how the parameters are set in the q-digest, two key-value pairs, {3:1, 4:1}, might get merged into one pair: {[3,4]:2}. In other words, we go from knowing that there is one copy of 3 and one copy of 4 to knowing that there are two copies in interval [3,4]. This idea is further applied to intervals with small counts. Intervals themselves can then be merged to save space if the elements in those intervals do not have high enough frequencies. The decision on what constitutes a high or a low count and the subsequent "blurring" step is determined by the compression parameter k. Remember that in a t-digest, we had scale functions; this is an analogous notion of something that will control the number of intervals. Next, we show how to construct and store a q-digest.

8.4.1   Constructing a q-digest from scratch

For the purposes of understanding how a q-digest works, we will envision an implicit tree T (a tree never gets stored.) The tree is a full binary tree with σ leaves (as big as your universe U), where the ith leaf from the left denotes the ith element from the universe U. In our simple example shown in figure 8.7, our universe is $U = [1,8]$, and

$\sigma = [1, 8]$

Figure 8.7   Original data and its frequencies represented through the leaves of an implicit tree

our dataset is $S = \{1{:}1, 3{:}5, 4{:}9, 5{:}2, 7{:}2, 8{:}1\}$. This frequency information for each element will be stored at each corresponding leaf of T. Each node v of T has an associated $count(v)$, and in the beginning only leaves have their $count(v)$ filled up.

To produce a q-digest from this implicit tree, we follow two rules:

1 For every internal node v in T that is not a root, $count(v) \leq {}^{n}\!/\!k$ (leaf and root nodes are allowed to break this rule).

2 For every node v in T that is not a root, $count(v) + count(v_s) + count(v_p) > {}^{n}\!/\!k$, where v_s denotes the sibling of v, and v_p denotes the parent of v. (The root node is allowed to break this rule.)

Here, we show the process of turning our implicit tree from figure 8.7 into a q-digest according to rules 1 and 2, in a couple of steps. In this example, we have that $n = 20$, and $k = 5$, so the maximum value allowed at the node is 4, and every "triangle sum" from rule 2 needs to be at least 5. Note that in the beginning of the process, rule 1 is not broken, as it does not refer to leaf nodes, and they are the only ones that contain values in the beginning.

The process begins at the leaf level, where, going left to right (as in a t-digest), we identify all "triangles" on the bottom level that break rule 2. Each time that happens, the values of v and v_s are summed, added to the value in v_p, and then deleted from v and v_s. For example, in the right-most triangle on the bottom of the first tree in figure 8.8, we sum 2 and 1, place 3 in their parent, and then delete 2 and 1. We continue in the same fashion with the next level, going again from left to right and finding problematic triangles. The process ends at the root, and the root is allowed to have indefinitely low or high values.

Using this process, we arrive at the final q-digest, represented by the last implicit tree in figure 8.8. The tree is never explicitly stored; only the nodes that have values in them. If we assign a level-by-level, left-to-right enumeration to nodes of the tree, then the resulting q-digest in figure 8.8 saves the following information: Q = {[1,8]:1, [5,6]:2, [7,8]:3, [3]:5, [4]:9}. If we enumerate each node and corresponding interval in a level-by-level left-to-right fashion, we get the following description: Q = {1:1, 6:2, 7:3, 10:5, 11:9}. We have gone from storing six key values when we had original data to now storing five of them—not that great. But with a larger universe and many low counts starting at the leaf nodes (typical of the Zipfian distribution exhibited by website time-spent data), the space savings become quite substantial.

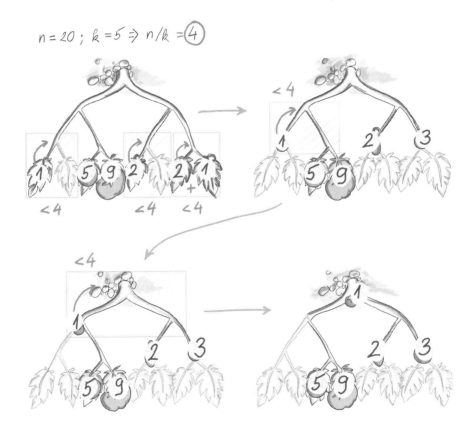

Figure 8.8 Building a q-digest from scratch

8.4.2   *Merging q-digests*

Q-digests were originally devised for the sensor-network and distributed setting, where q-digests can be locally computed and then later merged with q-digests at other nodes. The process of merging q-digests is fairly simple if both q-digests refer to the same universe. Given two trees T_1 and T_2, the q-digests can be merged by creating a tree T over the identical universe and summing the respective nodes from T_1 and T_2 into T. See the process in figure 8.9, where $n_1 = n_2 = 30$, $k_1 = k_2 = 6$. In the original T_1 and T_2, the maximum value at each node was 5.

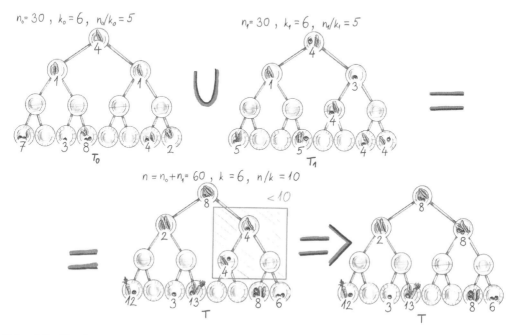

Figure 8.9 Merging two q-digests where $n_1 = n_2 = 30$, $k_1 = k_2 = 6$. Because the digests are of the same sizes, the resulting q-digest is of the same size, where the values at nodes are the sums at respective nodes. For example, the resulting q-digest has the value 8 at the root, because the q-digests participating in the merging operation both have the value of 4. However, this might lead to a q-digest that is not fully merged. In this example, the resulting q-digest has $n = n_1 + n_2 = 60$ and $k = k_1 = k_2 = 6$, so we are looking for triangles whose sum is 10 or less, and we propagate those values up to the parent, as before.

Once T is initially created from T_1 and T_2, it also needs to undergo the process of constructing a legal q-digest that respects both rules we mentioned earlier using the following parameters: $n = n_1 + n_2$, $k = k_1 = k_2$. If two q-digests being merged have roughly comparable or equal sums of observations, then the resulting q-digest's threshold (n/k) will be twice the size of the threshold for the earlier q-digests. In our example, the maximum node value for the resulting q-digest is 10. The two original q-digests being merged stored, in total, 16 key-value pairs, but the resulting q-digest uses only 8 key-value pairs, half as many.

8.4.3   *Error and space considerations in q-digests*

The maximum space used by a q-digest depends on the compression parameter k, and it equals $3k$. Denote the size of Q as $|Q|$ (measured in the number of key-value pairs). Then, from rule 2 we have that

$$\sum_{v \text{ in } T} count(v) + count(v_s) + count(v_p) > |Q| \times \frac{n}{k}$$

Also, it holds that

$$3 \times \sum_{v \text{ in } T} count(v) \geq \sum_{v \text{ in } T} count(v) + count(v_s) + count(v_p)$$

since in the right expression, the count of each node is being at most triple counted (each node appears once as a parent, once as a sibling, and once as itself; think about what's counted for the leaves and the root here). The left expression equals $3n$, hence $|Q| \times \frac{n}{k} < 3n$, which gives us $|Q| < 3k$.

As for the error rate, before we calculate the error when posing quantile queries, we need to observe how far a value within one node of the implicit tree T can be off. All nodes on the path between the root and node v can hold values potentially belonging to the interval specified by v. With that fact and the depth of the tree being $\log \sigma$, the total error within one node is $\log \sigma \times \frac{n}{k}$. If we observe this error in the relative term (as a percentage of n), we get that the error within one node is at most $\log \frac{\sigma}{k}$.

8.4.4   *Quantile queries with q-digests*

In order to perform quantile queries with q-digests, it is useful to sort the nodes of the implicit tree in a post-order traversal fashion. In other words, in the sorted sequence, we place the interval $i = [x, y]$ only after all its descendant subintervals have already been placed. Once we have done that and have provided a quantile query x, we sweep the array of key-value pairs, accumulating the values until x has been reached or overshot. The quantile reported is the right end of the interval where x was overshot. The example of a quantile query is given for the resulting q-digest from figure 8.9.

The post-order sequence of nodes in this tree with nodes enumerated in a level-by-level fashion is {8:12, 10:3, 11:13, 2:2, 14:8, 15:6, 3:8, 1:8}. This corresponds to right-sorted ranges {[1]:12, [3]:3, [4]:13, [1,4]:2, [7]:8, [8]:6, [5,8]:8, [1,8]:8}. Let's say we are given a query, $\phi = 0.5$; hence $x = n/2 = 30$ (i.e., we are looking for a median). Sweeping left to right and accumulating values in the list, we will accrue exactly the sum of 30 at $12 + 3 + 13 + 2 = 30$, and we will report the right end of our last node as the median. For the node containing 2, the right end of its range is 4. The reported median is 4. Similarly, say we are looking for $3n/4 = 45$. We again start from the left, accruing the sum $12 + 3 + 13 + 2 + 8 + 6 + 8 = 52$. With the last value, 8, we overshoot the value we are looking for, but our error will be commensurate with the max node values, so we report the right end of the interval corresponding to the key-value pair [5,8]:8, which is 8. Our returned result is 8.

The q-digest can be also used to answer many other types of queries, most notably range queries, inverse quantiles, and consensus queries. Provided the memory of m locations to build a q-digest, the error in the quantile query is at most $\varepsilon \leq (3\log\sigma)/m$. We obtain this by setting the compression factor k to be $m/3$.

8.5 Simulation code and results

To witness t-digests and q-digests in action, we devised a simulation scenario to showcase their empirical error behavior and compare their estimates of percentiles far in the right tail.

We drew 10 samples without replacement, each with 10^5 elements from our 2 GB of website data shown in figure 8.1. Since the q-digest works on integers only, we rounded the website data to the nearest millisecond. This way, we are able to use both algorithms on the same samples. The 10 samples, with 100 K observations each, that the code is using, as well as the total website data, are available in the code repository of the book.

To calculate our results, we used the `tdigest` library in Python and the version of q-digest implemented in Python from http://mng.bz/pOVw after validating the code on several small stream examples. The code to calculate and save results from the T- and q-digests, respectively, is shown. The code reads in 10 samples, and after each of the 10 is consumed by their own t-digest or q-digest object, a query is executed to get the 95th and 99th percentiles of the data. We end up with 10 estimates of the 95th and 99th percentiles:

```python
import pandas
from pandas import DataFrame
from tdigest import TDigest
import numpy as np
import os

df = pandas.read_csv('./test.csv')

resNinetyFive = np.array([])
resNinetyNine = np.array([])

columns = list(df)
for j in columns:
    tDigest = Tdigest(delta=1 / 200)

    tDigest.batch_update(df[j], w=1)

    resNinetyFive = np.append(resNinetyFive, tDigest.percentile(95))
    resNinetyNine = np.append(resNinetyNine, tDigest.percentile(99))

res = DataFrame({'NinetyFive': resNinetyFive, 'NinetyNine': resNinetyNine})
```

Read in 10 samples of length 100 K, each as a data frame. The .csv file can be found in the book's code repository.

Make empty arrays to save the results for the 95th and 99th percentiles.

For each of the 10 samples, make a t-digest with the reciprocal of $\delta = 200$ (the delta is parameterized differently in the implementation and the paper).

Let the digest consume the jth sample. w here means we are adding singletons with a weight of 1. For two different digests, these would be actual weights of the clusters.

Add the estimate of the 95th and 99th percentile to the results array.

After all 10 samples are consumed, make a data frame for the results.

```
os.chdir("./")
res.to_csv("Results_TD_WebsiteSample.csv", index=False)
```
**Specify the directory
and save the results.**

The efficiency of the implementation seems to be much better for the t-digest solution, so much so that it makes the efficiency comparison trivial:

```
import numpy as np
df = pandas.read_csv('/path/to/test/data')
```
**Read in 10 samples of length 100 K,
each as a data frame. The .csv file can
be found in the book's code repository.**

```
resNinetyFive = np.array([])
resNinetyNine = np.array([])
```
**Make empty arrays to save the results
for the 95th and 99th percentiles.**

```
columns = list(df)

for j in columns:
    universeSize = max(df[j])+1
    qDigest = QDigest(universeSize, 20)
```
**For each of the 10 samples,
make a q-digest with the size of
the universe as the parameter.
+1 is for the 0's.**

```
    length = len(df['sample1'])
    for i in range(length):
        qDigest.insert
```
**The q-digest class takes one element at a time
and consumes the jth sample one by one.**

```
    qDigest.compress()
```
**The q-digest gets reorganized after the whole sample has
been consumed to comply with the two triangle rules.**

```
    resNinetyFive = np.append(resNinetyFive,
      qDigest.quantile_query(([0.95])))
    resNinetyNine = np.append(resNinetyNine,
      qDigest.quantile_query(([0.99])))
```
**Add the estimates of the 95th and
99th percentiles to the results array.**

```
res = DataFrame({'NinetyFive': resNinetyFive, 'NinetyNine': resNinetyNine})
res.to_csv("/path/to/test/output", index=False)
```
**After all 10 samples are
consumed, make a data
frame for the results.**

**Specify the directory
and save the results.**

When it comes to the parameters chosen for creation of the two digests, we choose to make them approximately equal-sized. For the q-digest, we choose compression parameter = 20, while for the t-digest, we choose $\delta = 200$, which yields around 1 KB of each digest. For each sample, we found the maximum length of a visit, since it is required for the creation of a q-digest. For all 10 samples, maximums were between 2,742,437 milliseconds and 2,763,605 milliseconds; hence the universe sizes do not vary enough to prevent meaningful cross-sample evaluation of the results.

The error we are showing is calculated as follows: for each of the 10 samples, we can get the exact 95th and 99th percentiles because we can sort the data and find the actual values. These are the xs we hope to get. From the digests, we get zs, and we can check the difference between $R(x)$ and $R(z)$. In the case of the 95th percentile, $R(x)$ should be 95,000. If the digest returned the 94,990th element, then the absolute error we are showing is $|0.94990-0.95000| = 0.00010$. You can check this in the right graph; this is how close the t-digest comes. Figure 8.10 shows the resulting absolute empirical

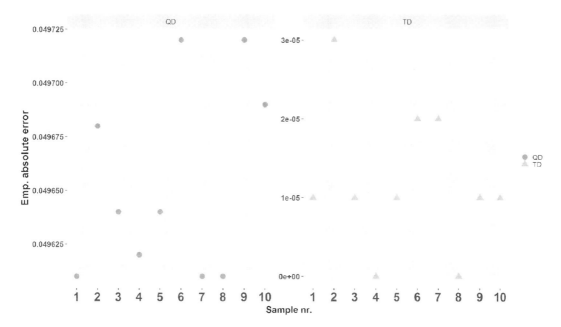

Figure 8.10 The graphs show the empirical absolute error that the q-digest (left) and t-digest (right) exhibit when estimating the 95th percentile. The error in estimating $q \in [0, 1]$ is calculated as follows: if the true rank of the answer (value) that a digest provides is r, then the absolute error is $\left| \frac{r}{n} - q \right|$ where n is the number of elements digested so far.

errors for estimations of the 95th percentile for each of the 10 samples. The first thing to notice is that we are not showing the absolute empirical errors on the same *y*-axis. The average absolute empirical errors of the q-digest are around 5,000 times higher than the average absolute empirical errors of the t-digest. We wouldn't be able to appreciate their within-group variability visually had we showed them both on the same axis. The average absolute error of the t-digest (triangles) is 1.2×10^{-5}, while the one for the q-digest shows an average of 4965.4×10^{-5}. It seems that the t-digest out-performs the q-digest, as judged by the absolute empirical error on this data, by the order of magnitude of 10^3.

To fully appreciate this difference, we need to first understand what it means to be off by 1.2×10^{-5} when estimating the 95th percentile. Since we created the data, we know the exact quantile for any $q \in [0, 1]$ (as long as the sample offers that fidelity; i.e., it is hard to get an exact 99th percentile of a sample with 10 elements). Hence, if the true rank of z that we get back from the digest when we ask for 95th percentile is r, then the absolute error becomes $\left| \frac{r}{n} - 0.95 \right|$, where n is the number of elements in the sample (or seen from the stream so far). So, if one is off by 1.2×10^{-5} from 0.95, this means that the t-digest delivers the 95,001st or 95,002nd website time spent, instead of the 95,000th. According to the same reasoning, the q-digest returns the 90,035th or 99,966th website time spent in their ordered sequence instead of the 95,000th.

Another thing to note is that we are not talking about milliseconds here, but the ranks that the lengths of visits occupy.

You can see the same pattern in figure 8.11, where we show analogous results for the 99th percentile. Although the difference in average absolute empirical error is seven times smaller than for the 95th percentile, the t-digest still errs by a single element, while the q-digest errs by close to a thousand. Nevertheless, the error bound claimed in the original paper on the q-digest is upheld. With our maximal universe size of 2,763,605 and $k = 20$, we can calculate that the error should be below 0.74. This is true for our case. An additive error bound for estimating the 95th percentile of 0.74 means that even giving the 22nd percentile as the answer would manage to keep the theoretical upper bound on the error.

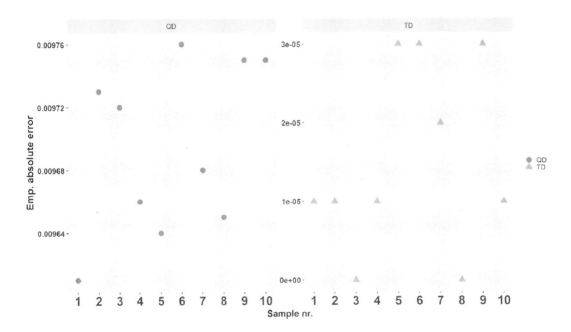

Figure 8.11   The empirical absolute error that the q-digest (left) and t-digest (right) exhibit for estimating the 99th percentile. The error in estimating $q \in [0, 1]$ is calculated as follows: if the true rank of the answer (value) that a digest provides is *r*, then the absolute error is $\left|\frac{r}{n} - q\right|$, where *n* is the number of elements digested so far.

According to our results, the t-digest clearly outperformed the q-digest when estimating high-end quantiles like the 95th and 99th percentile on this data. Since the t-digest does not come with any upper-bound error, we cannot claim that it stays beneath it, but judging by our empirical results, it certainly stays under the q-digest one for this data.

Summary

- Having ad hoc approximate quantiles any time in a streaming data application, especially one that is used to detect anomalies, is very important. Having efficient online algorithms that save small summaries of the whole data and deliver answers about quantiles with some error guarantee means being able to create a small sketch of the data distribution in the form of a histogram. This way, you can keep an eye on multiple quantiles at once and set sensitive thresholds.

- The error with which algorithms approximating quantiles work is either additive or relative (multiplicative). Additive error, εn, is the same no matter which quantile we estimate. Relative error, $\varepsilon R(x)$, is relative to the specific quantile we are interested in, so it is smaller for small quantiles and largest, εn, for the maximal value. Error in the data space instead of the ranks space is sometimes called relative error as well, but it has nothing to do with the relative (multiplicative) error we covered.

- The t-digest is a very popular heuristic algorithm for calculating approximate quantiles. We saw the mechanism for keeping small samples on the edges of quantile intervals and for keeping larger ones in the middle and how k-size regulation via scale functions makes sure of this. This results in better accuracy when estimating tail quantiles such as the 95th or 99th percentile, or even finer ones close to 1. We saw how the t-digest delivers very accurate estimates in those ranges on 10 samples of realistic website time-spent data.

- We learned what the q-digest algorithm is and how to build one from scratch, as well as how to merge two or more. The q-digest works for integers only, and you only need to be familiar with the universe the data is coming from to use it. This might not be true for streaming data. If we don't really know the range of data we are about to see, the q-digest is of limited use. The t-digest does not share that constraint and seems to perform better than the q-digest, with absolute empirical errors smaller by two to three orders of magnitude for estimating the same high-end quantiles.

Part 2

Data structures for databases and external memory algorithms

While parts 1 and 2 were concerned with squeezing and sampling data to make it fit into RAM, we can now finally breathe a sigh of relief—our data, all of it, is comfortably resting on disk. In the three chapters in part 3, we will learn how to effectively design algorithms and data structures for large datasets sitting on disk. This will include understanding how retrieval, insertion, and deletion work in different kinds of databases and how to efficiently sort large files on disk. We will also delve into differences in the design of indices between read-optimized and write-optimized databases. The first step in doing all of this will be understanding how the I/O cost (i.e., the cost of transferring one block of data from disk to main memory) dominates the cost of a CPU operation by three or more degrees of magnitude. Thus, the lens through which we will observe the algorithm efficacy will blur everything happening in RAM and zoom in on the data transfer between disk and RAM. Learning how to do Big-O analysis from the perspective of the disk transfer will be one of the major takeaways of part 3.

Introducing the external memory model

This chapter covers

- Introducing computer limitations that affect the design of data-intensive applications
- Introducing and describing the external memory model (DAM model)
- Building simple scanning, searching, and merging algorithms in external memory
- Reviewing use cases where data scientists and programmers work with huge files
- Using Big-O notation to measure I/O efficiency of the algorithms

This chapter introduces fundamental ideas that form part 3 of the book. We begin by introducing external memory algorithms and the external memory model [1]. This model will teach us how to view the efficiency of algorithms and data structures in the context of working with large datasets stored on disk.

Most applications maintain data on some type of local or remote storage, files and databases being prominent examples. Storage offers the flexibility of capturing large amounts of data persistently and very cheaply. Even when the system benefits from data summaries that quickly satisfy queries from RAM, we still want to preserve the original data on some slower and larger storage. As we have seen in the case of Bloom filters and Google's WebTable, when the query returns `Present`, we make a trip to disk to fetch the (`key,value`) pair and metadata or to establish that we have a false positive.

Data structures that are power relational (and other types of) databases take lessons from storage and memory design to offer optimal on-disk performance, and they are different from data structures that perform the same tasks optimally in RAM. As we will see, the worlds of in-RAM data structures and those on disk differ significantly. Through building analogies between two types of data structures and algorithm designs, our aim is to demonstrate common themes and algorithmic tools you may find helpful for solving any on-disk problem.

Before moving on, let's clarify what we mean when we say "disk." Depending on the context, data can be stored in different types of local or remote storage, such as a local solid-state drive (SSD), a local magnetic disk, a cloud, or some combination of the three. In this chapter, we will refer to all these storage devices simply as "disks," as the central issues we plan to address are shared by all the types of storage, the main one being the slow speed of access. There are many differences in access times between different storage technologies; for instance, SSDs have speed performance characteristics that are superior to magnetic disks in many respects, but the performance is not superior enough to make the problems we will delve into throughout this chapter go away entirely.

The specifics of computer design, such as the CPU performance gap, memory hierarchy, latency, and bandwidth, form an important foundation to understanding how to design efficient data structures for external memory. For a refresher on those topics, you might want to review section 1.4 in chapter 1. Following are the key peculiarities that make the issues surrounding the design of external memory algorithms new and unique:

- Main memory (RAM) is significantly smaller than a large dataset residing on disk and can only hold a small portion of the entire dataset at one time. Therefore, to solve a problem (say, to sort a file), data has to be brought in and out of main memory piecewise.
- Data from disk is fetched in consecutive chunks (i.e., blocks/pages). Bringing a block of data into main memory is an expensive operation, which is offset by having the chunk carry many elements. Whether we make use of just one or thousands of elements in the chunk, we pay the same cost of one data transfer.
- Performing a single input/output of a block, that is, an I/O transfer from disk to main memory, is very slow, and it can be up to a factor of 100–1,000 times slower than a typical computational operation in RAM.
- The sequential order of accessing data on disk is faster than the random order. The sequential access makes use of the high bandwidth, whereas the random access faces the penalty of high latency.
- Disk reads tend to be faster than disk writes.

The main takeaway from this chapter will be learning to zoom out of RAM and see the bigger picture of how data travels back and forth between the disk and main memory. Understanding that the data-transfer aspect is the bottleneck for many applications out there, while everything that happens in RAM (e.g., which internal memory algorithm or data structure we use) is often a second-order concern, is one of the key lessons of this chapter. Switching to this manner of thinking is not always easy, considering that we are used to counting comparisons, arithmetic operations, and other things that happens in RAM, as well to having an entire dataset available. We will continue to use the Big-O notation to characterize the runtime of algorithms, but from now on, the expressions inside the Big-O will reflect the number of data transfers, not CPU cycles. To anchor us in this new worldview, we next introduce the external memory model and show a couple of basic algorithmic examples to simulate it.

9.1 *External memory model: The preliminaries*

The external memory model, or the disk-access model (DAM), was first suggested in 1988, back when many large organizations started encountering their first massive data issues. Since then, it has proved to be an incredibly helpful tool for analyzing algorithms if you are working with data-intensive applications. Figure 9.1 depicts this model.

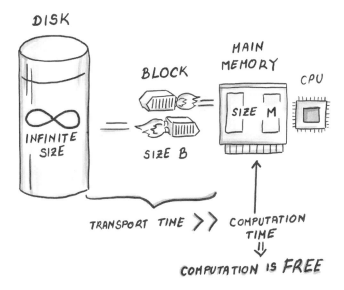

Figure 9.1 The external memory model. This model is suitable for analyzing massive data applications, where the cost of computation in RAM is subsumed by a much larger cost of transferring data from disk to main memory and back. Computation is not exactly free, but it is so much cheaper than the cost of transferring data that, in many applications, it is effectively free.

In the external memory model, the computer consists of external storage (disk) of infinite size, and the main memory of limited size M. Data originally sits on disk and is transferred between disk and main memory in blocks of size B. Once data arrives in the main memory, all computation on it, and whatever is done with it, are given out for free. For example, once you bring a block of data into memory, you can consider it sorted if you need it to be sorted. No sorting cost will be charged. You can consider any meaningful computation (that does not require overshooting the size of remaining memory!) already done. The only cost charged will be that of one I/O data transfer to RAM.

You may think of parameters M and B as values plugged into the algorithm. Different computers have different values for M and B, depending on the hardware setup. These parameters will also appear in the Big-O analysis of external memory algorithms, as they will be used to analyze efficiency. The place where each parameter appears in the bound will help us better understand the role that each plays. Our input size all throughout part 3 will be N, and it will denote the total volume of data (i.e., N unit-sized elements).

Keep in mind that even though in the Big-O analysis constants do not matter, and the values of B and M are constant for a given computer, we will view them as parameters that can grow and change, and the runtime of algorithms should be parameterized by them. For example, we will not simplify $O(N/B)$ to $O(N)$ even though B does not grow the same way we expect N, our input, to grow.

Does B stand for B bits, B integer variables, B 64-bit words, or something entirely different? If we pick the same unit consistently for N, M, and B, then the choice is not that important, as the relevant ratios remain the same; for instance, N/B (number of blocks the dataset takes up on disk) or M/B (the number of blocks that fit into the main memory).

Here, we will assume that the unit is the memory footprint of one particular data item in the dataset that we are working with, be it a string, an integer, a float, or some larger, more complicated object. For the sake of simplicity, we will also assume that in one dataset, all items are the same type and take up the same amount of space, even though the reality will defy us on this one. For example, experience and research show that records in databases can be of very different sizes, which can significantly impact the runtime of algorithms that blindly assume all records are the same size. Check out the research on B-trees for different-sized keys or sorting with size-priced information if you want to learn more.

But to get anything done in life, we need to make some simplifying assumptions. Either way, we proceed with the following parameters in mind:

- N = number of records in the dataset sitting on disk
- M = number of records that can fit into the main memory
- B = number of records that can fit into one block

The size of B is usually the size of a block transferred between disk and memory, and it is usually between 4 and 64 KB. On some SSDs, a block is on the order of a couple of

MBs. Either way, it is important to understand that one block carries thousands of elements consecutively placed on disk. Memory sizes also vary, and currently an average computer has somewhere between 8 and 32 GB. However, not all of that space can be used for computation, as the RAM holds all working programs, the operating system, and so on. The size of N also varies, but if we are talking about data sitting on disk, then we should be ready for some very big datasets. As an example, the creators of Teradata Relational Database Management system claim that they can host databases of up to 50 petabytes (PB) in size. In summary, it is correct to assume that in most situations, N is much larger than M, and M is still significantly larger than B even though the latter gap is much smaller. Let's put this model into action with a few examples.

9.2 Example 1: Finding a minimum

Quite commonly, we need to find a minimum value in a set of values. From the perspective of traditional algorithms, this requires a linear scan of elements in the list where the items are stored. Now consider an analogous external memory use case.

9.2.1 Use case: Minimum median income

Say you are working for a startup that is modeling demography and census data and visualizing it for their users (e.g., Social Explorer at www.socialexplorer.com.) There is a large number of tables that carry aggregated data, and for the income table data, the individual records are aggregated up to a demographic block (i.e., "A new kid on the block") level. We will differentiate the demographic and disk blocks by calling them *demographic blocks* and *blocks*, respectively. The US territory is divided into over 10 million demographic blocks, and for each demographic block, the table carries a substantial amount of information, all organized sequentially per block. One of the variables includes median income, and we are interested in finding the demographic block with the minimum median income in the entire US.

Effectively, what we are given is an unsorted array of N integer records on disk, and we need to find the minimum value. In the world of "regular" algorithms, a simple for loop requiring $O(N)$ comparisons will suffice. If we apply the analogous approach when data resides on disk, then we instead pick up blocks of data, starting from where the data begins to the last block containing any of our items. Consider the two patterns of how we read data in RAM and on disk in pseudocode.

How we read data in RAM:

```
min = INT_MAX
for i in range(N)
    if (A[i] < min)
        min = A[i]
```

How we read data from disk:

```
BLOCK_SIZE = 1024
min = INT_MAX
```

```
for i in range(ceil(N/BLOCK_SIZE))
    BLOCK = read_block(filename, file_start + i*BLOCK_SIZE, BLOCK_SIZE)
    for i in range(BLOCK_SIZE):
        if (BLOCK[i] < min):
            min = BLOCK[i]
```

The second block of pseudocode reads a block of data by specifying the filename (this tells us the starting position of the file), the offset, that is, the position within the file, and the size of a block to read starting from that position. This pseudocode makes a couple of simplifying assumptions, such as assuming that file_start occurs right at the block boundary, which might not be the case. Because the disk is partitioned into blocks of memory, and blocks tend to be fairly large, there is no guarantee that our file will begin at the beginning of the block. Our read_block function assumes that if the position we seek is in the middle of the block, then it should pick up the block containing the item we desire.

A few notes about programming in external memory: when working with large files in Python, for example, we can use a number of libraries that allow us to perform system calls such as open (to open a file), seek (to look up a particular position in the file), or write (to write to a specific position in the file). Roughly speaking, seek corresponds to the expensive I/O read we have been referring to, but it is difficult to track how blocks are being shuffled to and fro by the operating system. The operating system has a large number of built-in optimizations that work under the hood to address I/O issues. For instance, if the operating system observes that we have accessed a number of blocks in sequential fashion, it might fetch a number of blocks that follow it even before we request them, assuming this is what we might want to do next. Also, when we read in a block and modify it in main memory, the operating system might not want to immediately write it back. Instead, it might prefer to buffer it in RAM and write it back with a number of other blocks in sequence later.

This is a large and important topic, but what we aim for in the teaching of external memory algorithms is understanding the concepts from the abstract point of view and understanding the algorithmic tricks involved. To that end, we show examples in Python-like pseudocode where we physically pick up particular blocks to show the workings of the algorithm, even though this is not how this type of code is regularly written. We believe this simplified view aids the sort of understanding we're after.

Now, back to our example. As we sequentially scan blocks on disk, we input blocks one by one into the main memory. Once the block is read, we do not need it anymore, so at all times we need only one block in memory simultaneously and a min variable that we update accordingly. Figure 9.2 shows the process on a toy example where $N = 11$, $M = 6$, and $B = 3$. Because there are at most $N/B + 1$ blocks that our data occupies, the algorithm requires $O(N/B)$ memory transfers (or I/Os).

Here, we come to the first difference in runtimes between RAM bounds and external memory bounds (as shown in figure 9.3). In the external memory world, "linear-time"

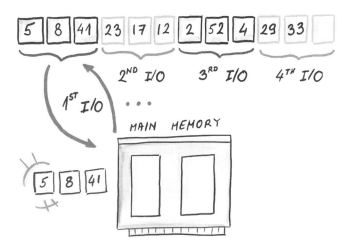

Figure 9.2 Finding a minimum in external memory. There is a total of 11 elements that occupy four blocks of size 3. The last block is not full. In this example, the beginning of the file is block aligned.

naturally becomes $O(N/B)$. This is the cost of a linear sweep over consecutively ordered data. It is good if we can achieve the $/B$ part, as, in the worst case, if data is not sequentially ordered, or if we are accessing it randomly, reading N elements might require up to $O(N)$ I/Os.

Figure 9.3 The difference in the way bounds look for an in-RAM algorithm (left) and an equivalent on-disk algorithm (right.) It is important not to directly compare them as they represent different units. The comparison in the way the bounds look is there to understand how algorithms change as the consequence of different design.

EXERCISE 9.1

Using Python's open, seek, read, write, close, and so on operations, create a file with 1 billion integers (one per line) and store it on disk.

Then use the same calls to complete the following tasks:

1 Compute the sum of the first 1 million integers.
2 Compute the sum of the randomly chosen 1 million integers.

For both 1 and 2, separately time the task of data transfer (such as the seek call) and the computational task (summing up data). Compare how much time is needed for each. Also, compare the amount of time required to read sequentially and randomly. If you feel like it, for task 2, time whether the seek call takes the same amount of time at every point of the experiment, and if not, think about why not.

9.3   *Example 2: Binary search*

Now let's see how we would adapt our good ol' binary search to disk. There are a number of important use cases for doing this—whenever we need to search in an ordered file for a particular value, binary search comes to mind. Because binary search jumps all over the file, it will be interesting to see how many different block transfers we incur. But first, consider the following use case.

9.3.1   *Bioinformatics use case*

You are working as a computer scientist for a bioinformatics startup, and you are working on the problem of DNA sequencing. In the particular problem you are given, you have been given a large number of K-mers (K-length substrings of a number of given DNA sequences). Each K-mer has its own string value, as well as a small number of key other properties important for further study. Data is laid out in the form of one (K-mer, property1, property2, ...) tuple per line. The file has grown to be over 1 TB. K-mers are sorted and deduplicated, and what you are interested in is locating particular K-mers in the file. Data is static, so you are not interested in modifying the file or reorganizing data in the file; you just want to be able to query the file in the fastest possible way, so you resort to binary search.

How would binary search work in RAM versus out of RAM? Let's see the pseudocode and figure 9.4.

Binary search in RAM:

```
binarySearch(arr, left, right, x)
  while left <= right:
     mid = left + (right - left) // 2
     if arr[mid] == x:
         return mid
     elif arr[mid] < x:
         left = mid + 1
     else:
         right = mid - 1
  return -1
```

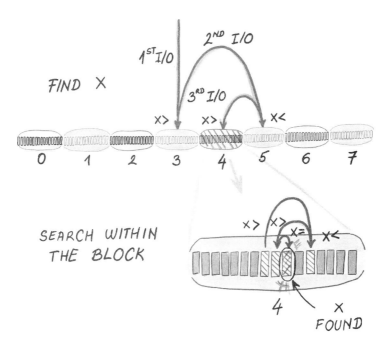

Figure 9.4   Binary search in external memory. The algorithm accesses a separate block for each pivot accessed, except from the last few pivots, which all reside in the same block.

Binary search on disk:

BLOCK_SIZE is the same as B in the text and runtime analysis.

```
BLOCK_SIZE = 1024
def binarySearchExtMem(filename, file_start, left, right, x):
    while left + BLOCK_SIZE <= right:
        mid = left + (right - left) // 2
        BLOCK = read_block(filename, file_start + mid, BLOCK_SIZE):
        if BLOCK[BLOCK_SIZE - 1] < x:
            left = mid + 1
        elif BLOCK[0] > x:
            right = mid - 1
        else:
            return binarySearch(BLOCK, 0, BLOCK_SIZE - 1, x)
    BLOCK1 = read_block(filename, file_start + left, BLOCK_SIZE)
    return binarySearch(BLOCK1, 0, BLOCK_SIZE - 1, x)
```

The in-RAM binary search performs $O(\log_2 N)$ comparisons as well as that many cell reads.

The external memory version of the same algorithm is only slightly modified. In essence, we still wish to perform the same sequence of comparisons, and we pick up blocks that contain items we wish to compare. (Again, here, we obviate many important details when we perform read_block(filename, file_start + mid, BLOCK_SIZE), because it will most certainly not be the case that `file_start + mid` is always at the block boundary. Once the block is in main memory, in the case that x is smaller than the smallest element in the block, we proceed with binary search on the left side of the array, and in the case that x is larger than the largest element in the block, we proceed on the right side. In the remaining case, we call the in-RAM binary search function to figure out whether the element is in the block.

However, the process proceeds only until the file size on which we perform binary search is larger than a block. Once the array size drops under the block size, we input the remaining data that fits into one block, and all remaining comparisons are performed in RAM using the original algorithm.

In the example from figure 9.4, we have that $N = 128$, $M = 64$, and $B = 16$. If we were to count only the number of comparisons in this identical binary search algorithm, we would need roughly seven comparisons to find the element we are looking for. Because we are mostly interested in counting block transfers, we need approximately 3 I/Os for the search in the worst case.

9.3.2 *Runtime analysis*

For most of the algorithm executions, in order to perform a comparison that will direct us to the left or the right side of the array, we spend 1 I/O, which amounts to $O(\log_2 N)$ I/Os. However, once the array becomes the size of a block, we perform just one more block input and thus have the last $\log_2 B$ comparisons all use 1 I/O. In total, we get $O(\log_2 N - \log_2 B + 1) = O\left(\log_2\left(\frac{N}{B}\right)\right)$ I/Os.

It is important to analyze what happens when the block enters the main memory. It does not help us, in the asymptotic sense, that we compare x against the two borderline elements of the block instead of just one element as in the original algorithm. Consider the first block input. Once the algorithm decides, based on two comparisons, to go to the left or the right side of the array, we are still left with $\frac{(N-B)}{2} \approx \frac{N}{2}$ elements. Still, examining the borderline elements in the block, or even sequentially scanning the whole block, is a smart thing to do considering we already have the block in memory. In practical terms, this tweak will likely make a difference in performance, even though it is not reflected in the asymptotic runtime.

Now that we've done things the somewhat clumsy way, here is a more natural way to view the binary search algorithm in external memory. We can consider the algorithm block based: instead of looking for the exact position of x in the array, we might think of locating the correct block where x is located (or where it should be, if it is not present). Therefore, the algorithm is performing binary search among the blocks, not among the elements. Once the element is within the outside boundaries of some input block, the algorithm execution ends. This also simplifies analysis. We have $O(\frac{N}{B})$ blocks, and each step of binary search costs 1 I/O. This gives us $O\left(\log_2\left(\frac{N}{B}\right)\right)$ I/Os, just like before.

In RAM, logarithmic runtime represents the optimal bound for searching, whether it be using binary search on a sorted array or traversing down a balanced binary search tree of logarithmic depth. The question presenting itself now, though, is whether the analogous binary search algorithm on disk that runs in $O\left(\log_2\left(^N/_B\right)\right)$ time is the optimal searching mechanism for files and databases on disk.

If data is simply laid out in a sorted array and we are not allowed to reorganize or regroup it in any way, then sure, binary search is the best way to go. But if we are allowed to preprocess data in some way (e.g., rearrange elements) to promote better query time, then we can do a lot better than binary search. Read on to find out how, but before moving on, try this small exercise.

EXERCISE 9.2

Create a file on disk with 1 billion ordered integers, one per line. Write a Python program to open the file and to run binary search on it. Use the `readline()`, `seek()`, and `tell()` system calls to complete this task. Run it on a few examples. Time different parts of the program and determine what the most time-consuming parts are.

9.4   *Optimal searching*

To understand why binary search is not our best bet for an optimal external memory searching algorithm, just consider any block input that takes place during binary search. Even though we are performing a really expensive I/O operation that brings thousands of elements into main memory, we are effectively only using one or only a couple of elements from it. It's like hiring a bus to take you (and only you) to work. We can do better than that.

To see how, see figure 9.5a and N sorted elements in it. Given a block size, $B = 3$, what is the best choice of elements to pack into the block we intend to bring into memory first? Well, the three elements that divide the array into four equal parts are, in this specific example, elements 15, 31, and 40. If we created such a block, then after bringing it in, we would be left with, not an $N/2$-sized array to search, but $^N/_{(B+1)}$. We can recursively continue in the same fashion with each remaining subarray by selecting B equally spaced pivots. To understand how to build these blocks, consider building an implicit binary search tree on top of the sorted array (figure 9.5b), and then, starting from the top of the tree, clumping in top B nodes in the tree to form one node (figure 9.5c). This way, we create a searching data structure such as the one in figure 9.5d, where a node allows us to branch into $B + 1$ (in this example four, but in the real world, thousands) different directions, based on just one block input. The higher the branching, the fewer the levels in the tree. Each level represents one I/O we need to perform, so a higher branching factor brings down the number of memory transfers.

To understand the difference in this small example, the number of comparisons we need to perform during a binary search is equivalent to the depth of the binary search tree in 9.4b, which is four comparisons. Because the last two levels of the tree will be in the same block, then we need $4 - 2 + 1 = 3$ block inputs if using a common binary search. But if we use the new structure shown in figure 9.4d, we need just two block inputs, as this structure has just two levels.

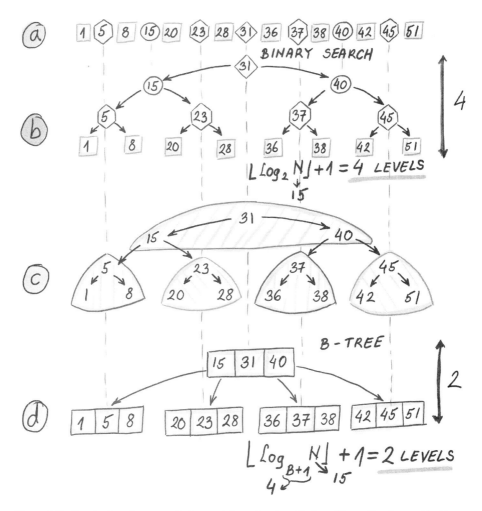

Figure 9.5   How to transform a sorted array into a structure that enables optimal searching in external memory (a *B*-tree). An optimal searching data structure in RAM looks something like d, where each node has one pivot based on how it has decided to continue down the tree. The optimal searching data structure in external memory has large nodes (the size of a block) that have many elements because we pull data into memory block by block.

The difference seems trivial because our dataset is small, and, more importantly, because our B is small. The difference, in fact, is enormous: while the number of I/Os for binary search is $O\left(\log_2\left(\frac{N}{B}\right)\right)$ I/Os, the number of I/Os we need using the structure from figure 9.5d is $O\left(\log_2\left(\frac{N}{B}\right)\right)$ I/Os.

Usually, the base of the logarithm is irrelevant asymptotically if both bases are constants. However, here, the base of the logarithm being B makes a tremendous difference.

Consider a dataset of size 1 billion ($\approx 2^{30}$) and a block that can fit 1,000 ($\approx 2^{10}$) elements. For example, the block size is 64 KB, and each element takes 8 bytes. This means that with a binary search, we need ≈ 20 block inputs, whereas with our new structure, we need only 3.

The structure from figure 9.5d is the cartoon version of what is known as a *B*-tree. The *B*-tree forms the backbone of database indices for the majority of large relational databases. Despite their massive data size, *B*-trees rarely exceed a depth of five or six, thereby limiting the number of I/Os we need to do to perform a query (see figure 9.6).

In the next chapter, we will see many more details of *B*-trees, their different reincarnations, and other data structures that power relational databases.

Figure 9.6   Another difference in the way bounds can look in the RAM model and the external memory model. Often, the runtime with a logarithm of base 2 can turn into a logarithm of base *B*, as we can examine *B* different elements simultaneously with the help of a single block. Base 2 does not always turn into base B, as we will see later.

Notice that, thus far, the memory size was not extremely important, as long as it could hold at least one block and some extra space to keep a few variables. While scanning, binary searching, or *B*-searching, we needed to input many blocks, but we needed only one at one time. However, there are other problems where memory size is important, and where the external memory algorithm can efficiently make use of it.

9.5   *Example 3: Merging K sorted lists*

Let's consider how we merge data in external memory. A popular problem when merging data from different sources, for example, comes down to merging multiple lists. In main memory, this is often solved with the help of a heap that repeatedly extracts the minima from particular lists. Now we will see how the problem of merging *K* sorted files can be solved in external memory and what this teaches us about the nature of merging many lists simultaneously in RAM versus external memory. This will prove important later when we start adapting merge-sort to external memory.

9.5.1   *Merging time/date logs*

You are working for a company whose product is a load balancer that supports high-traffic multiserver applications. The application also has a significant security component, and it collects traffic data at many different sites. You are interested in whether there is any connection between the times and dates when certain attacks occur, so you are analyzing a large number of event logs collected at different sites, each sorted by time/date. The key step is merging the files in the ascending order of the time/date into one gigantic file. Your local computer has 16 GB of memory, and the total size of files is 1 TB, shared between 16,000 different files.

The problem translates into merging K sorted lists. Let us assume that all lists together have N items. Before starting on the version where files to be merged sit on disk, let's recall how to solve this problem in RAM.

RAM VERSION

To most effectively merge K sorted lists in RAM, we can employ a min-heap that holds one representative from each sorted list (so, in total, K items) and extract minimum elements one by one. Once an element leaves the heap as its minimum, an element from its list is supplied back into the heap. Individual operations on the heap of size K cost $O(\log_2 K)$, and because each element has to be both inserted into a heap of size, at most, K at some point, and also removed from it, in total we need $O(N \log_2 K)$ comparisons to solve this problem.

EXTERNAL MEMORY VERSION

Now, let's consider what happens if N is too large to fit into RAM. In this example, we will assume that even though the total size of every file, and even each individual file, might be too large to fit into RAM, the number of files is small enough to accommodate one block of data from each file in RAM and still leave half of the memory available. In other words, we assume that $K \le M/2B$. This is not a very strict assumption, as it tolerates up to a million lists in some common hardware setups.

We are going to make use of this fact by reserving one block of memory for each file. In the beginning, we will read in the first block of each file.

Now we can employ the in-RAM solution on the blocks we just read in. We start by having each block insert its minimum into the min-heap. Then we begin extracting minima from the heap. Every time we extract a minimum, we supply the next element to the heap from the same block from which the minimum came from. Once we run out of one block, we supply the next block from that same file, until we reach the end of the file. Figure 9.7 shows the process, and the pseudocode shows more details.

In the pseudocode, a list, `file_names`, contains the names of files and allows us to access the starting positions of each file, and `files_loc` is a list containing the current position we are at within each file. The list `buffer_in` stores individual blocks into main memory (K of them), and each block can be indexed as a list of `BLOCK_SIZE_ELEMENTS` number of elements, so one way to think of `buffer_in` is as a two-dimensional list. The list `buffer_out` stores already merged elements ready for output, and as soon as it

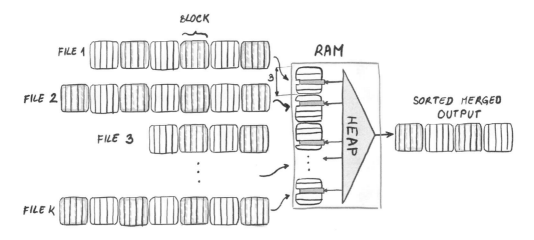

Figure 9.7 *K*-way merging of sorted files. Each file has one block of data allotted in main memory, and through that block, each file sends its remaining minimum elements into the heap. Minima are repeatedly extracted from the heap and sent to the output. This scheme works independently of the total accumulated file size, as long as $K = O(M/B)$.

contains `BLOCK_SIZE_ELEMENTS` number of elements, we write that block out to the `file_dest` location of `outfile_name` that holds the output file name.

The list `file_processed` indicates each file we are merging and whether we have already used up all of its elements. The list `merge_pos` denotes the element we currently point to while merging K block-sized mini lists in RAM. Once the counter reaches the maximum elements in the block, we trigger for the new block to be read from the corresponding file, unless we were already at the end of the file:

```
BLOCK_SIZE = 1024
ELEMENT_SIZE = 64
BLOCK_SIZE_ELEMENTS = BLOCK_SIZE / ELEMENT_SIZE

buffer_in = []
buffer_out = []
file_processed = []
merge_pos = []
file_dest = 0
for i in range(K)
    file_processed[i] = False
    files_loc[i] = 0
    buffer_in[i] = readBlock(files_names[i], files_loc[i], BLOCK_SIZE)
    files_loc[i]+=BLOCK_SIZE

for i in range(K)
    H.insert(tuple(buffer_in[i][0], i))
    merge_pos[i]=1

while(!H.empty())
    element, i = H.extractMin()
```

K is a number of sorted lists we are merging.

Read the first block of each list into main memory.

Advance the position within the file.

Heap H store (element, list index) pairs.

If there is
a full block
of merged
elements,
flush the
block.

```
buffer_out.append(element)
if buffer_out.size == BLOCK_SIZE_ELEMENTS:
    flushBlock(outfile_name, file_dest, buffer_out, BLOCK_SIZE)
    file_dest+=BLOCK_SIZE
    buffer_out.clear()
if(!file_processed[i]):
    H.insert(buffer_in[i][merge_pos[i]])
    merge_pos[i]+=1
    if merge_pos[i] == BLOCK_SIZE_ELEMENTS && files_loc[i]!=EOF:
        readBlock(files_names[i], files_loc[i], BLOCK_SIZE)
        merge_pos[i] = 0
        files_loc[i]+=BLOCK_SIZE
    elif file_loc[i] == EOF
        file_processed[i] = True
```

**The case where we did
not use up the file**

**The case where we reached
the end of a read-in block,
but not the end of file**

Note that in this problem, we make use of a large main memory to simultaneously merge a large number of files. The runtime is fairly simple to analyze, as we perform only 1 I/O for each block. This gives us $O(N/B)$ I/Os, including all the blocks written out.

This is an interesting artifact of external memory, because in internal memory, we could never merge more than a constant number of sorted lists in linear time. In external memory, we can merge a large (up to M/B) number of sorted lists in one linear pass over data (see figure 9.8).

What happens when we cannot allot one block per file in the main memory? We will leave this case for chapter 11, where we will revisit merging many lists as the backdrop for the optimal external memory sorting algorithm.

Figure 9.8 Difference in the bounds between merging many sorted lists in main memory and in external memory. In external memory, we can merge many sorted lists with just one sweep over the input data. In internal memory, merging more than a constant number of lists results in more than linear cost in a number of comparisons. This same internal memory cost remains in our external memory *K*-way merging algorithm; it is just not the most important cost.

We hope that seeing a couple of examples of how things change when we move from RAM to external memory helps you develop an intuition about the aspects of performance captured by the external memory model. However, this model fails to show some important aspects of I/O-related issues. In next section, we discuss where the differences are and how much they matter for the correct prediction of the efficiency of a real online application.

9.5.2 *External memory model: Simple or simplistic?*

One of the primary things that visually springs to mind when looking at the depiction external memory model (figure 9.1) is that it only contains two levels of memory: RAM and disk. As we know, the computer hierarchy is much more complex and contains many levels of memory. This should not dishearten us, however. Whatever our dataset size, we can always find the smallest level where data can fit and term that "the disk," while all other smaller levels can form the RAM. Block size B and memory size M are the parameters that will be affected by where our dataset size fits inside memory hierarchy. For instance, if our data fits in main memory but cannot fit in cache, then data between those two levels is transferred in cache lines, which are smaller than disk pages/blocks.

The original external memory model also allows for the possibility of a database being shared among many disks and, in that sense, allowing parallel data transfer. In most algorithms, if there are P disks, we can divide the entire performance cost by P.

Some of the simplifying assumptions of the external memory model, such as that disk space is infinite and that computation is entirely free in RAM, do not reflect reality. However, the disk space is extremely cheap, and neglecting the CPU performance will not affect us nearly as much as doing unnecessary disk seeks.

One important drawback of the external memory model is disregarding the sequential versus random performance. Whether we read x consecutive blocks or x blocks in very different locations of disk, the cost remains x I/Os. This is far from the truth for most storage technologies. Part of the reason for this is the way things work in hardware, but also various operating system optimizations. For instance, oftentimes, if we are doing a sequential read of a number of blocks, the operating system will notice this happening and try to pre-fetch the next block. Despite its imperfections, the external memory model remains the most popular model to date for analyzing the performance of algorithms in data-intensive contexts.

9.6 *What's next*

In this chapter, we started answering the question of how to optimally query on disk and began introducing the general idea of B-trees. However, their different implementations and variants are left for the next chapter. Specifically, we plan to answer questions such as the following:

- What variants of B-trees exist and are implemented in real-life systems?
- How can we add, delete, and modify items in a B-tree, and what are the mechanics of doing that?

- How can we know that the *B*-tree search is optimal in external memory?
- Is the *B*-tree an optimal data structure for inserts and modifications as well as lookups?

This question of whether *B*-trees are optimal for inserts will also motivate the introduction of two other data structures we will learn about: B^ε-trees and LSM-trees, two data structures oriented toward write-optimized databases.

Summary

- Many data-intensive applications maintain large amounts of data on disk. Large files and databases residing on disk need a different set of structural data and algorithmic tricks to function efficiently.
- The external memory model is a useful tool for analyzing algorithms for large datasets that cannot fit into main memory. This model assumes that all data initially resides on a disk of infinite size, and in order to perform computation, chunks of data are brought to and from the main memory of a limited size.
- The external memory model forgoes the computation cost of an algorithm in order to emphasize the cost of data transfers that tend to be up to 1,000 times more expensive than computation operations in RAM.
- When scanning sequential data, the external memory algorithm will tend to have a $/B$ part, suggesting that we packed items into consecutive blocks.
- Unlike in internal memory, binary search is not the optimal searching algorithm in external memory, as it does not make very good use of block inputs and outputs. A better runtime can be achieved by repackaging blocks and building a data structure called a B-tree.
- One major advantage of having a large main memory is that we can simultaneously merge a large number of sorted list/files in just one linear sweep, independently of how large the total file sizes are. This process is also a base for the optimal external memory sorting algorithm we study later.

Data structures for databases: B-trees, B$^\varepsilon$-trees, and LSM-trees

This chapter covers

- Learning how database indices work under the hood
- Exploring data structures that live underneath MySQL, LevelDB, RocksDB, TokuDB, and so on
- Learning what *B*-trees are and how lookups, inserts, and deletes in B-trees work
- Understanding how *B*$^\varepsilon$-trees work and how buffering helps writes
- Learning how log-structured merge trees (LSM-trees) work and their performance benefits

Choosing the right database for one's application requires some understanding of the way in which different database engines are built. Specifically, most databases implement indices to speed up the search of their large and frequently queried tables. Commonly, an index is placed on one of the columns to speed up the searches on that column. To understand all the performance ramifications of creating an index, we need to understand how different databases build and maintain their indices.

In the most basic terms, an index is a data structure, usually separate from the database table itself, that helps to efficiently route the query to the correct row back into the table. Without an index, the search operation boils down to a linear scan of keys in a given column. When dealing with systems that record 10 billion new rows daily or more (or less!), it is safe to say that the linear search will not cut it.

In this chapter, we will learn about the three most common data structures used to build indices in modern storage engines. Each data structure is optimized for a different kind of workload in terms of a ratio between lookups and inserts/deletes and other important operations. As usual, the costs of these operations will be at odds with each other. External memory data structures lie at the heart of efficient databases, and, in our opinion, they are a wonderful example of all the algorithmic tricks and tradeoffs involved when working with data on disk. But before diving into deeper, more technical levels of database design, let's first see the basics of how indexing works.

10.1   How indexing works

An index is most useful when built on a column on which we frequently query. The query we pose might need to return the entire row where the key matches the query key, but to locate the record, we only need the key—a value from the designated index column.

Consider the following simple example of building indices, shown in figure 10.1. We are given a table that stores the information about employees in a particular department store. In order to speed up the search, we can build an index on the Name column, and to do that, values in this column need to be unique. In other words, if we search for John, the index should give us one place where the row with a name equal to John can be found in the table (which is why Name, on its own, is a poor choice of a column to build an index on.)

When no single column has unique values, we can use a combination (i.e., concatenation) of columns and build an index on that. We can also build multiple indices to speed up searches on two or more independent columns, as shown in figure 10.1.

One of the ways to implement an index is to build a data structure separate from the table itself, where keys are lexicographically sorted so the lookup is fast (e.g., a search tree). The key in the data structure is the column we are building the index on, and the value is the location of the row in the table that contains the given key, as shown in figure 10.1. The query then works by first quickly locating the key within the index and then using the location provided by the value to instantly fetch the corresponding row from the table.

What we just described is sometimes called an *unclustered index*, where the actual table data is not being rearranged when building an index. When there are multiple indices, like in our example, then they must be unclustered. A *clustered index*, on the other hand, orders data inside the table when an index is being built, so there can be only one clustered index per table.

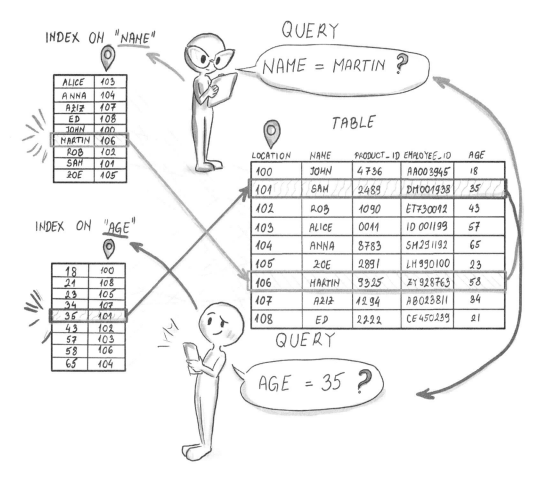

Figure 10.1   Building two indices on top of two different columns in a table

As you might imagine, having one index helps speed up the search on one column, but it is completely useless when we search on some other criteria. In our example from figure 10.1, if we want to query by employee age, we need a whole new index. Technically speaking, we could build an index on each table column just to be safe, but having many indices quickly reaches the point of diminishing returns. Namely, each time the table is updated (i.e., a row is inserted or deleted, or a value in a key column is modified), the index needs to be updated as well. Indices speed up the searches, but they slow down all other operations that modify the contents of the table. Having many indices per table is a safe bet only when we know that data will not often be modified, when search speed is much more important than the update speed, or when there isn't enough data to worry about speed.

The need to update an index along with the table teaches us the first important lesson of databases: the cost of lookups is closely intertwined with the cost of inserts and deletes. This should come as no surprise, as we have seen similar tradeoffs take place with in-RAM indices/dictionaries.

However, in databases, this relationship will be much more complex than what we have seen thus far. As explained in some of the more recent literature [1], the insert operation in many systems contains an embedded lookup. For instance, when performing deduplication, an insert operation first asks whether there is a record with a particular key present and inserts only if the key is not found. In this situation, the worst-case total cost of insert is the cost of a lookup in addition to the modification cost of insert. So, if we tuned the system to have blazingly fast inserts at the cost of incredibly slow lookups, we might be very disappointed in our ultimate insert performance when we see that it includes the lookup cost. Finding the optimal performance in many real-life cases such as this becomes a delicate balancing act.

10.2   *Data structures in this chapter*

In this chapter, we give the most attention to *B*-trees [2], as they form the backbone of the largest number of the most popular database engines out there, such as PostgreSQL (https://www.postgresql.org/docs/13/index.html) and MySQL (http://mng.bz/OG8n). *B*-trees are a lot like binary search trees, but with huge nodes whose node size corresponds to that of a page/block on disk. Because such nodes can fit a large number of keys, *B*-trees have a large branching factor (the number of children a node has is also sometimes referred to as fan-out), which guarantees small depth and thus excellent search performance. Aside from learning the mechanics of *B*-tree operations, in this chapter we will mathematically show that *B*-trees exhibit optimal performance for searching in external memory. It is no wonder, then, that since the time they were devised in the 70s, *B*-trees have remained the most popular choice when it comes to designing database engines.

B-trees are universally hailed for their fast searches, but it is possible to have a data structure with only slightly slower searches and substantially faster insert and delete performance than a *B*-tree. The B^ε-tree [3] is an alternative data structure behind storage engines such as TokuDB that have more recently become popular due to their superior insert/delete performance. With data becoming more dynamic, many applications need to maintain a much faster insert/delete throughput rate than what *B*-tree-based databases can offer, while maintaining fast lookups. For these types of workloads, B^ε-trees are an ideal data structure. B^ε-trees manage to keep the same asymptotic cost of lookups while improving (asymptotically) on the cost of inserts/deletes. In other words, the slowdown in their lookups is felt somewhat, but the speedup in inserts and deletes is felt much more.

The secret sauce in the B^ε-tree performance is that the inserts and deletes are not executed in an immediate fashion, like in *B*-trees, where a sole insert/delete/modify immediately travels down to the leaf of the tree and modifies it (*B*-trees just take life way too seriously.) In B^ε-trees, inserts and deletes act as messages that are buffered and delayed on their way to the leaves. The idea behind delaying operations is collecting enough insert/delete messages at one node that are headed in the same direction and then sending them together in one memory transfer, an idea not dissimilar to carpooling. By carpooling inserts and deletes, a B^ε-tree can make great use of its I/Os to process as many inserts and deletes as possible. This is in contrast to B-trees, where a single element descending down the tree triggers many expensive I/O operations solely for its own benefit.

Lastly, we discuss LSM-trees [4]. LSM-trees are the data structures behind LevelDB, RocksDB, Cassandra [5], and some other engines that care only about high-performance inserts that run faster than even those in B^ε-trees. The benefit of LSM-trees is that they make use of a very fast sequential-scan feature of disks. While B-trees and B^ε-trees access random blocks while descending the tree, LSM-trees organize their data in sequential runs that are occasionally merged, as in merge-sort. Merging two runs can be done at the speed of scanning (N/B for all elements, or $1/B$ per element) which is optimal, and occasional merging between runs makes sure that we do not end up with too many runs to have to query when time comes. Regardless, the lookups in this data structure do take a hit, but this can be somewhat improved by Bloom filters.

10.3 B-trees

B-trees are a natural extension of binary trees to external memory: where binary search trees use one key per node to direct the search/insert/delete in two different directions to the next level of the tree (<key and >key), B-trees use many more keys per node. In the rest of the text, we sometimes use the term *pivot* interchangeably with the key in a B-tree node.

Specifically, a B-tree of order d has in each node at least d keys (with the branching factor $d + 1$) and at most $2d$ keys (with the branching factor $2d + 1$). Branching factors of nodes can differ depending on how many keys they house. The only node that does not need to obey the requirement on the minimum number of keys is the root, which can have fewer than d keys, but not more than $2d$ keys.

The value of d in a B-tree node determines the size of the node, as the node always has the space to accommodate $2d$ keys and $2d + 1$ pointers to the subtrees below, regardless of how many keys it actually stores. As we will see, nodes will commonly have some empty space.

To understand the internal structure of B-tree nodes, see figure 10.2, which shows two nodes in a B-tree of order 2. On the left, we see a minimally filled node with two keys and three pointers to children that are non-null. On the right, we see a full node, with four keys and five pointers to children that are non-null.

Each key inside a B-tree node, aside from the value used to route the query to the next level, also contains a pointer to the row location into the table, as we showed in figure 10.1. We hide this detail from figure 10.2 onward and only show the key, as we will not refer to original database tables in the remainder of the chapter. We will simply assume that the moment we locate a key in the node of the tree that is the answer to the query, we will have the necessary information to automatically jump to the table

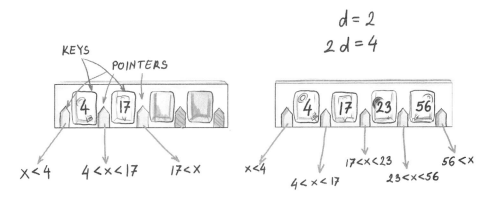

Figure 10.2   A structure of a node in a *B*-tree. Each node has space to accommodate 2*d* keys and 2*d* + 1 pointers, no matter how full it is. The pivots direct the search; that is, when searching for the element *x*, we compare it with the pivots, and the next node (i.e., pointer to it) is chosen based on the value of the key. The node on the left is minimally filled, and the node on the right is maximally filled.

to fetch the rest of the record. However, it is important to understand that there is a great deal of bookkeeping and wiring that takes place within each node of a *B*-tree that consumes a large fraction of its space. These considerations are important when choosing the node size. Generally, throughout this chapter, we will assume that node size is related to the block size B, so d can be considered some fraction of block size (e.g., $B/2$, $B/4$, etc.).

Consider the case when the block size $B = 1024$. If pointers leading to the next level of the tree take up roughly half of the space, then the remaining half is left for the keys and pointers to the table. Let us assume that this space is again evenly split, so keys take up $B/4$ space, and pointers into the table take up the remaining $B/4$. Even though the original node houses 1,024 words and could theoretically store 1,024 keys, it in fact stores up to 256 keys. This is still a bargain, considering that such a B-tree with all nodes at full capacity can in four levels store over 4 billion keys in the leaf level. In practice, many *B*-trees have much larger nodes, sometimes on the order of megabytes.

10.3.1 *B-tree balancing*

To maintain a low search cost, just like with balanced binary search trees, we need to be sure that no single root-to-leaf path in a *B*-tree becomes too long. *B*-trees have this problem nicely solved, in that every root-to-leaf path is always of the same length. A *B*-tree is flat from the bottom (i.e., all leaves reside on the same level).

Insert and delete operations can violate the size limitations of a node, such as when inserting into a full node or deleting from the minimally occupied node. When this happens, we might split an overly full node in two and redistribute the keys, or we might join two nodes that do not have enough keys. This might trigger the changes up the tree, requiring splits/merges on upper levels, where in the extreme case the tree could ultimately grow or shrink from the top. That is, we might end up splitting the root into two nodes and imposing a new root above, or we might bring down the existing root to the lower level, merging it with nodes below it.

If this sounds confusing, don't worry; we will visualize and describe these operations in detail soon. For now, it is important to understand that *B*-tree depth grows and shrinks from the top, while leaves all stay on the same level on the bottom. Contrast this with the binary search trees, where a new element is inserted as a leaf on the bottom of the tree, without requiring that all leaves be at the same level. Now we'll look at the mechanics of lookup and insert/delete operations.

10.3.2   Lookup

The lookup algorithm is fairly simple and mimics the logic of a lookup in a binary search tree. To perform the lookup, we first read in the root node of the *B*-tree and find where the query key belongs in the sorted order among the root keys. In case our key equals one of the root keys, we return `True`; otherwise, we follow the appropriate pointer down the tree and apply the same algorithm recursively until we either return `True` or reach a `null` pointer and return `False`. If the element is found before reaching the leaves, then there is no need to go further down the tree. Depending on the implementation, we might prefer to have a stored value returned instead of a Boolean, but the idea is the same.

Because the upper levels of the tree are often small enough and reside in RAM, we might save some I/Os while searching the upper levels of the tree. Most keys, however, will reside in the lower levels, so the probability of the queried key being in one of the nodes in RAM is fairly small.

In the worst case of a lookup, we might need to read in every block on the root-to-leaf path, making the lookup cost $O(\log_d N)$ for the *B*-tree of order d. Because we will generally make an assumption that $d = \theta(B)$, that means our worst-case lookup cost will be $O(\log_B N)$. The fact that some nodes will be emptier than others will not disturb the asymptotics, as the branching factor will still be $\theta(B)$.

The worst case will happen when an item we are searching for is in the leaf level, so we need to examine every block on the root-to-leaf path to the element in order to find it. The worst case occurs often when you consider that the majority of elements reside in leaves and that the worst case also occurs when the lookup reports the element as not present.

10.3.3   Insert

Insert is somewhat more involved than a lookup. First, we perform a lookup to find the leaf where a given element should be inserted (we always insert into a leaf). If the leaf is not full (has < 2*d* keys), then the element is simply added to the right position in the appropriate leaf, and the modified node is written back to disk. Consider the example shown in figure 10.3, where 80 is inserted into a *B*-tree of order *d* = 2. Aside from adding the element to the leaf, no other changes to the tree are required.

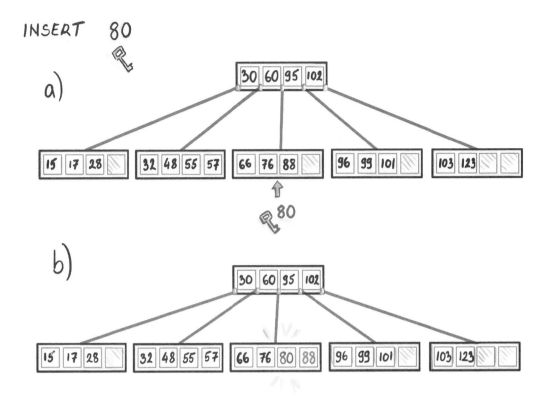

Figure 10.3   Insertion into a B-tree when the designated leaf is not full

However, it might happen that the designated leaf is full (it already has $2d$ keys), in which case, after the new key is placed, the node will have $2d + 1$ keys. Because it now violates the size limit, the overfull leaf is broken into two leaves in the following way: the left leaf will contain the smallest d keys, the right leaf will contain the largest d keys, and the median key will be inserted into the parent node to serve as the separator of the two newly created nodes. This process might trigger further splits up the tree. For example, if all nodes on the given root-to-leaf path are full, all nodes will be split going up to the root, including the root, and the tree will grow in height by 1.

Such is the example shown in figure 10.4, where we insert 69 into the *B*-tree of order $d = 2$. After 69 is placed into the leaf, the leaf has five elements, and it splits into two leaves that will be separated by the median 76; two elements go to the left leaf, and two elements go to the right leaf, and 76 is inserted into the parent to serve as a separator between the two newly formed leaves. In this case, the parent is the root of the tree, and it is also full, so the insert triggers a new split. The root splits into two nodes, each with two keys, and the median gets promoted to a newly created root.

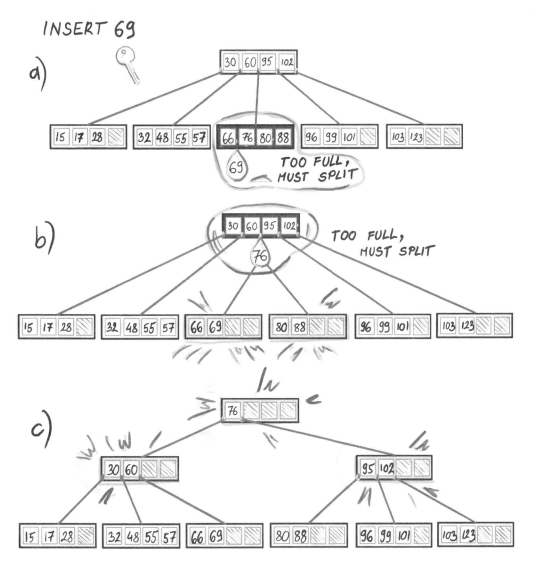

Figure 10.4   Insertion into a full node that results in B-tree growing in depth by 1

What is the cost of the insert operation? We can divide the total cost of the insert into the lookup cost—the cost required to find the place where to insert—and modification cost, including the node splits, redistributing the keys, and so on. The lookup cost is always $O(\log_B N)$ I/Os, as we need to reach the leaf every time when performing a lookup required by an insert. The modification cost varies depending on how far we need to perform splits up the tree, but in the worst case, this cost is $O(1)$ I/Os per level of the tree. Creating a new node and moving over some of the keys does not require more than access and writing to a constant number of blocks. Therefore, in the worst case, the modification cost does not asymptotically degrade the total insertion cost, as it is also, at most, $O(\log_B N)$.

Note, though, that because the *B*-tree has very large nodes, the gap between a minimally filled node (*d* keys) and a full node (2*d* keys) is quite large. This means that node splits triggered by inserting into a full node do not happen quite as often. Some insertion patterns might trigger many node splits; for example, a lot of inserts into the same leaf will make a *B*-tree suffer. This is why many practical *B*-tree implementations attempt to recognize when these inserts take place and treat them differently (they are inserted in one big batch, etc.).

10.3.4 *Delete*

Deletion of an element from a *B*-tree is somewhat analogous to the insert. Deletion, however, has the two following cases:

- We are deleting a key from an internal node.
- We are deleting a key from a leaf.

The deletion algorithm reduces both cases to the second case in the following manner: if the key to be deleted sits at an internal node, it gets removed from its node, and its successor is placed in its location. As a reminder, the successor of an element *x* in the tree is the smallest element in the tree that is larger than *x*.

You might want to stop here and assure yourself that every key in a non-leaf node in a *B*-tree must have a successor and that the successor of an arbitrary key in an internal node must reside in a leaf. We can find a successor of a key *x* in an internal node by following the pointer *p* just right of the key and finding a minimum of the subtree pointed to by *p*. Visually, by following *p*, we make one right, and then we keep making lefts until we reach a leaf. The left-most (smallest) key in that leaf is *x*'s successor.

By replacing an element with its successor (the way 60 gets replaced by 66 in figure 10.5), we maintain the same number of keys in the internal node from which the deleted element comes, and we also uphold the lexicographical order of elements in the tree, so there are no problems there. However, we just lost an element from a leaf.

How do we delete from a leaf? If the leaf *y* contains more than *d* keys, then the element can be safely removed from the leaf, and that's it (see the example of deleting 99 in figure 10.5).

On the other hand, if the leaf *y* has *d* keys, removing a key will cause an underflow. We then turn to the left/right neighbor of *y* to see whether we can borrow some keys from it. If the left or the right neighbor has more than *d* keys, then we can borrow at least one key to make up for an underflow.

Ideally, if one of the neighbors has ample keys, we want to evenly split keys between that neighbor and leaf *y*, but rearranging elements among leaves causes the separator

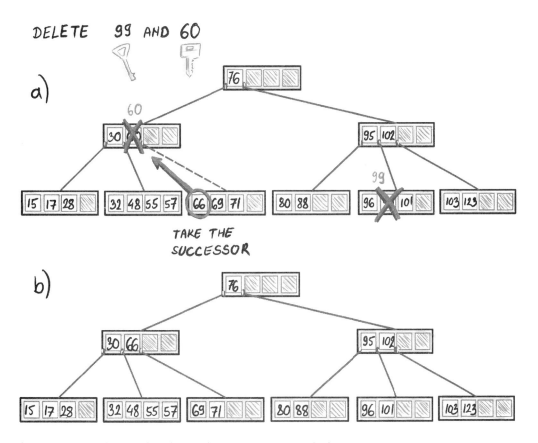

Figure 10.5   Handling deletions from an internal node versus a leaf

to also change. In the example shown in figure 10.6 where we delete 69, after 69 is removed, the left node contains 32, 48, 55, and 57, the separator is 66, and the right node contains 71. We rearrange these elements so that the left node contains 32, 48, and 55, the separator becomes 57, and the right node's contents become 66, 71.

It might not be apparent on a *B*-tree of order $d = 2$, but redistributing elements evenly between two leaves is very important (e.g., consider nodes that have thousands of keys). By redistributing evenly, we are pushing the next potential redistribution of keys further into the future.

It might happen that both neighbors are at their minimum capacity and cannot lend any keys. In that case, we concatenate leaves. We concatenate the leaf y (now it contains $d-1$ keys) with a neighbor of our choosing (contains d keys) and the earlier separator between the two leaves to form a new node that contains $2d$ keys, thus forming a full node. By bringing the separator down, we effectively delete a key from an

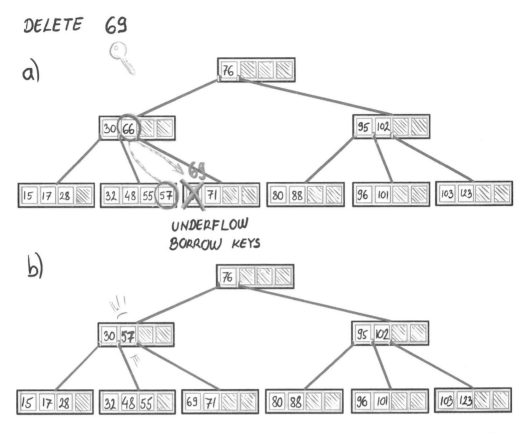

Figure 10.6 Deletion of an element can cause an underflow. If neighbors are not at their minimum capacity, the node borrows keys from one of the neighbors.

internal node, which might trigger further redistribution of keys or node concatenations up the tree.

Consider the example in figure 10.7 where the deletion of 88 causes concatenation at the leaf level. Once the leaf is concatenated with its right neighbor, the previous separator of the two leaves (95) comes down into the new concatenated node. That triggers an underflow on the second level of the tree, causing another concatenation to happen, and ultimately reducing the depth of the B-tree by 1.

The deletion, just like insertion, requires a lookup of a key to be deleted, and potentially may require node modifications. Similar to insertions, the modification cost to the tree during a deletion does not asymptotically endanger the total cost, and it amounts to $O(\log_B N)$.

Even though we analyze operations asymptotically in a B-tree, the depth of a B-tree is rarely above 6 or 7. The upper levels of a B-tree can also often fit in main memory. For instance, for the node where $d = 512$, and the total node size is on the order of a couple of kilobytes, a standard RAM memory might fit two or three top

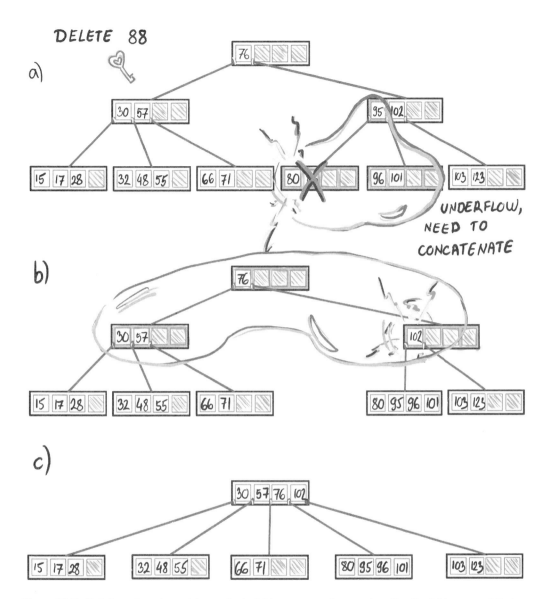

Figure 10.7 Deletion of an element from a leaf might cause a node concatenation if neighbors are at their minimum capacity. The concatenations can propagate up the tree and ultimately reduce the tree height by 1.

levels of the tree. This saves us I/O access to be used for the lower two to four levels of the tree only.

10.3.5 B⁺-trees

Most implementations of *B*-trees in use today are in fact *B⁺*-trees. The main difference between the plain *B*-trees we just described and the *B⁺*-trees is that *B⁺*-trees hold all their data in leaves. The internal nodes contain keys whose main purpose is to route the query to the correct leaf, but they do not necessarily reflect the contents of the actual dataset. This also means that all queries cost $O(\log_B N)$, as even if we encounter a queried key in an internal node during search, we still continue the search all the way to the leaf.

There are a couple of reasons why we benefit from this design. First, the leaf level is organized in a linked list, as shown in figure 10.8. This allows fast sequential access over the sorted order of data and fast range queries. Consider how, in a classical *B*-tree, a range query or a need to scan all data in the sorted order triggers an in-order traversal of a tree, which jumps up and down various tree levels. If the tree is laid out on disk in a level-by-level fashion, then switching between levels invokes inevitable random access. Range queries and the need to output all data in one fast scan are important in systems such as databases and filesystems. Therefore, the ability to provide fast traversals in a B^+-tree becomes particularly handy.

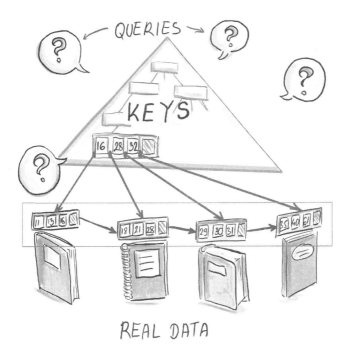

Figure 10.8   A B^+-tree organization. Internal nodes are simple and contain keys that route queries to the leaves, where more detailed information on each key is contained.

In addition, not maintaining pointers to the actual data in the internal nodes frees a lot of space to store more keys. This gives a higher branching factor and a lower depth, thus resulting in a smaller number of I/Os for common operations than in the classical *B*-tree.

10.3.6 *How operations on a B⁺-tree are different*

Initially, a B^+-tree can be built so that keys from internal nodes are duplicated versions of actual data keys. In other words, in the beginning, all the items existent in the leaves are also existent in the internal nodes. However, when an item is deleted, it is deleted only from a leaf and stays in the internal node as a guidepost (unless there is no longer a need for that separator key due to node merge, etc.) For example, if item 28 was to be deleted from the B^+-tree in figure 10.8, it would be removed from the leaf level but would stay as a separator between the two leaves in the internal node.

Similarly, during a more complicated insert, a node is split into two, and a key from the leaf is promoted to the internal level; in a B^+-tree, it is duplicated so that it still stays on the leaf level and is promoted to the internal node level to serve as a separator.

Searches always go all the way down to the leaf level of the tree, so we cannot have a case where a search incurs zero I/Os because the element was found in one of the higher levels of the tree that were cached in RAM. On the other hand, once a particular element is found, the successor operation runs in amortized $O(1/B)$ time, because for every $\theta(B)$ operation, we fetch a new block, and at all other times, the successor operation is free. As we will see later in this chapter, a B^+-tree is a useful component for building larger data structures where components are occasionally merged. In this case, the ability to quickly scan down all the data of two components and merge them in a merge-sort-like fashion significantly boosts performance.

10.3.7 *Use case: B-trees in MySQL (and many other places)*

B-trees form the foundation for many database engines, such as PostgreSQL, MySQL, and many others. File systems, such as Apple's filesystem HFS+ (http://mng.bz/YgoN) and BTRFS by Linux (http://mng.bz/GGYq), all use B-trees. If your company is running some kind of database, most likely it is a B-tree-based database. Many of these implementations are actually B^+-trees.

As an example (and for a change), consider an online application that does not deal with an enormous dataset. The website contains the information on all self-storage facility records in the United States. The database contains about 50,000 self-storage facilities, but each facility has a large number of storage types that can be rented (different categories of storage dimensions; different features, such as whether the facility is climate controlled, whether there is elevator access, or whether there is a promotion on the price), so in effect, we have about 10 million individual records, including historical records.

Users can go to the site to check the availability of particular types of storage in their neighborhood, and they can filter using various criteria (e.g., by ZIP code, storage size, etc.). Every day, over 100,000 new rentals are signed, so we can assume an even larger number of queries are posted to the site.

On the other hand, modifications to the database do happen, but not nearly at the same pace as queries; for instance, a facility might close, or a new one might open; also, pricing information can change, but all this happens at the rate of a couple of times a week. To make searches fast, we should store the database as a *B*-tree, and we can build indices on different columns in the table (e.g., ZIP code).

In the next section, we touch on the mathematical foundations of optimality behind *B*-tree searches. This section is primarily intended for mathematically curious readers and can otherwise be skipped.

10.4   Math bit: Why are B-tree lookups optimal in external memory?

To determine the optimal way to query in external memory, let's back up to RAM and optimal searching in RAM. We know that binary search trees (as well as binary search on a sorted array) can perform queries optimally in $\sim\log_2 N$ comparisons; in other words, the lower bound for searching in RAM is $\Omega(\log_2 N)$ comparisons. But how do we know this? In other words, how do we know that someone won't come along one of these days and invent a new algorithm that is faster than binary search?

To answer this, we need to produce a lower bound argument that places all potential algorithms under one umbrella of procedures that performs a sequence of comparisons (e.g., $a < 3$?) whose answers can be yes or no and analyze the amount of information we learn from each answer. That is, we are operating in the world of algorithms that can only perform comparisons (otherwise, hash tables can beat our searching lower bound). Then we compute the minimum number of questions that this generally defined procedure has to ask in order to solve the problem.

To illustrate the point, let's turn to a children's game that might be familiar: say that you imagine a number x between 1 and 1,000,000, and your friend is trying to guess the number. They are allowed to ask questions such as "Is x smaller, larger, or equal to 30,000?" and you need to give them a truthful answer. If x equals the number they mention, the game stops; otherwise, you respond that their guess is too high or too low, and the game continues until they guess correctly. The goal is for them to guess the right number in the smallest number of questions possible.

You can conclude that the best choice for a first question is whether x is smaller, larger, or equal to 500,000. This way, even in the worst case, the space of potential options is reduced from 1,000,000 to 500,000. If your friend chose a smaller or a larger number, that would be of benefit to you but not to your friend, as you can cater your responses to whichever options leaves more candidate numbers while remaining consistent in your answers (e.g., if they ask whether the number is smaller, equal, or larger than 900,000 as the first question, you will definitely answer "smaller").

The conclusion is that one question/comparison helps us cut down on the number of options by at most a factor of two; a question might cut down on the number of options by a smaller factor or none at all if it is not designed well, but the most that it can help us to reduce options is by a factor of two. This means that to go from the search space of N to 1, we need to ask at least $\Omega(\log_2 N)$ questions, so with $N = 1,000,000$, our game is called "20 Questions." Now let's translate this analogy into external memory.

While in RAM we count the questions (i.e., the number of comparisons the algorithm has to make to solve the problem), in the external memory model, we count I/Os. Consequently, we need to compute the maximum benefit possible (i.e., how much information we learn from one memory block input).

Because a memory transfer contains at most B elements, inputting one block is like changing the game to let our friend ask a bit more complicated question involving B values. An example of such a question with $B = 4$ could be "Where would you place x between the following four numbers: 23, 31, 56, and 88?" If x equals one of the numbers, the game stops; otherwise, you would have five options for your answer ($x < 23$, $23 < x < 31$, $31 < x < 56$, $56 < x < 88$, and $x > 88$), and the game would continue until one of the offered numbers equaled x. What would be the optimal first question for our friend if, say, $B = 4$? It would be four evenly spaced-out numbers so that whichever of the five options we choose, the space in between is equal. This prevents us from prolonging the game.

In theoretical computer science, this proof technique is called an *adversary argument*. In our game, we are the adversary, because provided with some B elements, we will always choose to place x in the subspace that allows the game to go on the longest. This is how we test the worst case of an algorithm. The only way to decidedly win against the adversary is for the algorithm to make all subspaces of equal size. When we deploy our algorithms into the real world, we do not have real-life adversaries; rather, the adversary metaphor is there to help us realize the asymptotic complexity of a problem.

So, the best that could happen is if B elements in the block help reduce the number of options by a factor of $B + 1$. Again, note that our friend can make up a bad block, which would enable us, the adversary, to cut down on space by a factor smaller than $B + 1$ (see figure 10.9 to see how one can make a good/bad block).

Because each I/O helps us reduce the total number of options by at most $B + 1$, we need $\Omega(\log_{B-1} N) = \Omega(\log_B N)$ I/Os to perform a search in external memory, and B-tree lookup meets this lower bound.

10.4.1 Why B-tree inserts/deletes are not optimal in external memory

Now that we know that B-trees are optimal with respect to queries, let's look at modify operations, such as inserts and deletes that require the same asymptotic number of memory transfers as the lookup.

Inserts and deletes, however, are essentially different from lookups, because an insert operation does not require an immediate proof that a new element has been stored into a leaf. Similarly, a delete operation does not need an immediate confirmation that an element has been physically removed from the tree. The only confirmation comes as a result of a later lookup, when it should result in a yes on an inserted element and a no on a deleted element. Lookup is the only operation that requires immediate feedback, and as such, it cannot be delayed. Inserts and deletes, on the other hand, can be delayed and buffered. This way, a data structure can process these

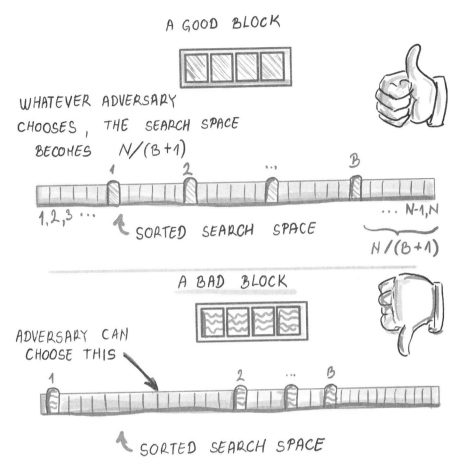

Figure 10.9   The lower bound calculation assumes good blocks

operations more efficiently in batches. We will see two such data structures in the rest of the chapter: B^ε-trees and LSM-trees.

10.5 B^ε-trees

The B^ε-tree was devised by Brodal and Fagerberg [6] as a data structure that embodies the tradeoff between the speed of inserts and lookups in external memory. The tradeoff is reflected in the range of values of parameter $\varepsilon = [0,1]$ that can be tuned, and when $\varepsilon = 0$, the data structure is fully optimized for inserts/deletes; when $\varepsilon = 1$, it is fully optimized for lookups (it is a B-tree).

However, when we talk about B^ε-trees in this chapter, we will commonly refer to the "middle-ground" data structure that occurs at $\varepsilon = 1/2$. This value of ε is interesting because, at that point of the spectrum, we get a data structure with lookups that are only a constant-factor worse than B-trees and inserts that are asymptotically better than B-trees. This means that for write-optimized workloads, the B^{ε}-tree is a significantly better fit than a B-tree and maintains asymptotically optimal lookups.

10.5.1 B^{ε}-tree: How it works

The key design feature of B^{ε}-trees is that, aside from keys, each internal node features a buffer. The purpose of buffers is to temporarily store inserts and deletes that act as messages on their way to the designated leaf. A delete operation in a B^{ε}-tree does not work the way it works in a B-tree, by directly going to the location of the element and physically removing it. Instead, a tombstone message "Delete x" is initially inserted into the buffer of the root node, and it gradually moves down the buffers along the root-to-leaf path to the leaf that stores x. Once the tombstone message reaches the leaf containing x, x is physically removed from the tree along with the tombstone message. The analogous process exists with inserts.

Like in a B^{+}-tree, in a B^{ε}-tree all items reside in leaves, so all inserts and deletes eventually affect the leaves, and keys in internal nodes are there only as pivots to direct the search. Insert/delete messages wait in the buffer until enough other messages have been collected to be flushed together to one of the children in just one I/O. This is in contrast to B-trees, where a single insert/delete uses one I/O to descend to the next level of the tree and, consequently, a number of I/Os to complete the operation. By delaying operations in a B^{ε}-tree, we can make them run faster in the amortized sense. Later we will see how keeping all these messages around affects our lookup algorithm.

The internal structure of a node in the B^{ε}–tree is as follows: each node contains B^{ε} keys, and the remaining $B - B^{\varepsilon}$ space is used for a buffer (see figure 10.10 for a node where $B = 16$ and $\varepsilon = 1/2$). For our common setup of $\varepsilon = 1/2$, we have $\sqrt{B}$ keys and $B - \sqrt{B}$ buffer space. The buffer, therefore, occupies most of the node space. Also note that the depth of the B^{ε}-tree is dictated by the node structure, where $\sqrt{B}$ keys per node gives us the tree depth of $\log_{\sqrt{B}} N = 2 \log_B N$. Even though the number of keys is significantly smaller, the depth of the tree is only twice that of a B-tree. This will slightly affect the performance of lookups, as we have sacrificed node space to accommodate buffers, but the asymptotic lookup cost will remain equal to that of a B-tree.

10.5.2 Buffering mechanics

One may think of a buffer as a single area in the node where messages accumulate, and once the buffer becomes overly full, we flush it. That is, we only flush the elements destined for the child that has the most pending updates. Perhaps a cleaner way to think of a buffer visually is by splitting it into $B^{\varepsilon} + 1$ different sub-buffers, where each sub-buffer holds the messages destined for one particular child based on the keys' values (such as in figure 10.10). We do not explicitly partition the space between sub-buffers, and different sub-buffers can share each other's space so that the flush is

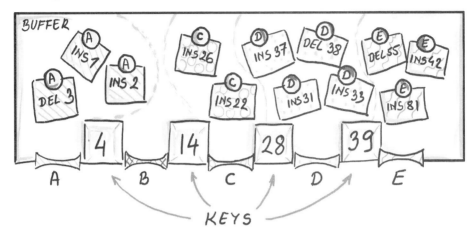

$B = 16$

$\sqrt{B} = 4$ (KEYS)

$B - \sqrt{B} = 12$ (BUFFER SPACE)

Figure 10.10   A node in a B^ε-tree has keys and buffers. Currently, the buffer is full and cannot accommodate more updates.

triggered only after the whole buffer has been filled. However, once the buffer is full, only the fullest sub-buffer gets flushed. The buffer is usually implemented as a balanced binary search tree, where we can quickly add and traverse the items and keep them in the sorted order. If we are implementing sub-buffers as separate binary search trees, we should worry only about their total size so as not to overshoot the buffer capacity, not the individual sizes of sub-buffers.

Figure 10.11 shows the moment a buffer overflows after a new update (Del 8) and gets flushed. Messages from the fullest sub-buffer get flushed and distributed to appropriate sub-buffers at the child. Other messages from the buffer stay in the buffer (for instance, Del 8, which triggered the flush, does not get flushed.)

In figure 10.11, the child node already had some of its earlier updates waiting in the buffer (Del 29 and Ins 36); however, together with the incoming messages, it does not overshoot the buffer capacity, so the process stops here. One important detail not shown is that each update message has a timestamp associated with it. The timestamp helps us reconstruct the history, and thus perform the lookup algorithm correctly.

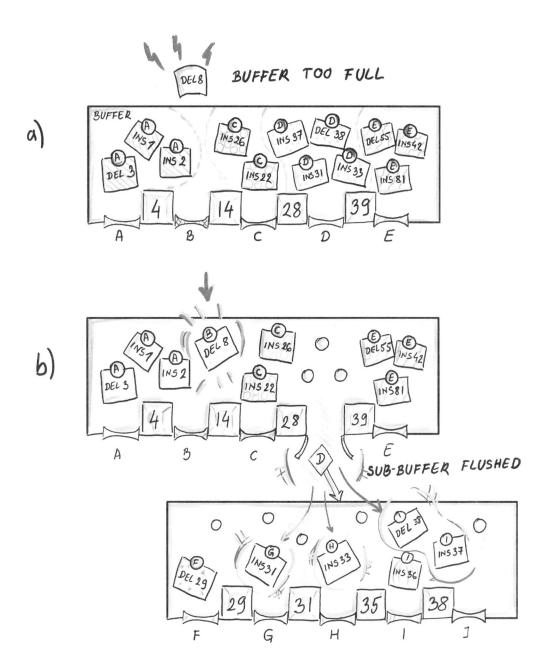

Figure 10.11 When a buffer becomes too full, we flush the fullest sub-buffer to the appropriate node.

10.5.3 *Inserts and deletes*

Now that we have the buffering mechanism under our belt, let's see the whole insert/delete process through. An insert/delete message is initially placed in the buffer at the root of the tree. If the message does not trigger any buffer overflows, we are done. Otherwise, if the message triggers the root buffer to flush, we flush it, and we perform any cascading flushes down the tree, potentially going all the way down to the leaf level, with appropriate inserts/deletes at the leaf.

If a leaf level is reached during flushes, we perform an insert/delete of messages that have arrived at the leaf level by physically inserting/adding an element, like we do in a B^+-tree, and by eliminating those insert/delete messages from their buffer. Nodes in a B^ε-tree have the same sort of "order d" property as B-trees. When a leaf overflows its capacity, it splits in the same way it is done in B^+-trees. When it becomes too empty, it gets merged in the same way as in B^+-trees. So, a typical insert/delete that progresses down buffers and eventually reaches the leaf might then trigger a split/merge operation at the leaf that might, in turn, trigger new splits/merges up the tree. This whole process works just like we described it for a B-tree, except that now we split/merge the keys and redistribute the messages in buffers.

10.5.4 *Lookups*

The searches in the B^ε-tree operate similarly to those in a B-tree, in that they follow the root-to-leaf path to the leaf that might contain the queried element. However, a B^ε-tree lookup also has to be mindful of the insert/delete messages it encounters along its path, as they affect the final lookup result.

For instance, let's say we are looking for an element, 10, that was inserted in the past; however, a delete operation was recently issued for it. If no other operations were issued in regard to 10 since, our lookup should report the element not present. However, the element might still exist in the leaf of the tree, as the tombstone message may not have reached it.

For this reason, a lookup operation has to collect all messages (with their timestamps) that relate to the queried element on the root-to-leaf path to the element. Then, when it determines whether the element is present in the leaf, it applies any potential insert/delete messages in the correct chronological order. In figure 10.12, a lookup of an element, 7, collects messages on its root-to-leaf path, and upon reaching the leaf level and applying all the messages, it concludes that 7 is present.

Keep in mind that a lookup never triggers the flushing of any buffers. It internally collects relevant messages so that it can correctly answer the query. All the work in relation to flushing buffers is left to the insert/delete operations.

10.5.5 *Cost analysis*

In this section, we analyze the cost of lookup, insert, and delete operations in the B^ε-tree. We focus on the analysis for the middle-ground data structure that is of interest to us ($\varepsilon = 1/2$,) even though it is easy to generalize for any value of ε.

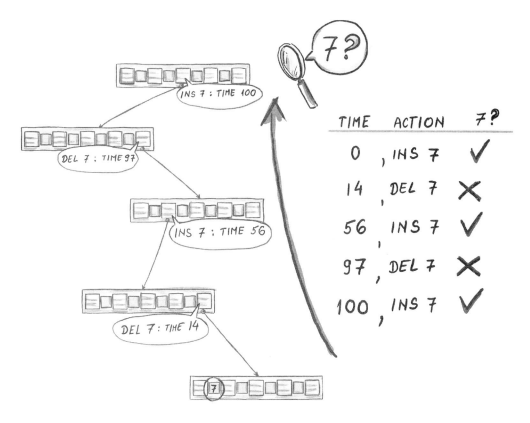

Figure 10.12   Insert and delete messages on the root-to-leaf path to item 7.

A B^ε-tree has $O(\log_B N)$ levels, so the lookup has to read in $O(\log_B N)$ nodes on its root-to-leaf path. In that sense, a lookup costs asymptotically the same as that of a lookup in a B-tree. More precisely, it is twice as slow because the B^ε-tree is twice as deep.

Inserts and deletes can be analyzed together, as they work similarly. First, we need to analyze how much it costs for one message to descend from one level of the tree to the next. This depends on how many elements travel together in one I/O when the buffer is flushed. When the buffer becomes full, the fullest sub-buffer is at least as full as all other sub-buffers; hence it contains at least $(B-\sqrt{B})/(\sqrt{B}+1) \sim \sqrt{B}$ messages. This means that in 1 I/O, we transport roughly $\sqrt{B}$ updates to the next level of the tree; therefore, each update costs $O\left(1/\sqrt{B}\right)$ per level. The tree has $O(\log_B N)$ levels, so one insert/delete costs $O\left((\log_B N)/\sqrt{B}\right)$ I/Os overall, a factor of $\sqrt{B}$ cheaper than in a B-tree! An example of this is shown in figure 10.11, where $B = 16$, but we flushed four elements (the fullest sub-buffer has four items), so, per item, we used ¼ of an I/O. If we consider that B is often expressed in thousands or even millions, being a factor $\sqrt{B}$ cheaper can represent a significant reduction in cost.

Other than the buffering cost, there is also the classic cost of physical splits and merges of nodes that are like those in a B-tree. But this time around, we need to analyze this cost more carefully, considering that we do not want to overshoot $O\left((\log_B N)/\sqrt{B}\right)$ insert/delete cost. In other words, with a B-tree, we can be more loose with the analysis and assume that in the worst case, one split or merge happens per level, and that cost will still be covered by an already existing insert/lookup cost of just traversing down the tree. With the B^ε-tree, we need to be more frugal. Luckily, the number of expected splits and merges works in our favor.

Consider the worst possible workload of all inserts headed toward one leaf; this workload maximizes the number of node splits. Starting from the tree of order $d = \theta(\sqrt{B})$ whose nodes are minimally filled, every $\theta(\sqrt{B})$ inserts, and we need to make a node split. After $\theta(\sqrt{B})$ such splits, which also constitute inserts into a higher level, we need to make a split on one level above. That is, we would only affect the level above the leaf level after $\theta((\sqrt{B})^2)$ insert/deletes. However, that cost is already covered by the cost of much more frequently occurring splits on the leaf level. We could continue to make an argument for higher levels, but the bottom line is that the cost incurred by splitting and merging is negligible and is constant-I/O cost amortized. This means that the cost of splits/merges in a B^ε-tree is dominated by the cost of flushing and transporting messages down the tree.

10.5.6 *B$^\varepsilon$-tree: The spectrum of data structures*

As mentioned before, depending on how ε is chosen, we might get either a better lookup or a better insert performance than in our common setup when $\varepsilon = 1/2$. Figure 10.13 shows three points on the spectrum: (a) a B-tree (all keys, no buffers), (b) a B^ε-tree at $\varepsilon = 1/2$ (some keys and majority buffer space), and (c) a buffered repository tree (one key and all buffer space).

A buffer repository tree is an interesting data structure that allows us to optimize insert/delete performance even more than a B^ε-tree with $\varepsilon = 1/2$. Because the buffer is large and messages at each node can be directed in only two different directions, $\theta(B)$ items can carpool to the next level, bringing the insert performance down to $O(1/B)$ per level, and $O\left((\log_2 N)/B\right)$ I/Os in total (the buffer repository tree has the $O(\log_2 N)$ levels, just like binary search tree, which makes it infeasible for the lookup performance).

10.5.7 *Use case: B$^\varepsilon$-trees in TokuDB*

B^ε-trees have been implemented by the Percona TokuDB storage engine for the Percona server for MySQL. Similarly, there have been implementations of file systems that run B^ε-trees underneath, such as BetrsFS [7]. Because B^ε-trees help inserts get better, this can help make index maintenance easier and faster, thus allowing multiple indexes to coexist without inserts becoming too slow. So, somewhat ironically, the story is that we make lookups worse to help the inserts, that, in turn, help lookups.

A typical use case where B^ε-trees might prove useful is in highly dynamic applications where both inserts and searches need to be fast. Consider the following highly

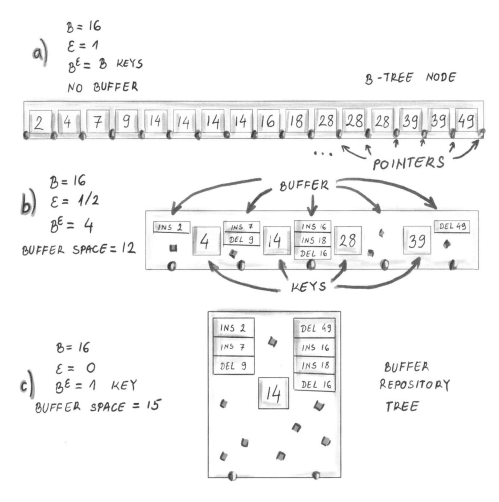

Figure 10.13 The spectrum of *Bᵉ*-tree data structures, from most read-optimized to most write-optimized

performant application: your company hosts web requests for the largest publisher of online magazines. Users constantly load new content and react to that content (e.g., by adding new comments), and at the same time, a large amount of new content and articles is posted, modified, and simultaneously queried.

The challenge of this type of application is to post new content that is up to date, but not at the cost of slowing down customers' reading experiences. Similar use case scenarios arise with social networks, where new content should be ingested at a high rate; however, the content needs to be quickly loaded to users as well.

10.5.8 *Make haste slowly, the I/O way*

One of the major differences between *B*-trees and B^ε-trees is that *B*-trees perform in-place updates; that is, when, for example, a modify/insert/delete operation arrives, the change is immediately incorporated right where the relevant element resides. B^ε-trees, on the other hand, perform out-of-place updates, where a modify/insert/delete message is incorporated into the data structure in a different place from the one where the element in question resides. There is no rush to immediately find the element and apply the needed change to it. Note that out-of-place updates increase the amount of space required by the data structure, in that the number of items in a data structure is measured not by the number of distinct elements but by the number of updates to it. We store items and the messages in relation to those items.

However, note that the out-of-place feature is exactly what helps the modify/insert/delete operations be faster than in a *B*-tree. In order to perform an update, we do not need to search for the exact location of the element immediately and burn a lot of I/Os in the process. Updates take their time to travel down the tree when it's cheapest to descend. Inserts/deletes wait longer to be applied but for that reason are faster; this is because we do not measure the efficiency of operations in the time taken to apply the operation but in the number of I/Os required for the change to be applied. In the next section, we will see a data structure that takes the notion of fast writes (and out-of-place writes) even further than B^ε-trees.

10.6 *Log-structured merge-trees (LSM-trees)*

To understand how LSM-trees came about, let's start by developing a simple write-optimized data structure ourselves. What is an optimal way to implement an external memory index with blazingly fast out-of-place inserts/deletes without regard to the speed of lookups?

Simply logging insert/delete messages in one sequential log comes to mind. One way to envision such a data structure is to have an in-memory buffer where messages carrying inserts, deletes, or modifications to records are accumulated. Once the buffer is full, we flush it in a sequential fashion to a location on disk. Then we again fill the in-memory buffer with writes (when we say *writes*, we mean inserts, deletes, and modify operations) and flush the memory contents by appending the new stuff to the end of the log.

This simple system guarantees an ideal insert/delete performance of $1/B$ per item. This is the amortized cost of writing the items to disk, so it is not hard to see why we cannot do better than that. Of course, queries would be terrible, as we would need to scan the whole file on disk to answer a query (N/B I/Os).

Now let's try to slightly modify this idea without hurting the write performance. Let's say that every time the memory buffer gets filled up, we internally sort all the items in the memory buffer. To do this, a buffer can be some sort of a balanced binary tree and flush the sorted range to a separate file or a table on disk. The next time the buffer gets filled up, we again sort all in-memory data and flush it to another table next to the first table, and so on. Now we have a somewhat more organized system, with many separate tables of data, and each table is internally ordered. The inserts/deletes still run optimally in $O(1/B)$ amortized per element, as buffer sorting takes place in internal memory and does not need any additional I/Os. Queries are not astronomically better: now we have to examine each table to locate updates related to an item of interest. If the table size is similar to the main memory size M and the total number of updates is N, we will have a total of N/M tables. Because each table is sorted, we can use binary search to guide the search within individual tables, which helps us avoid a full linear scan of a table. This gives us $O\left(\frac{N}{M} \times \log_2\left(\frac{M}{B}\right)\right)$ I/Os in cost per query.

Let's slightly improve our simple design: considering that tables are immutable (we will not modify them after flushing to disk), why not build a B^+-tree index on top of each table and improve the query performance to $O\left(\frac{N}{M} \times \log_B\left(\frac{M}{B}\right)\right)$ I/Os? Our resulting data structure is shown in figure 10.14.

Over time, a growing number of tables will exacerbate an already poor lookup performance. Maintaining a number of Bloom filters in RAM (a use case covered in chapter 3), one per table, can help eliminate the disk lookup on tables that do not contain updates for the queried element. However, as you'll recall, Bloom filters also grow linearly with the total size of data, so before we know it, we will be inundating the RAM with a ton of mini Bloom filters. Bloom filters buy us time, but not for long if we are dealing with ridiculously high insert rates.

The log-structured merge tree (LSM-tree) is a data structure devised in 1996 that embeds the idea of our simplified write-optimized structure and adds to it a mechanism that limits the number of tables on disk by occasionally merging and compacting them. The LSM-tree has been successfully implemented in a number of write-optimized databases such as LevelDB, used by Google, RocksDB, Facebook, and others. Let's see how LSM-trees work.

10.6.1   *The LSM-tree: How it works*

There are a number of variants of the basic design of an LSM-tree, as well as many different implementations [8]. Originally, the LSM-tree was made out of k components $C_0, C_1, ..., C_{k-1}$, where C_0 is in internal memory and all other components are on disk. However, there are a couple of important differences from our simplified data structure from before: in an LSM-tree, we assume that the size of C_0 is on the order of memory size M, and C_1 is by a factor f (usually $f \geq 2$) larger than component C_0. In fact, the ratio f is maintained between the sizes of any two consecutive components, so the component sizes, in increasing order, are M, fM, f^2M, and so on.

On-disk components were originally envisioned as B^+-trees, but as we will see, in modern implementations different data structures are used, such as skip lists or simple sorted key-value tables and files. The exponential increase in sizes between components guarantees that we will have a manageable number of components to query

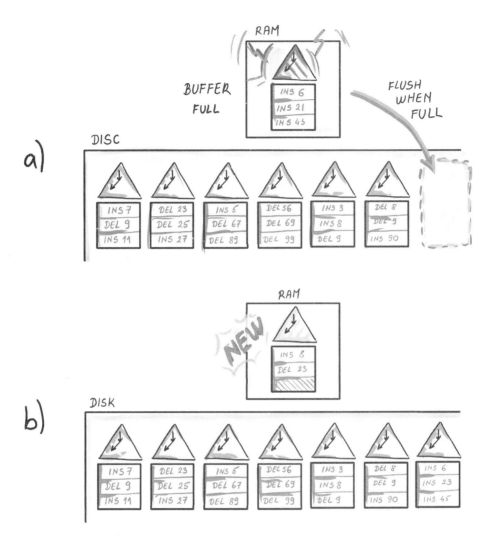

Figure 10.14   Our simple write-optimized data structure that is not the LMS-tree

later. The largest component should be able to store all N elements, so the total number of components is $k = O\left(\log_f {}^{N}\!/_{M}\right)$, if the smallest component is of size $\theta(M)$.

Each component sits at its own level, and each level has a limit on its maximum capacity. When the upper capacity threshold is violated at one level, the corresponding component C_i gets merged into the component C_{i+1}. This in turn might fill up the component C_{i+1} and cause cascading merges with levels below. In the original LSM-tree design, this was achieved by merging the range of keys from the smaller component into the larger component. Modern LSM-tree implementations favor the approach where once written, components (also called *runs*) are immutable. So, even if the final effect of merging level C_i into C_{i+1} is the same as in the original LSM-tree merging approach, modern merging policy between levels never mutates the structures once written. Instead, it creates a new merged component and garbage-collects the old ones. Figure 10.15 shows an example of an LSM-tree and the merging policy we just described, commonly known as *leveling merge policy*, obviating the details of how things are physically merged on disk.

In the example in figure 10.15, we set $M = 4$ and $f = 2$. On the left side of the figure, we capture a snapshot of the data structure at some point in the workload processing. The component C_1 is full and has to be merged into C_2. To merge C_1 into C_2, we sequentially scan the range of items in C_1 and C_2 and merge them in the fashion in which they would be merged during merge-sort. We can do this because items inside individual components are sorted. Before the merge, C_2 had 8 items, and now it has 16 (the right side of the figure). The component C_2 will also be merged into C_3, as it has reached the maximum capacity.

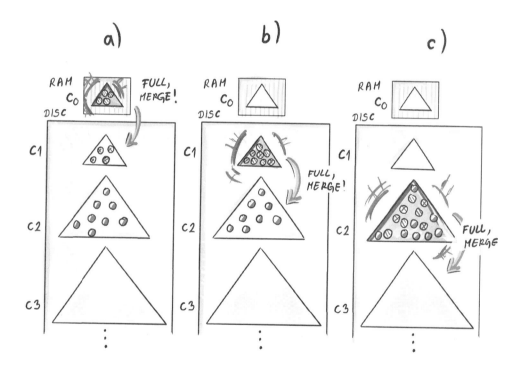

Figure 10.15 Merging a smaller component into a larger one in a leveling merge policy of an LSM-tree. The example shows B^+-tree-like unit components at each level, but modern LSM-tree implementations use various data structures or even simple tables and files instead of B^+-trees.

Note that when we merge in this way, for one element to descend to the next level, we write that piece of data many times: once when it is being merged into the lower level and then later when other items are being merged into its level. This process gets repeated for each level, and this so-called *write amplification* effect is more pronounced with larger growth factors, as we need to merge the smaller component f times into the larger one in order to fill it up. Write amplification is a term used to measure how much data is written inside the data structure per unit item inserted. It is safe to say that with leveling merge policy, write amplification is fairly high.

Tiering merge policy is another popular mechanism for the component compaction in modern LSM-tree implementations. In this policy, tiers are equivalent to levels, except that each tier contains f components of the same size. Once f components at tier i fill up, they all get merged into one new component in the tier $i + 1$. This way, to descend to a new tier, each item gets written only once. See an example of tiering merge policy in figure 10.16, where we use sorted runs instead of B^+-trees as components, and $f = 2$. In this example, two tables at tier 1 become full and get merged into one table at tier 2. This process of merging is done in a fast, sequential manner. It is not shown in the figure, but now two full components at tier 2 will get merged into one component at tier 3.

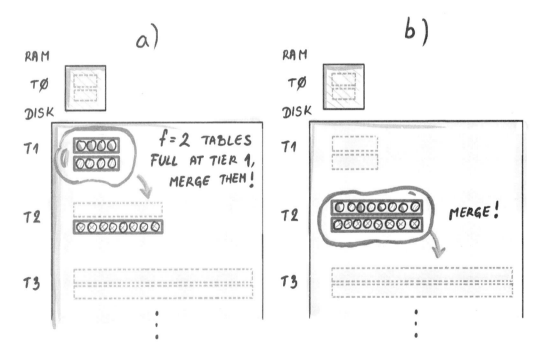

Figure 10.16 Tiering merge policy in an LSM-tree with $f = 2$. When f components at tier i get filled up, they merge into one component at tier $i + 1$.

10.6.2 LSM-tree cost analysis

Note that with both merging policies, we lose some of the initial $O\left(\frac{1}{B}\right)$-type write performance during compaction. In leveling merge policy, because each item is written about $O(f)$ times in order to descend one level, the total cost for one item to descend one level below is $O\left(\frac{f}{B}\right)$, and the total cost to descend to the bottom of the LSM-tree is the cost accumulated over all levels: $O\left(\left(\frac{f}{B}\right)\log_f \frac{N}{M}\right)$ I/Os. In tiering merge policy, we only need $O\left(\frac{1}{B}\right)$ per level, and accumulated over all levels we need $O\left(\log_f \frac{N}{M}\right)$ I/Os, a factor f less than in leveling merge policy.

Queries, however, tell a different story. Without regard to the size of the component itself, we need about a constant number of I/Os per component to check the presence of an item. This can be achieved even if the component itself or a run is much larger than a block. An example is string-sorted tables (SSTs) that contain sorted key-value pairs of data, as well as a small index of keys. If we first want to find out where a potential item might lie in the table, we fetch the index of the individual table (component) that is small enough to fit in a block. By learning where the item resides, we then need just one more I/O to fetch the item. So, overall, one component needs one I/O.

In leveling merging policy, because we have the number of components equal to the number of levels, we need $O\left(\log_f \frac{N}{M}\right)$ I/Os for a lookup. In tiering merge policy, we can have up to a factor of f more components to check, which increases the query cost. However, the biggest gains in the query performance come with the use of Bloom filters that help redirect the query to the right table, thus bringing the query performance to $O(1)$ in most cases. This is the optimization that can be applied to both merging policies, and it works this time because the total number of components is logarithmic in the total size of the dataset; thus, maintaining those Bloom filters in main memory is quite manageable. Range queries are not as lucky as they cannot benefit as well from Bloom filters as point queries.

10.6.3 Use case: LSM-trees in Cassandra

LSM-trees have been implemented in a number of large database engines, such as Cassandra, LevelDB, RocksDB, and so on. Specifically, Cassandra's tiering merge LSM-tree uses Bloom filters to avoid unnecessary disk seeks. Figure 10.17 is a throwback to chapter 3, where we hailed applications of Bloom filters in distributed storage contexts. The tables in the figure show an LSM-tree whose components are tables. You can envision that with $f = 4$, tables SST 1–4 are tier 1, SST 5–8 are tier 2, and so on.

A typical business case for an LSM-tree is an application that needs blindingly fast write performance. An example of such an application is a backup product that takes data snapshots of data at regular intervals and stores petabytes of data, but rarely revisits history. Another use case is a traffic-monitoring network application that witnesses hundreds of millions of requests per hour. The requests are stored in the database, but there is rarely a case of an explicit search for a particular request.

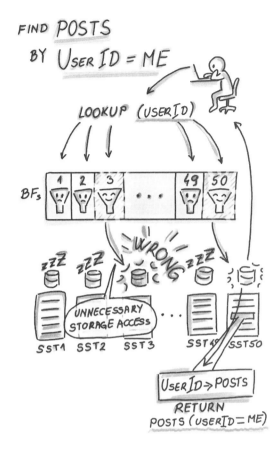

Figure 10.17   LSM-trees use Bloom filters to eliminate unnecessary disk seeks to tables that do not contain queried items.

Summary

- A database index is a data structure built on top of a database table meant to speed up query performance for large tables. Indices are built using data structures that can perform efficient searches in the external memory setting.

- *B*-trees form the backbone of the most widespread storage engines, such as MySQL. A *B*-tree is an optimal data structure for performing lookups on disk. *B*-tree nodes are large and are usually related to the block size. All operations in a *B*-tree are logarithmic with the base of *B*. When nodes in *B*-trees become too full/too empty, nodes can be split/merged, and the tree grows upward.

- *B*-trees are read optimized, and there are other data structures that are better suited for writing heavy workloads. Inserts and deletes are operations that, unlike searches, can be delayed or processed in batches together. Write-optimized data structures use this idea to delay and buffer insert/delete operations to achieve much faster inserts than *B*-trees.

- A B^ε-tree is a write-optimized data structure whose inserts/deletes are asymptotically faster than B-trees, and with lookups that are by a constant factor slower than B-trees. B^ε-trees employ buffers at their nodes to temporarily store insert/delete messages so that they can, at a convenient moment, be processed in a batch. The value of a parameter ε determines the extent to which the data structure prefers writes over reads.
- An LSM-tree is a write-optimized data structure that consists of sorted runs that occasionally get merged in a fast sequential fashion. LSM-trees can achieve extremely fast updates at the cost of lookups that are slower than both those of a B-tree and B^ε-tree.

External memory sorting

This chapter covers

- Understanding the importance of efficient sorting on disk
- Revising the two most classical in-RAM sorting algorithms: merge-sort and quick-sort
- Learning how external memory merge-sort works
- Understanding how external memory quick-sort works
- Understanding the relationship between searching and sorting in internal versus external memory

In the previous chapter, we learned about different ways to design indices in databases. Indices embody the fundamental problem of searching in computer science. Another fundamental problem that crops up in databases—and pretty much everywhere else—is sorting. Just think of how many times you've used the function sort() in your code to order a set of data.

Aside from obvious applications of sorting, there is a large number of algorithms that use sorting as their subroutine. For instance, in chapter 2, we discussed the problem of deduplication (i.e., eliminating duplicates) and talked about various efficient hashing solutions. Hashing gives a good average-case performance; however, if we are aiming at the best worst-case performance involving actual element comparisons (not matching via hashing), eliminating duplicates requires sorting data. This does not mean that the optimal algorithm for deduplication must explicitly sort, but it needs to perform at least the amount of work required to sort—so we might as well solve it by sorting and then scanning the array for duplicates. Another slightly different version of this problem is the element distinctness problem that takes an unordered array as an input, and asks to output "Yes" if all elements are distinct in an array and "No" otherwise. Element distinctness also requires sorting in a similar way to deduplication in that the optimal algorithm for this problem will have a runtime at least as high as that of sorting ($\Omega(n \log_2 n)$).

In this chapter, we will first talk about different contexts where sorting comes up and the challenges that arise when sorting large files with a main memory of limited size. Then we will explore two well-known sorting algorithms, merge-sort and quicksort; more specifically, we will explore how to adapt them to external memory. We will do so gradually so as to demonstrate algorithmic tricks that can be useful in other sorting-like problems. Lastly, we will show how to analyze lower bounds for sorting in internal and external memory. Using this tool, we will be able to ascertain that external memory merge-sort is an optimal algorithm for sorting in external memory.

11.1 Sorting use cases

Sorting is common across applications in many domains. In the world of geometry, sorting points by coordinates is quite common and is needed for many fundamental routines, such as computation of the closest pair of points in a 2D plane, sweep line algorithms, and others. Consider the following application of sorting in computational geometry and robotics.

11.1.1 Robot motion planning

Imagine you are designing a robot that needs to move around the kitchen table avoiding obstacles (let's say the robot needs to pick up crumbs from the table). The robot has a map of objects and their 2D footprints in its neighborhood, which should aid the robot in moving seamlessly around the table without crashing into objects on it. Objects can be of various shapes, and the actual footprints might be complicated shapes that can make the motion planning difficult, so to simplify computation, instead of actual footprints, the robot computes what we call the *convex hull* of the 2D footprint of each object, the smallest convex polygon that contains the footprint (see figure 11.1 for clarification).

Many convex hull algorithms use sorting, where they sort the points along x and y coordinates. One way to visualize one popular convex hull algorithm is to imagine wrapping gift paper around the 2D footprint of an object. The process of figuring out which corner to wrap around next involves sorting the angles from the current corner

Figure 11.1   Robot motion planning algorithms often involve computing convex hulls of nearby objects.

to other corners of the footprint. For more details, see the Jarvis March algorithm, also known as the giftwrap algorithm for convex hulls. (Many other algorithms for computing convex hulls, without giftwrap in their name, also use sorting.)

Databases also use sorting extensively to create indices to perform group-by operations, sort query outputs, and so on [1]. Aside from using sorting to implement basic database operations, large databases commonly need to order data according to some criteria that involve computations on a number of different columns. Consider an example of a bioinformatics database as an application of sorting.

11.1.2   *Cancer genomics*

You have a large database of genomes (a complete genetic code of an individual) that you would like to order according to proclivity to a particular type of cancer. You are using your database to test a hypothesis from a recent study that the frequency of certain sequences, X and Y, within the genome play a role in cancer incidence, and sequence X does so twice as much as sequence Y. To do so, we order genomes according to the evaluation score that uses the number of occurrences of said sequences and use the evaluation score as the input to the comparison function, as shown in figure 11.2.

When sorting, it is common to provide a customized comparison function, which we used to define the notions of less than and equal than. This is especially helpful with nonprimitive data types, where the ordering between items is something context specific and more complex. Python's sort function, for example, allows one to pass in a customized comparison function.

Given particular ranges and types of data, the size of a dataset, and many other parameters, a different sorting algorithm might apply. Research on sorting and different implementations of sorting algorithms are quite extensive. A comprehensive review of sorting deserves a chapter or a book of its own, and with the exception of a

	SEQUENCE X #	SEQUENCE Y #	EVALUATION SCORE $2 \cdot X + Y$	RANK
ACTGGGTCACCGTGCA...	52	4	$2 \cdot 52 + 4 = 108$	2
GGCCTATTGCGCGTGCA...	33	3	$2 \cdot 33 + 3 = 69$	3
AGAGCCTTCTCCTTTTGA...	12	23	$2 \cdot 12 + 23 = 47$	5
GCTTATCGCGAGCTAAA...	$\emptyset$	12	$2 \cdot \emptyset + 12 = 12$	6
GCTTGCTCGCTCATCTTC...	27	90	$2 \cdot 27 + 90 = 144$	1
TCAAAGCGCAATCTCCTT...	19	10	$2 \cdot 19 + 10 = 48$	4
GATCATGCTAGCTGATCC...	1	8	$2 \cdot 1 + 8 = 10$	8
CGATTGACCTATTTCTAG...	5	1	$2 \cdot 5 + 1 = 11$	7

Figure 11.2   In bioinformatics, genomes are often ordered according to various criteria. In this particular case, we are ordering genomes by the number of times sequences X and Y have occurred. Sequence X's presence is valued as twice as that of sequence Y's presence.

couple of algorithms that we will review in this chapter, we will not discuss many intricacies of sorting.

We will focus on the aspect of sorting when data becomes too large to fit into RAM. When we have a large file to sort that sits on disk and only a small chunk can fit into the main memory at one time, the main issue becomes how we define the high-level sorting procedure that will sort the whole file while being able to work with only a small portion of data simultaneously. Specifically, figuring out how to do this while minimizing the number of disk transfers is the focus of this chapter.

11.2   *Challenges of sorting in external memory: An example*

Imagine working for a hosting company that collects data on web requests for its clients. Say you want to order all requests from the past month to determine the distribution of access times and find the requests that took the longest. Your company collects a lot of data, and data is organized into one large table where each row represents one request and all its associated information: IP address, browser, access time, and so on. In total, you have a file of roughly 512 GB that needs to be sorted, but you dispose of only 4 GB RAM.

The first thing that comes to mind is that we can sort 4 GB of data at one time. If we partition the original file into chunks of 4 GB and read each whole chunk into the main memory, then sort it and write it back, we get a partially sorted dataset.

This step of creating mini-sorted lists is, in fact, a great starting point for applying the merge-sort algorithm in external memory only. We will sometimes use the term *two-way merge-sort* to refer to the traditional merge-sort algorithm as a means of contrasting it with the multiway merge-sort we will develop for the external memory. Let's see how two-way merge-sort (or just merge-sort) works when blindly translated to external memory.

But first, a quick review: Two-way merge-sort in RAM works by trivially partitioning the array into small sub-arrays from the top down to a size of 1 and does all the work by merging those arrays from the bottom up, one pair at a time. Merging is, effectively, sorting. This recursive merging turns n sorted lists of size 1 into $n/2$ sorted lists of size 2, $n/4$ lists of size 4, and so on, and then, at last, 1 list of size n. Merge-sort runtime is described using the following recursive formula $T(n)$, that, when the recursion is unrolled, represents the number of comparisons required by merge-sort:

$$T(n) = 2T\left(\frac{n}{2}\right) + O(n)$$

The $O(n)$ term represents the time required to merge at one level (e.g., $n/2$ lists of size 2 into $n/4$ lists of size 4). The base case of recursion is $T(1) = 1$ because sorting a list of one element is trivial. Unwrapping this recursion using the master method, or a simple tree built by unraveling the recursion, we determine that the merge-sort runtime is $O(n \log_2 n)$.

11.2.1 *Two-way merge-sort in external memory*

Before we start thinking about how to adapt two-way merge-sort to external memory, let's review the parameters we use for the analysis of algorithms in external memory. The value of N represents the input size (the number of records), M represents the total size of the main memory, and B is the block size.

The benefit of external memory when it comes to sorting is that with one sweep over all data (N/B block transfers), we can get N/M sorted lists of size M, so trivially partitioning into lists smaller than M does not make much sense. Naturally, this will translate in the base case of our algorithm. After creating N/M sorted lists, each of size M, the algorithm works analogously to internal merge-sort, where we merge pairs of lists (see an example involving sorting cards in figure 11.3a).

When merging two sorted lists, we are often unable to hold both lists in their entirety in the main memory simultaneously, but all we need to perform merging is to have one block of each of the two lists in the main memory and pick out the smallest remaining element among the two blocks until one is fully exhausted; then we read the next block from the list. The process is similar to merging k sorted lists, as in figure 9.7, a figure we repeat here (figure 11.4), but in two-way external merge-sort, $k = 2$.

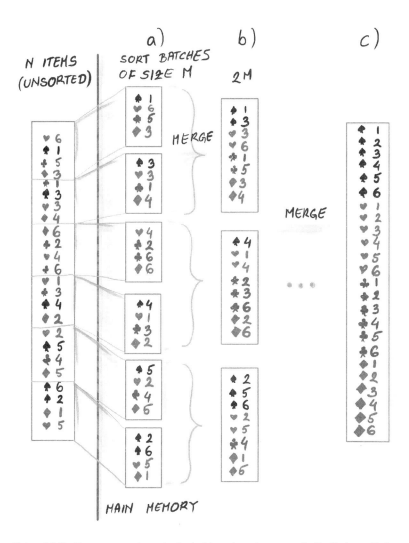

Figure 11.3   Two-way merge-sort adapted to external memory. In the first run, *N* elements are processed in *N/M* batches of size *M*, where each batch of size *M* is sorted. This is our "base case" for external memory merge-sort (internal memory merge-sort ordinarily begins from lists of size 1). Then, one by one, pairs of lists of size *M* are processed and merged into lists of size 2*M*, then 4*M*, and so on. Eventually we arrive at the final list of size *N*.

This means that the runtime of two-way external merge-sort is

$$T_{2ext}(N) = 2T_{2ext}\left(\frac{N}{2}\right) + O\left(\frac{N}{B}\right)$$

and the base case is $T_{2ext}(M) = O(M/B)$, the number of transfers required just to read the data. The total sorting cost dominates the linear cost of creating initial sorted lists of size M, so we do not include it in the formula. To understand what happens in two-way external merge-sort, it is important to understand that each read of all of data costs N/B transfers. Each sweep over the entire data that increases the list size by a factor of 2 (and cuts the number of lists by a factor of 2) needs N/B I/Os. To get from N/M lists of size M to 1 list of size N by doubling the list size every run, we need $O\left(\log_2 {N/M}\right)$ such sweeps. This analysis (as well as the unwrapping of the recursion) gives us $O\left({N/B} \log_2 {N/M}\right)$ I/Os.

To check your knowledge of how blocks travel back and forth during two-way external merge-sort in external memory, first solve the following exercise.

EXERCISE 1

Analyze the number of block requests needed to sort the request data from an earlier example using two-way merge-sort in external memory. Some of the common block sizes are 8 KB–64 KB.

We can do better than two-way external merge-sort, so let's go back to merging K sorted lists simultaneously. Figure 11.4 is instructive as to how to merge sorted lists whose total size cannot fit into RAM.

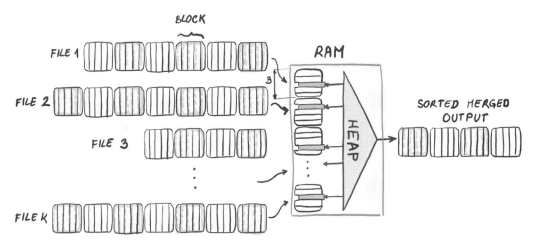

Figure 11.4   Merging *k* sorted lists in external memory. Each list has one representative buffer block residing in memory at all times. The minimum of each block is initially inserted into a heap, from where minima are repeatedly extracted. Every time an element is extracted from the heap, the next element in line from the same block where the minimum came from gets inserted into the heap. When we run out of elements of one block, we bring in the next block of the same list.

According to this figure, we can have up to $O\left({M/B}\right)$ lists merged at one time, as every list needs just one block to represent it in RAM. Merging many lists at one time produces significant gains, as we can turn M/B lists of size x into 1, and to do this, we use the same number of memory transfers as two-way external merge-sort uses to turn M/B lists of size x into $M/2B$ lists. Introducing the idea of merging many lists to the two-way external merge-sort gives way to the most popular external memory sorting algorithm, external memory M/B-way merge-sort.

11.3 External memory merge-sort (M/B-way merge-sort)

External memory, or M/B-way merge-sort, first introduced back in the 1980s [2], employs the idea of merging many lists at once. It begins by creating the base case M-sized sorted lists to be further merged. Then it proceeds by merging M/B lists at once into one list, thus increasing the list size between runs by a factor of M/B. In other words, we begin with lists of size M, then M^2/B, then M^3/B^2, and so on, until we reach one list of size N. See figure 11.5 for an example.

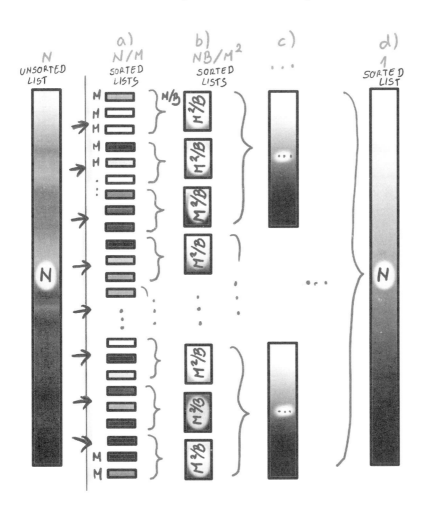

Figure 11.5 In M/B-way merge-sort, we begin by creating, in one run, N/M sorted lists of size M. Then these lists are further merged, M/B at one time, to eventually create one sorted list.

The algorithm is like the classic internal merge-sort in that it is recursive, so it trivially partitions the lists until they are of size M, sorts each one individually, and proceeds by recursively merging the lists. The recursive formula that describes M/B-way external merge-sort is as follows:

$$T_{(\frac{M}{B})ext}(N) = \frac{M}{B}T_{(\frac{M}{B})ext}\left(\frac{N}{\frac{M}{B}}\right) + O\left(\frac{N}{B}\right)$$

The base case is the same as for the two-way external merge-sort, $T(M) = O(M/B)$. Let's unwrap this recursion. To get from lists of size M to a list of size N by always increasing list size by a factor of M/B, we need $\log_{M/B} N/M$ steps. Each step needs one sweep over the entire data, each of which costs $O\left(N/B\right)$ I/Os. Thus, the total cost of the M/B-way external merge-sort is $O\left(N/B \log_{M/B} N/M\right)$ I/Os.

Mere expressions for runtimes might not mean much, but if we visually compare the formula for M/B-way external merge-sort and the two-way external merge-sort, the key difference appears in the base of the logarithm (2 versus M/B). How big of a difference is this really? We are used to neglecting the base of the logarithm, as it is usually a difference in a constant factor. However, here we have the parameters M and B involved, and we do not treat these as constants. The two runtimes differ by a factor of $\log_2 M/B$. For many common choices of memory size and block size, the factor of difference might even be up to 30. See for yourself by solving the following exercise and comparing the results with those in exercise 1.

EXERCISE 2

Calculate how many block transfers are used by the M/B-way external merge-sort algorithm for our request data example. Remember that memory size is 4 GB, and the total dataset size is 512 GB. Use the same block size you used for exercise 1.

Now that you have solved exercise 2, you have a good understanding of the number of I/Os required by the sorting algorithm. However, even though in the M/B-way external merge-sort we attempt to optimize disk-related costs, the internal memory should not be neglected. The way we handle operations in main memory greatly affects the final execution of the algorithm. Our merging example from chapter 9 that describes how heap can be used in the main memory to merge k sorted lists serves as an example of a good use of memory in this type of algorithm. Specifically, in external merge-sort, we can maintain an M/B-sized heap to maintain the minima from each block representing its list. This way, we can achieve both external and internal memory optimality.

11.3.1 *Searching and sorting in RAM vs. external memory*

Let's step back for a moment and think about the connection between searching and sorting and how it changes when we go from internal to external memory. In internal memory, searching and sorting are highly related in the following sense: a balanced binary search tree, a data structure built for efficient searches (such as an AVL tree, red-black tree, etc.), can also be used to sort data optimally. Insert (as well as lookup and delete) in a balanced binary search tree costs $O(\log_2 n)$, so n inserts into the tree effectively sort the data in $O(n \log_2 n)$ comparisons, and one in-order traversal can output data in a linear order into an array. The per-element cost of sorting is then equal to the per-element cost of searching, $O(\log_2 n)$.

Transferring that analogy to external memory, if we attempt to sort using a B-tree, we get performance that is far from the optimal sorting algorithm: N inserts into a B-tree cost $O(N \log_B N)$ I/Os, or, if we think of the top levels of a B-tree as residents in the main memory, then $O\left(N \log_B {}^N/_M\right)$ I/Os. The per-element cost of sorting for M/B-way external merge-sort is only $O\left({}^1/_B \log_{M/_B} {}^N/_M\right)$ I/Os, which is substantially less than the time to insert into a B-tree. In other words, the per-element cost of sorting is much less than the per-element cost of searching in external memory. That is, we cannot transfer the analogy to external memory.

This difference is important because it shows that for batched problems, such as sorting, we can make good use of a large memory (merging many lists is a good example). By batched problems, we mean problems where you need to process a ton of data and only provide the result at the very end. Batched lookup, for example, means getting a group of queries and reporting answers to those queries once at the end. In the batched version of the lookup problem, we are optimizing the total amount of time to solve the entire problem, and when this is the goal, we can think about the problem of multiple queries as a whole (i.e., answering one query might help us answer another query, etc.). In this setup, processing a lot of data at once can be very helpful, and a large main memory can help us do that.

This is essentially different than if we are given the same queries but need to report answers one by one and are optimizing the sum of times taken to answer each query. This latter version feels more like the sequence of classical searching problems, and that sort of searching cannot make good use of a large memory except for storing top levels of a B-tree into the main memory, because the outcome of comparison to elements from one block determines the next block that should be brought in.

If the last two paragraphs feel like too much philosophy, you're probably right. But this is our last chapter, and we feel entitled to wax philosophical to some degree. The point is, in sorting and other related problems, we truly benefit from having a large main memory, whereas in some other problems, increasing the main memory size might help, but not that dramatically. You can assure yourself of this by looking at the runtimes of sorting versus searching and seeing how much the I/O-cost improves if the main memory doubles (i.e., M becomes $2M$).

There are many other batched problems that can benefit from a large memory in the same way sorting does. So far, we have seen only the example of merging many lists as a benefit of large memory. Next, we will study the external version of quick-sort and see how large memory allows us to speed up ordinary two-way quick-sort (that is, pivot selection).

11.4   What about external quick-sort?

Let's begin with a brief review of internal quick-sort. Unlike merge-sort, quick-sort does most of its work from the top down by carefully partitioning data. The partition happens based on a chosen pivot, where data is further divided into elements smaller than or of equal size to the pivot and elements larger than the pivot. Once the arrays to be partitioned become size 1, quick-sort's work is effectively done.

In internal memory, quick-sort has a better reputation than merge-sort, and sort libraries more often employ quick-sort than merge-sort. This might seem unusual considering that quick-sort does not offer optimal worst-case guarantees the way merge-sort does. Deterministic quick-sort that selects an arbitrary pivot at a fixed point (say, always from the first position in the array) can range from $O(n \log_2 n)$ to $O(n^2)$, and so does the randomized quick-sort that selects the pivot at random. Yet, randomized quick-sort is a much safer choice, as it effectively handles the case of almost sorted data, or any pattern in the data that might prove unfavorable for a fixed point choice of a pivot.

It is possible to force quick-sort to sort in $O(n \log_2 n)$ by using the median-of-medians worst-case linear-time selection algorithm [3], but this algorithm has various practicality issues; on the other hand, to obtain the asymptotically optimal runtime, we do not need perfect medians.

One of the main benefits of quick-sort is that it is an in-place algorithm, so all recursive calls work on the same part of the memory, the original array to be sorted. This means that we do not spend time copying over data and allocating extra memory, the tasks that slow down merge-sort. Saving space also saves time for the internal memory quick-sort, but let's see whether those effects translate into external memory.

To understand how to effectively translate quick-sort to external memory, our first exercise is to directly translate the ordinary two-way quick-sort, without any significant modifications to the algorithm.

11.4.1   External memory two-way quick-sort

The direct adaptation of (randomized) two-way quick-sort to external memory is fairly straightforward. We randomly choose a pivot location, bring in the block containing the pivot, and then sweep the whole file through memory, block by block, deciding for each element whether it is smaller than, equal to, or larger than the pivot. There are two buffer blocks in the main memory that accumulate elements belonging to the two groups, and when a block is full on one side, we write it back to disk to its appropriate "side." After a linear number of memory transfers, we have performed one level of partitioning (see figure 11.6).

The partition step illustrated in figure 11.6 requires $O(N/B)$ I/Os. Then we recursively run the same algorithm on two separate pieces of files. Our base case occurs when the size of the file to be sorted is a size of memory (M) or less. In that case, we pull the whole file, sort it in memory, and write it back.

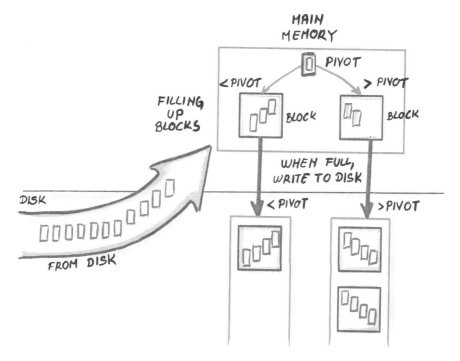

Figure 11.6 A snapshot during a partition in external memory two-way quick-sort. Data is sequentially input through the main memory, and each element is compared to the pivot. We have one block of buffer space to accumulate elements smaller than the pivot, and one block of buffer space to accumulate elements larger than the pivot. Once any of the buffer blocks are full, they are written back to a particular location on disk, where either the left or the right side of the array is being appended. It is important for the recursive calls that will be done later that the elements that are smaller or larger than the pivot are all contiguously placed.

Let's assume for a moment that the pivot chosen always splits data into two equal halves. Then the recursion describing the runtime of two-way external quick-sort is identical to that of two-way external merge-sort, and it gives $O\left(\frac{N}{B}\log_2\frac{N}{M}\right)$ as the runtime.

11.4.2 *Toward external memory multiway quick-sort*

Following the analogy of merge-sort, to improve on the parallelism in this algorithm, we might think about increasing the number of pivots we find, and doing an M/B-way partition instead of a two-way partition. Let's indulge this idea for a moment. Assume that in $O(N/B)$ I/Os, we can find $O(M/B)$ pivots that partition the data into $O(M/B)$ sub-arrays. That will take us from this sort of recursion for two-way external quick-sort

$$T_{2qext}(N) = 2T_{2qext}\left(\frac{N}{2}\right) + O\left(\frac{N}{B}\right)$$

to this type of recursion

$$T_{\left(\frac{M}{B}\right)qext}(N) = \frac{M}{B}T_{\left(\frac{M}{B}\right)qext}\left(\frac{N}{\frac{M}{B}}\right) + O\left(\frac{N}{B}\right)$$

which will lead us to the runtime equivalent to that of M/B-way external merge-sort. But not so fast: the conversion from two-way external quick-sort to multiway external quick-sort is not that straightforward.

The main issue we are facing is that it is not obvious how to find $O(M/B)$ good pivots and partition in a linear number of block transfers. We can do this if we resort to randomized pivots, but randomized pivots will not yield good partition.

Another idea is to utilize the median-of-medians algorithm that when transferred to external memory requires $O(N/B)$ transfers to find one median. When applied recursively, this algorithm can find $O(M/B)$ medians in $O\left(\frac{N}{B}\log_2 \frac{M}{B}\right)$ I/Os; this messes with our earlier plan where we promised the partition work (the non-recursive part of the recursive formula $T_{\left(\frac{M}{B}\right)qext}(N)$ would be $O(N/B)$). There is, however, a way around this.

11.4.3 *Finding enough pivots*

It turns out that there was a loophole in our thinking in the previous section. We said that to achieve the runtime of M/B-way merge-sort using quick-sort, we would need to do an M/B-way partition (i.e., be able to find M/B well-distributed pivots in N/B I/Os). We can get away with much fewer pivots, and here's why: whatever we achieve runtime-wise with $O(M/B)$ pivots, we can also achieve (asymptotically speaking) with $(M/B)^c$ pivots for some constant c, $0 < c < 1$. So, finding $\sqrt{M/B}$ pivots or even $\sqrt[3]{M/B}$ pivots still gives us the runtime asymptotically equal to that of $T_{\left(\frac{M}{B}\right)qext}(N)$. Having $\sqrt{M/B}$ pivots will double the depth of the recursion tree, but this will not asymptotically affect the runtime. This will be our first relaxation of the problem: find $\sqrt{M/B}$ pivots instead of M/B pivots.

The second relaxation will be something that we should have known from internal quick-sort: the partition does not need to divide data into exactly equally sized sub-partitions for the sorting algorithm to perform asymptotically optimally. To make our lives easier, we will translate this idea into external memory and try to find pivots that do not have to have exactly spaced-out ranks. They will be good enough in that they will separate data into $O(s)$ sub-arrays, where $s = \sqrt{M/B}$, and all sub-arrays will be within a constant-factor size of each other. Some sub-arrays might be two or three times the size of other sub-arrays, and that's fine.

Let's take a second to understand why this will not be a problem. If we zoom back to the regular internal quick-sort, recall that if every time we choose a pivot, the pivot falls exactly in the middle of the ordered array, then we will get the performance of $O(n\log_2 n)$. If a pivot always falls somewhere in the middle half of the ranks (i.e., it is never in the smallest 25% or the largest 25% of data), then the worst-case runtime is described using the following recurrence:

$$T(n) = T\left(\frac{n}{4}\right) + T\left(\frac{3n}{4}\right) + n$$

This also gives us $O(n \log_2 n)$. In fact, even if a pivot separates data into 1% and 99% of ranks, the runtime generated by the recurrence

$$T(n) = T\left(\frac{n}{100}\right) + T\left(\frac{99n}{100}\right) + n$$

still results in $O(n \log_2 n)$. As long as the partitions are within constant sizes of each other, this should not give us the asymptotically worse performance than that given by perfect partitions. We will make use of this fact while finding s approximate pivots for external multiway quick-sort (now we can call it $\sqrt{M/B}$-way quick-sort).

11.4.4 *Finding good enough pivots*

We will split the original set of N elements into N/M chunks and sort each chunk. Then, from each chunk, we will select each αth element. Take $\alpha = \sqrt[8]{4} = \sqrt{M/B}/4$. We will call the set of these selected elements $R \subseteq N$ (i.e., representatives); the set will have a cardinality of $\sim N/\alpha$. Now we employ the median-of-medians selection algorithm recursively to find s pivots in R.

First, we need to prove that it is possible to do this in a linear number of memory transfers. When the median-of-medians algorithm is applied recursively to the set of size N/α to find $s = 4\alpha$ pivots recursively, it costs $O\left(\frac{N}{\alpha B} \log_2 4\alpha\right)$, which in total does not cost more than $O\left(\frac{N}{B}\right)$ I/Os.

Next, we need to show that the s medians chosen from R are approximate medians in N. The s medians partition R into $\sim s$ partitions of size $k = \frac{N}{s\alpha}$, and each of these elements is a representative we chose from some chunk of size M in the original set. However, the chunks are not mutually ordered, so one partition could have elements from different chunks. For instance, the first partition (one containing the smallest elements) might have one representative from the first chunk, five representatives from the second chunk, four from the third chunk, and so on. Either way, these representatives carry the elements that come before and after them in the original set.

The maximum number of elements that k representatives from a partition can carry with them is, for each representative, α elements that come after, and, for the first element in a chunk, the elements that come before it. This equals at most

$$C_1 = k \times \alpha + \left(\frac{N}{M}\right) \times \alpha = \frac{N}{s} + \frac{N\alpha}{M}$$

elements from the original set, and the least that one partition can carry is similarly

$$C_2 = k \times \alpha - \left(\frac{N}{M}\right) \times \alpha = \frac{N}{s} - \frac{N\alpha}{M}$$

Because $s = q(\alpha)$, then $C_1 = C_2$, thus showing that s medians found in R are approximate and good enough medians for the original set N (http://mng.bz/zQva).

11.4.5 *Putting it all back together*

Now that we know how to find pivots in linear time, let's see how this version of external $\sqrt{M/B}$-way quick-sort will work (see figure 11.7).

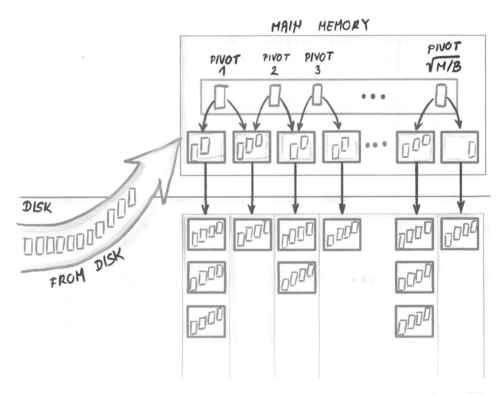

Figure 11.7 Snapshot of external memory multiway quick-sort. Instead of one pivot, we find $O(\sqrt{M/B})$ pivots and pull the entire dataset through memory. Based on comparisons with the pivots, each element is routed to the correct buffer block. Once the buffer block of any partition is filled, it is written back to memory, and the buffer is emptied. After all data is pulled through main memory, we created $O(\sqrt{M/B})$ partitions that quick-sort can again recurse on. Once a partition is of size M, the entire partition is read into the main memory, sorted, and written back.

It is important that we can simultaneously fit s pivots into the main memory, along with $s + 1$ blocks that act as buffers for collecting elements. Once each block fills up, it is written back to disk. Once all elements have been processed, we recursively continue onto $s + 1$ partitions.

The runtime of this algorithm equals that of external M/B-way merge-sort, $O\left(\frac{N}{B} \log_{M/B} \frac{N}{M}\right)$ I/Os. In the next section, we will see that this bound is optimal for any external memory sorting algorithm.

11.5   Math bit: Why is external memory merge-sort optimal?

To understand why $\frac{M}{B}$-way merge-sort and $\sqrt{M/B}$-way quick-sort in external memory are optimal, it is important to first settle this question in internal memory. How do we know that the bound of $O(n \log_2 n)$ is optimal for sorting?

In the very beginning, when data is given to the sorting algorithm, we do not know which permutation of data represents the correct sorted order. One way to analyze the complexity of the sorting problem is to think of how much one comparison can help us eliminate some permutations that do not represent the sorted order. For example, say we have a dataset of only three elements. There are $3! = 6$ potential permutations that might give us the final sorted order: (a_1, a_2, a_3), (a_1, a_3, a_2), (a_2, a_1, a_3), (a_2, a_3, a_1), (a_3, a_1, a_2), and (a_3, a_2, a_1).

Say we compare a_2 to a_3 and learn that $a_2 < a_3$. This means that three permutations listed, where a_3 comes before a_2, should be eliminated as potential outcomes. Because permutations are symmetric in this sense, we can assume that a good comparison can eliminate at most half of the remaining permutations. Note that if our algorithm is not good, a comparison might not cut down as much, or at all (imagine posing the same comparison over and over again). But in the event that the algorithm poses meaningful comparisons, we need at least $\log_2(n!)$ comparisons to get to one permutation. Simplifying this expression, we get that the lower bound for the sorting problem is $\Omega(n \log_2 n)$.

How does this work in external memory? Our unit operation here is a block transfer, so the question becomes how much one block transfer can help us reduce the number of candidate permutations. This will largely depend on the contents of a block being brought in and the contents of main memory. But for the lower bound, we are interested in the *most* that one block can help us during sorting. When one block is input, it has at most B elements, and the memory has at most $M - B$ resident elements (see figure 11.8).

To simplify the computation, we will assume that each individual block is sorted. This reduces the total number of permutations from $N!$ to $\frac{N!}{(B! \frac{N}{B})}$. Now that the block being brought into the main memory is sorted, and the memory itself is sorted, the total number of options for where the B elements might land is (M choose B). Based on these two quantities, we obtain that the lower bound for sorting in external memory is

$$\log_{\binom{M}{B}} \frac{N!}{B!^{\frac{N}{B}}}$$

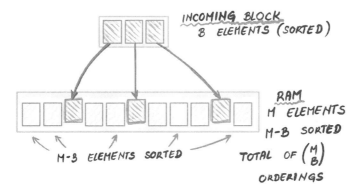

Figure 11.8 To understand how much one block transfer can help in sorting, we analyze how many potential orderings of B elements (contents of one block) there are inside a memory full of elements. There is a total of (*M* choose *B*) orderings, and this is a factor by which one memory transfer can reduce the total number of permutations remaining to be examined.

which, after some algebraic manipulation, comes out to $\Omega\left(\frac{N}{B} \log_{M/B} \frac{N}{M}\right)$, the bound that matches our external memory sorting algorithms. This analysis has been adapted from Erickson (http://mng.bz/zQva), which you can consult if you wish to understand more details about the algebraic manipulation of this lower bound and lower bounds in general.

11.6 Wrapping up

We have arrived at the end of this book. Whether you picked up this book because you are trying to implement probabilistic data structures to solve a problem in a specific domain or you are beefing up your large-scale system and algorithm design know-how for an interview at a big data company, we hope this book was a good investment of your time. If not, we hope you at least enjoyed the illustrations.

If you're only getting started in the field of massive-scale algorithms, our hope is that after reading this book, you have a better understanding of the range of algorithmic problems that large datasets introduce in modern-day systems—and, more importantly, that you find them exciting. We hope we convinced you that problems such as set membership, searching, sorting, cardinality estimation, sampling, and database indexing for massive datasets are intriguing and challenging problems and that thinking about ways of solving them helped you develop or deepen a new, more nuanced view of efficiency and performance.

Ultimately, resulting tradeoffs from limited space and time when working with large data forces us to think more creatively about problems than ever before and to embrace error and imperfection. Working with massive datasets teaches us that we can't have it all (not that we needed massive datasets to teach us this!). With a growing gap between our resources and the size of data that applications process, it is clear that the success of many applications today will be determined by how well they grapple with scalability challenges. To successfully do that, we need engineers who can wear many hats and are able to combine algorithmic and programming know-how with the domain knowledge and mathematical underpinnings of data structures and algorithms. This book represents our small contribution to the education of such a versatile engineer.

Summary

- Sorting is one of the best-known problems in computer science, and there is a large body of research optimizing sorting algorithms for different contexts.
- When data cannot fit into main memory, the sorting algorithm needs to bring in small pieces of data into main memory and sort chunk by chunk.
- M/B-way external merge-sort is the algorithm of choice for when data is too large to fit into RAM. This algorithm merges many lists at once, thus making use of a large available memory.
- Analogously, it is possible to adapt quick-sort to work optimally in external memory by choosing a larger set of pivots and thus partitioning data into many individual sub-partitions instead of just two.
- Batched problems like sorting have a cheaper per-element cost than searching in external memory. This is an important difference between RAM and external memory: in RAM, we can optimally sort by inserting into a search structure, while doing that in external memory results in a suboptimal algorithm.
- To understand whether a sorting algorithm is optimal, it is important to understand how sorting lower bounds works. With internal memory, the key is understanding how much one comparison can contribute to eliminating permutations that are not the sorted order; in external memory we do the same, but by analyzing how much one block input can help us eliminate the permutations.

references

Chapter 1

1 A. Aggarwal and J. S. Vitter, "The Input/Output Complexity of Sorting and Related Problems," *Communications of the ACM*, vol. 31, no. 9, pp. 1116–1127, 1988.

2 B. Ellis, *Real-Time Analytics: Techniques to Analyze and Visualize Streaming Data*, Wiley, 2014.

3 G. Andrii, *Probabilistic Data Structures and Algorithms for Big Data Applications*, *Books on Demand*, 2019;
B. Ellis, *Real-Time Analytics: Techniques to Analyze and Visualize Streaming Data*, Wiley, 2014;
C. G. Healey, *Disk-Based Algorithms for Big Data*, CRC Press, 2016;
A. Rajaraman and J. D. Ullman, *Mining of Massive Datasets*, Cambridge University Press, 2011;
M. Kleppmann, *Designing Data-Intensive Applications*, O'Reilly, 2017;
A. Petrov, *Database Internals*, O'Reilly, 2019.

4 J. L. Hennessy and D. A. Patterson, *Computer Architecture: A Quantitative Approach* (5th ed.), Morgan Kaufmann, 2011.

5 C. Terman, "MIT OpenCourseWare," Massachusetts Institute of Technology, Spring 2017, https://ocw.mit.edu/courses/electrical-engineering-and-computer-science/6-004-computation-structures-spring-2017/index.htm.

6 D. A. Patterson, "Latency Lags Bandwidth," *Communications of the ACM*, vol. 47, no. 10, pp. 71–75, 2004.

7 J. L. Hennessy and D. A. Patterson, *Computer Architecture*.

8 D. A. Patterson, "Latency Lags Bandwidth."

Chapter 2

1 B. Debnath, S. Sengupta, and J. Li, "ChunkStash: Speeding up Inline Storage Deduplication Using Flash Memory," in *Proceedings of the 2010 USENIX Conference on USENIX Annual Technical Conference*, p. 16, 2010.

2 S. Schleimer, D. S. Wilkerson, and A. Aiken, "Winnowing: Local Algorithms for Document Fingerprinting," in *Proceedings of the 2003 ACM SIGMOD International Conference on Management of Data*, pp. 76–85, 2003.

3 T. H. Cormen, C. E. Leiserson, R. L. Rivest, and C. Stein, *Introduction to Algorithms* (3rd ed.), The MIT Press, 2009.

4 A. Pagh, R. Pagh, and M. Ruzic, "Linear Probing with Constant Independence," in *Proceedings of the Thirty-Ninth Annual ACM Symposium on Theory of Computing*, San Diego, California, pp. 318–327, 2007.

5 python/cpython, "Python Hash Table Implementation of a Dictionary," February 20, 2020, https://github.com/python/cpython/blob/master/Objects/dictobject.c.

6 D. K. Targer, E. Lehman, T. Leighton, R. Panigrahy, M. Levine, and D. Lewin, "Consistent Hashing and Random Trees: Distributed Caching Protocols for Relieving Hot Spots on the World Wide Web," in *Proceedings of the Twenty-Ninth Annual ACM Symposium on Theory of Computing*, El Paso, Texas, 1997;
G. Valiant and T. Roughgarden, "CS168 The Modern Algorithmic Toolbox," April 1, 2019, https://web.stanford.edu/class/cs168/l/l11.pdf.

7 I. Stoica, R. Morris, D. Liben-Nowell, D. R. Karger, M. F. Kaashoek, F. Dabek, and H. Balakrishnan, "Chord: A Scalable Peer-to-Peer Lookup Protocol for Internet Applications," *IEEE/ACM Transactions on Networking*, vol. 11, no. 1, pp. 17–32, 2003.

8 G. DeCandia, D. Hastorun, M. Jampani, G. Kakulapati, A. Lakshman, A. Pilchin, S. Sivasubramanian, P. Vosshall, and W. Vogels, "Dynamo: Amazon's highly available key-value store," *SIGOPS Review*, vol. 41, no. 6, pp. 205–220, 2007.

Chapter 3

1 B. H. Bloom, "Space/Time Trade-Offs in Hash Coding with Allowable Errors," *Communications of the ACM*, vol. 13, no. 7, pp. 422–426, 1970;
A. Broder and M. Mitzenmacher, "Network Applications of Bloom Filters: A Survey," *Internet Mathematics*, pp. 636–646, 2002.

2 F. Chang, J. Dean, S. Ghemawat, W. C. Hsieh, D. A. Wallach, M. Burrows, T. Chandra, A. Fikes, and R. E. Gruber, "Bigtable: A Distributed Storage System for Structured Data," *ACM Transactions on Computer Systems*, vol. 26, no. 2, pp. 4:1–4:26, 2008.

3 S. Lebresne, "The Apache Cassandra Storage Engine," 2012, https://av.tib.eu/media/39995.

4 M. A. Bender, M. Farach-Colton, R. Johnson, R. Kraner, B. C. Kuszmaul, D. Medjedovic, P. Montes, P. Shetty, R. P. Spillane, and E. Zadok, "Don't Thrash: How to Cache Your Hash on Flash," in *Proceedings of the VLDB Endowment (PVLDB)*, vol. 5, no. 11, pp. 1627–1637, 2012.

5 L. Fan, P. Cao, J. Almeida, and A. Z. Broder, "Summary Cache: A Scalable Wide-Area Web Cache Sharing Protocol," *IEEE/ACM Transactions on Networking*, vol. 8, no. 3, pp. 281–293, 2000.

6 A. Gervais, S. Capkun, G. O. Karame, and D. Gruber, "On the Privacy Provisions of Bloom Filters in Lightweight Bitcoin," *Proceedings of the 30th Annual Computer Security Applications Conference*, pp. 326–335, 2014.

7 L. Fan, P. Cao, J. Almeida, and A. Z. Broder, "Summary Cache: A Scalable Wide-Area Web Cache Sharing Protocol," *IEEE/ACM Transactions on Networking*, vol. 8, no. 3, pp. 281–293, 2000.

8 J. Bruck, J. Gao, and A. Jiang, "Weighted Bloom Filter," Proceedings of *IEEE International Symposium on Information Theory*, pp. 2304–2308, 2006.

9 M. A. Bender, M. Farach-Colton, M. Goswami, R. Johnson, S. McCauley, and S. Singh, "Bloom Filters, Adaptivity, and the Dictionary Problem," in *IEEE 59th Annual Symposium on Foundations of Computer Science (FOCS)*, pp. 128–193, 2018.

10 M. A. Bender et al., "Don't Thrash: How to Cache Your Hash on Flash."

11 D. E. Knuth, *The Art of Computer Programming, Volume 3: Sorting and Searching* (2nd ed.), Addison Wesley Longman, 1998.

12 M. A. Bender et al., "Don't Thrash: How to Cache Your Hash on Flash."

13 B. Fan, D. G. Andersen, M. Kaminsky, and M. D. Mitzenmacher, "Cuckoo Filter: Practically Better Than Bloom," in *Proceedings of the 10th ACM International Conference on Emerging Networking Experiments and Technologies*, Sydney, Australia, 2014.

14 M. A. Bender et al., "Don't Thrash: How to Cache Your Hash on Flash."

Chapter 4

1 T. Roughgarden and G. Valiant, "The Modern Algorithmic Toolbox Lecture #2: Approximate Heavy Hitters and Count-Min Sketch," Stanford University, 2020, https://web.stanford.edu/class/cs168/l/l2.pdf.

2 M. Charikar and N. Wein, "CS369G: Algorithmic Techniques for Big Data, Lecture 7: Heavy Hitters, Count-Min Sketch," Stanford University, 2015-2016, https://learn.fmi.uni-sofia.bg/pluginfile.php/200059/mod_resource/content/2/Heavy_hitters_-_count-min_sketch.pdf.

3 G. Cormode and S. Muthukrishnan, "An Improved Data Stream Summary: The Count-Min Sketch and Its Applications," *Journal of Algorithms*, vol. 55, no. 1, pp. 58–75, 2005.

4 D. Jurafsky and J. H. Martin, *Speech and Language Processing* (2nd ed.), Pearson, 2009.

5 A. Goyal, H. Daume, III, and G. Cormode, "Sketch Algorithms for Estimating Point Queries in NLP," in *Proceedings of the 2012 Joint Conference on Empirical Methods in Natural Language Processing and Computational Natural Language Learning*, pp. 1093–1103, 2012.

6 G. Cormode and S. Muthukrishnan, "An Improved Data Stream Summary: The Count-Min Sketch and Its Applications," *Journal of Algorithms*, vol. 55, no. 1, pp. 58–75, 2005;
Charikar and Wein, "CS369G: Algorithmic Techniques for Big Data, Lecture 7."

Chapter 5

1 S. Skiena, *The Algorithm Design Manual* (2nd ed.), Springer, 2008.

2 P. Flajolet, E. Fusy, O. Gandouet, and F. Meunier, "HyperLogLog: The Analysis of a Near-Optimal Cardinality Estimation Algorithm," *AOFA: Proceedings of the 2007 International Conference on Analysis of Algorithms*, pp. 137–156, 2007.

3 S. Heule, M. Nunkesser, and A. Hall, "HyperLogLog in Practice: Algorithmic Engineering of a State of the Art Cardinality Estimation Algorithm," *Proceedings of the 16th International Conference on Extending Database Technology*, Genoa, Italy, pp. 683–692, 2013.

4 P. Flajolet and G. N. Martin, "Probabilistic Counting Algorithms for Data Base Applications," *Journal of Computer and System Sciences*, vol. 31, no. 2, pp. 182–209, 1985.

5 M. Durand and P. Flajolet, "Loglog Counting of Large Cardinalities," *European Symposium on Algorithms (ESA)*, pp. 605–617, 2003.

6 P. Flajolet et al., "HyperLogLog: The Analysis of a Near-Optimal Cardinality Estimation Algorithm."

7 K. Y. Whang, B. T. Vander-Zanden, and H. M. Taylor, "A Linear-Time Probabilistic Counting Algorithm for Database Applications," *ACM Transactions on Database Systems*, vol. 15, no. 2, pp. 208–229, 1990.

8 C. Estan, G. Varghese, and M. Fisk, "Bitmap Algorithms for Counting Active Flows on High-Speed Links," *ACM Transactions on Networking*, vol. 14, no. 5, pp. 925–937, 2006.

Chapter 6

1 Partly adopted from A. Rajaraman and J. D. Ullman, *Mining of Massive Datasets*, Cambridge University Press, 2011.

2 R. Sebastiao and J. Gama, "A Study on Change Detection Methods," *Proceedings of the 14th Portuguese Conference on Artificial Intelligence: Progress in Artificial Intelligence*, pp. 353–364, 2009.

Chapter 7

1 F. Olken and D. Rotem, "Simple Random Sampling from Relational Databases," *Proceedings of 12th VLDB Endowment*, 1986.

2 J. S. Vitter, "Random Sampling with a Reservoir," *ACM Transactions on Mathematical Software*, vol. 11, no. 1, 37–57, 1985.

3 P. J. Haas, "Data-Stream Sampling: Basic Techniques and Results," in M. Garofalakis, J. Gehrke, and R. Rastogi R. (Eds.), *Data Stream Management: Processing High-Speed Data Streams*, pp. 24–27, Springer, 2016.

4 J. Von Neumann, "Various Techniques Used in Connection with Random Digits: Monte Carlo Methods," in A. S. Householder, G. E. Forsythe, and H. H. Germond

(Eds.), *Monte Carlo Method*, vol. 12, pp. 36–38, US Government Printing Office, 1951.

5 C. C Aggarwal, "On Biased Reservoir Sampling in the Presence of Stream Evolution," *Proceedings of the 32nd International Conference on Very Large Data Bases*, pp. 607–618, 2006.

6 B. Babcock, M. Datar, and M. Rajeev, "Sampling from a Moving Window Over Streaming Data," Annual ACM-SIAM Symposium on Discrete Algorithms, pp. 633–634, 2002.

7 P. J. Haas, "Data-Stream Sampling: Basic Techniques and Results," in M. Garofalakis, J. Gehrke, and R. Rastogi R. (Eds.), *Data Stream Management: Processing High-Speed Data Streams*, pp. 30–31, Springer, 2016

8 M. Hahsler, M. Bonalos, and J. Forrest, "Introduction to stream: An Extensible Framework for Data Stream Clustering Research with R," *Journal of Statistical Software*, vol. 76, no. 14, pp. 1–50, 2017.

Chapter 8

1 M. Blum, R. W. Floyd, V. Pratt, R. L. Rivest, and R. E. Tarjan, "Time Bounds for Selection," *Journal of Computer and System Sciences*, vol. 7, pp. 448–461, 1973.

2 J. I. Munro and M. S. Paterson, "Selection and Sorting with Limited Storage," *Theoretical Computer Science*, vol. 12, no. 3, pp. 315–323, 1980.

3 N. Shrivastava, C. Buragohain, D. Agrawal, and S. Suri, "Medians and Beyond: New Aggregation Techniques for Sensor Networks," *Proceedings of the 2nd International Conference on Embedded Networked Sensor Systems*, pp. 239–249, 2004.

Chapter 9

1 S. Aggarwal and J. S. Vitter, "The Input/Output Complexity of Sorting and Related Problems," *Communications of the ACM*, vol. 31, no. 9, pp. 1116–1127, 1988.

Chapter 10

1 M. A. Bender, M. Farach-Colton, W. Jannen, R. Johnson, B. C. Kuszmaul, D. E. Porter, J. Yuan, and Y. Zhan, "An Introduction to *B*-trees and Write-Optimization," vol. 40, no. 5, 2015.

2 D. Comer, "The Ubiquitous B-Tree," *ACM Computing Surveys*, vol. 11, no. 2, pp. 121–137, 1979; R. Bayer and E. M. McCreight, "Organization and Maintenance of Large Ordered Indices," in *Proceedings of the 1970 ACM SIGFIDET (Now SIGMOD) Workshop on Data Description, Access and Control*, pp. 107–141, 1970.

3 G. S. Brodal and R. Fagerberg, "Lower Bounds for External Memory Dictionaries," in *Proceedings of the Fourteenth Annual ACM-SIAM Symposium on Discrete Algorithms*, pp. 546–554, 2003.

4 P. O'Neil, E. Cheng, D. Gawlick, and E. O'Neil, "The Log-Structured Merge-Tree (LSM-tree)," *Acta Informatica*, vol. 33, no. 4, pp. 351–385, 1996.

5   C. Luo and M. J. Carey, "LSM-Based Storage Techniques: A Survey," *VLDB Journal*, vol. 29, pp. 393–418, 2020;
    Y. Matsunobu, S. Dong, and H. Lee, "MyRocks: LSM-Tree Database Storage Engine Serving Facebook's Social Graph," *Proceedings of the VLDB Endowment*, vol. 13, no. 12, pp. 3217-3230, 2020.

6   G.S. Brodal and R. Fagerberg, "Lower Bounds for External Memory Dictionaries"; M.A. Bender et al., "An Introduction to B-trees and Write-Optimization."

7   W. Jannen, J. Yuan, Y. Zhan, A. Akshintala, J. Esmet, Y. Jiao, A. Mittal, P. Pandey, P. Reddy, L. Walsh, M. Bender, M. Farach-Colton, R. Johnson, B. Kuszmaul, and D. E. Porter, "BetrFS: A Right-Optimized Write-Optimized File System," in *Proceedings of the 13th USENIX Conference on File and Storage Technologies*, vol. 11, no. 4, pp. 1–29, 2015.

8   C. Luo and M.J. Carey, "LSM-Based Storage Techniques: A Survey."

Chapter 11

1   G. Graefe, "Implementing Sorting in Database Systems," *ACM Computing Surveys*, vol. 38, pp. 1–37, 2006.

2   A. Aggarwal and S. J. Vitter, "The Input/Output Complexity of Sorting and Related Problems," *Communications of the ACM*, vol. 31, no. 9, pp. 1116–1127, 1988.

3   M. Blum, R. W. Floyd, V. Pratt, R. L. Rivest, and R. E. Tarjan, "Time Bounds for Selection," *Journal of Computer and System Sciences*, vol. 7, no. 4, pp. 448–461, 1973.

index

Grokking Algorithms
by Aditya Y. Bhargava

ISBN 9781617292231
256 pages, $44.99
May 2016

Advanced Algorithms and Data Structures
by Marcello La Rocca

ISBN 9781617295485
768 pages, $59.99
May 2021

Math for Programmers
by Paul Orland

ISBN 9781617295355
688 pages, $59.99
November 2020

Spark in Action, Second Edition
by Jean-Georges Perrin
Foreword by Rob Thomas

ISBN 9781617295522
576 pages, $59.99
May 2020

For ordering information go to www.manning.com

Hands-on projects for learning your way

liveProjects are an exciting way to develop your skills that's just like learning on the job.

In a Manning liveProject, you tackle a real-world IT challenge and work out your own solutions. To make sure you succeed, you'll get 90 days of full and unlimited access to a hand-picked list of Manning book and video resources.

Here's how liveProject works:

- **Achievable milestones.** Each project is broken down into steps and sections so you can keep track of your progress.

- **Collaboration and advice.** Work with other liveProject participants through chat, working groups, and peer project reviews.

- **Compare your results.** See how your work shapes up against an expert implementation by the liveProject's creator.

- **Everything you need to succeed.** Datasets and carefully selected learning resources come bundled with every liveProject.

- **Build your portfolio.** All liveProjects teach skills that are in demand from industry. When you're finished, you'll have the satisfaction that comes with success and a real project to add to your portfolio.

Explore dozens of data, development, and cloud engineering liveProjects at www.manning.com!